The Year of the Cicadas

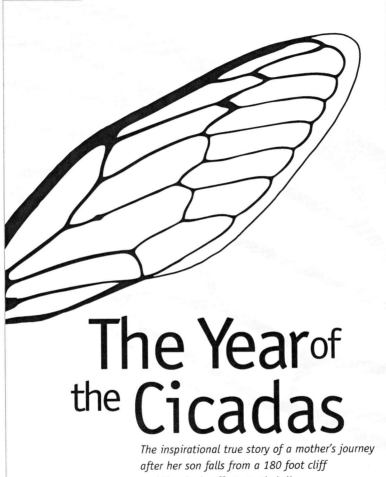

The Year of
the Cicadas

The inspirational true story of a mother's journey
after her son falls from a 180 foot cliff
and the ripple effects to their lives.

Catie Hartsfield

The Year of the Cicadas
by Catie Hartsfield

Crooked Tree Publishing
PO Box 54793
Cincinnati OH 45254

www.theyearofthecicadas.com

Published 2012 by Crooked Tree Publishing

Printed in United States of America

ISBN 978-0-9884567-0-9

Cover design by Lisa Muller-Jones
Book design and layout by Blaire Price

FIRST PAPERBACK EDITION

10 9 8 7 6 5 4 3 2 1

Dedications and Heart Felt Thanks

This book was written for my grandchildren and my great-grandchildren to come. I did not want this story to pass away along with me. I want you to know from whom you came. I hope when the time comes, and it will come, you find the strength and courage within yourself to face what life will send your way. Know I love you and will be watching over you from the other side.

To my husband and my life partner. I love you with all of my heart and soul. To my children, my love for you is eternal and thank you for letting me share your stories with the world and for your help with this book. Thank you for assisting me in accomplishing my dream. Your courage to always *put it all on the line* continues to amaze me. Most of all my appreciation goes to James, Ace, Bryant and the Boy Scouts. Without your will, determination and tenacity, this would be a completely different story.

These events took place in our mid-western home state, which for privacy I cannot disclose. I had to go away for a while to find the strength to write this story. It was within the quiet serenity and beauty of my surroundings that I was finally able to let this story, and the tears that came with it, pour out of me. This book in its entirety was written while looking out over the beautiful Casco Bay in Portland, Maine. Thank you to the special ladies who spurred me on with encouragement when I didn't think I could finish. Thank you for the many hours of editing and encouragement Moe, Lisa, Jill, Michelle, Shirley, Laurie, Marcia, Lynn, Pat and Sue. Thank you Mojo for the beautiful book cover and Sandra for our final edit. Thank you Dave, Rusty and Blaire for formatting and preparing our book for print.

Grandpa Bryant, if that was you on the other side, spurring Bryant on....
Thank you, thank you, thank you.
Here's to our jubilation!

Forward

It took four years for me to start to write this down, three additional years to pick it up again, and a year to finish my book. It has been almost eight years since *The Accident*, as we now refer to that day. I was unable to speak about it to anyone for the first two years, finally telling a small group of people from my church. They were all in tears and strongly suggested I write every memory down to share. You see, it was a really painful time for me, and I must relive the time to write it down. I still cry every time I think about it but I needed to get it out of me and onto paper. I think they call this a "missive," at least that is what it has become for me. I believe in my heart this is God's story; He wanted me to tell it. Perhaps there is another person out there who can relate and maybe learn from my journey. That is my hope.

This is the story told from my vantage point. I am sure for everyone involved there is another viewpoint, a completely different story, their story. This is mine and mine alone. I cannot tell someone else's story.

These are the facts as I know them; either lived by me or told to me. These were my feelings at the time. I am older and wiser now so, I would respond differently today. Please accept my apologies if I paint someone in a not-so-bright light, it could have been the lenses through which I was looking. I was in a negative place in my life and thought that everyone else needed to change, not me.

My husband and I started keeping a journal while in the ICU. We recorded as many conversations and facts as we could, which was our way of keeping in contact with each other while travelling along our separate paths. When the accident occurred we were man and wife, each of us going about our marriage as two separate individuals. This is about to change, one agonizing minute at a time.

Maybe this missive will enlighten you to either a deeper understanding of me, of yourself, or of the struggle of a family dealing with a traumatic brain injury and its ripple effects. It is my hope to inspire you. This is a story of change, transformation, hope and miracles.

It is written for all of the victims and caregivers of a Traumatic Brain Injury and for those who can and cannot tell their story. My wish is that by Bryant allowing me to share his journey and struggles that it will resonate with you, give hope and allow for a deeper understanding of the daily struggles you face.

It is written for all of the parents, spouses, and loved ones who are there for a handicapped person day in and day out, hour-by-hour, minute-by-minute for their entire lives. I had a small peek into this world. They are the true heroes, but they don't have the time to write their story; this is my journey into their world.

I had been praying for change: my marriage, my family, and we were all in trouble. I did not see a way out. I could not see the forest for the trees. Be careful for what you pray, you just may get it, but not the way you think! Everyone associated with this story has changed; it's called the Ripple Effect. No one is left the same; God works miracles, both big and small.

This is a true account of the journey, the best I can tell it. I changed the names and the locations, to offer a small degree of privacy to my family. I hope you understand.

Table of Contents

————————————————— Section Three: Recovery

Section Four: New Beginnings

Section One
The Accident

"There comes a time in life when
everything you have known,
tolerated and loved is suddenly shattered;
All that is before you is an empty frame
and broken glass on the floor.
You can't even imagine how to tape or
glue it back together,
all you can do at that moment
is breathe........"

- Maureen Momm

Chapter 1
The Phone Call

"Obstacles are opportunities to learn more about ourselves and the world in which we live. Life would certainly be boring, and we would not grow, if there were no disagreements, conflicts, and unexpected traumas in our lives."
– RaMa

I had a terrible dream a few weeks ago about my son falling. I saw him falling and falling, a long way down. Then later that same night I had a second dream, I saw him from a distance, alive but somehow...different. I wanted to trade places with him. I was walking in line to trade places with him but he headed out in the other direction. He did not recognize me. It was my son, I was sure about that, but he wasn't the same. I felt a strong sense of responsibility, and then...it all faded away. It had left me with an uneasy feeling, and a strong sense of anxiety. I feel so out of control right now, and I just hate this feeling. Usually I don't remember my dreams, but this one stuck. I tell myself, *how many times have I worried and how many times has everything been fine?*, I also tell myself, *not often but on occasion my dreams have come true, what if this is one of those times?*

The heavy sense of anxiety left over from this dream caused me to beg Bryant not to go camping at the Gorge this weekend. At his age, he does what he wants. I can make suggestions to him but I can't tell him what to do anymore. I begrudgingly agreed to let James his younger brother go with him yesterday morning. This is James' first trip to the Gorge, and I am hoping with his younger brother tagging along Bryant will be more into the hiking and camping.

I lectured Bryant the day before about no alcohol. Although he is twenty-one, James is barely seventeen and not allowed to drink. Alcohol made my childhood difficult. I am really strict in this regard, probably too strict. It is a matter of contention in our family. Focusing on them not drinking has backfired with the two older boys. The focus, negative or positive, has still been alcohol. They tell me all college kids do it, but I don't like it. I worry about them.

I didn't sleep at all last night. I had a sick discomforting feeling listening to the rain. Usually it has a calming effect on me, but not last night. We have not heard from the boys, but expect to hear from them any time now. Their phones do not work in the Gorge, but Bryant usually calls on his way home, which hopefully will be soon.

After the rains last night, the morning has dawned blue and beautiful. I love the color of spring green, a bright new green only found in young nature. It is probably the beautiful weather keeping them from getting on the road. Who can blame them? Certainly they will call soon. I take another breath, concentrating on my breathing, trying to relax.

Today is one of those late days in May that makes one feel like she is emerging from a cold damp cocoon. I have been waiting for a beautiful weekend like this one, all through the dark, gray, cold winter. I love all the seasons, including winter, but the second week of February always finds me combing through the gardening catalogs, dreaming of days like today. Spring is probably my favorite season everything is new and fresh.

These thoughts are swirling through my mind as I swim around our pool. Gently parting the water in front of me with my hands, I paddle around. The water feels good, just the right temperature. The pool is surrounded by a thick hedge protecting it from cool breezes, allowing for the added bonus of an extended swimming season. It also helps that it is directly in the sun. Even with all of that, I am running the heater to keep the chill off the water. More company will be arriving any day now. I want the water to be swimmable for the younger kids coming for the double graduation party. The yard looks good, the house is clean, tables are even set up on our inside porch room, inside because the Cicadas are predicted.

"How bad could they really be?" I have decided to make it as much fun as possible. This is the year of the Cicadas. I do not really know what that entails. We were not living here the last time the Cicadas arrived. They come every seventeen years, and we have only lived here ten. We have all been laughing about it, I even made up T-shirts for the party. They say: "I survived the year of the Cicadas."

My uneasiness slowly escalated into a mild panic earlier this morning. I even found myself, before my in-laws arrived, pulling out old picture albums and looking through them. I need my boys home so I can relax.

The phone rang fifteen minutes ago, and my husband Steve, jumped out of the pool to answer it. I urged him to hurry since maybe it was the boys. He has not come back out and if it were the boys, he would have told me. He knows how worried I am.

It must be his office calling. It is like him to occupy himself with work and leave me out here with his dad. Steve is always travelling, talking on the phone, and in constant contact with work.

Just your average workaholic, I think to myself.

I am still swimming around. I do not want to get out of the water without Steve here to distract his dad. In my bathing suit, I feel a little more hidden in the water.

What the heck is taking so long, I wonder? My in-laws arrived early this afternoon. They came a week early to bring additional food for the parties. Since I do not have adequate freezer space, they left the food in their motor home at the casino. My mother-in-law, Rose, loves to cook and is on a gourmet level. It makes her feel really good to be the "Head Cook." Although I cook every day, knowing it makes her feel important, I always let her take over my kitchen. I believe she means well, but somehow our relationship has gotten side-ways.

My favorite all time Rose quote is, "Grandma's here. You're finally going to get a decent meal." I find it hard to get that one out of my head.

Elizabeth is shopping with her grandmother to look for a dress to go under her graduation gown. She will be graduating from high school next week and Paul, our oldest son, will be graduating from college the week after. We are planning one large party to celebrate both at the same time. I saved this task for Rose. I know she likes to shop, and I hate it with a passion. She likes spending time with Elizabeth. Who wouldn't, she is such an easy-going dependable girl.

With everyone else gone, I now find myself alone with my father-in-law, Bernard, a former FBI agent from the Hoover days. His profession was to make judgments and assumptions as to people's character. I am not sure if the job made him that way or if he fit the profile of the job. He retired long ago, but his attitude of supremacy still remains. Rose is old-fashioned and serves him hand and foot. Compared to today's women, I am pretty old school myself, but not enough for him. He has had no problem over the years letting me know where I am lacking. I think my husband Steve is torn between us. I believe he wants to support me, but somehow he always seems to come up short in the support department. My children and husband adore both of them.

It is difficult for them to grasp Bernard's harsh treatment of me. They are part of his click, and when you are included into his arena, he is a warm, kind, giving and loving man. I once was a member, so I know what it feels like to be there. Somewhere along the way, I was removed, and am now considered an outsider by him, unworthy of inclusion, and he regularly disapproves of me.

My father-in-law is sitting on a lawn bed by the pool. He is eighty-two and in great shape for his age. He still does aerobics and push-ups every day. His mind is still sharp, but so is his temper. It is clear that I am his least favorite daughter-in-law. I focus on the water, my breathing and on the warm sun on my skin. It feels so good.

I have gained weight over the past ten years. I believe that many people from his generation see fat as a real weakness of character. Bernard does not approve of fat women, and he tells me often in more ways than one. Here is my favorite: "You will not want to be remembered this way, Catie. You were so beautiful when you were younger. We will wait for you to lose weight before we take your picture."

They have not displayed a photo of me taken in the past ten years. Family photos of all of their sons, daughters-in-law and grandchildren fill the rooms of their home; photos of me are clearly missing. I know they are right, I do need to lose weight, and keep the weight off. It is really hard for me. Every morning I vow to stick to my diet, and most nights I lay in bed feeling like a failure. It is an area of contention for us and I struggle with them because of my own self-image and as a result I have developed an "attitude."

I think it is safe to say this is not the best my relationship with my in-laws has been. I take another slice out of the water with my hands. After tossing and turning all night, I am trying to ease my mounting worry by telling myself it is their visit that is bothering me. The boys will be fine it's only a short day and a half trip.

Now I find myself swimming in the pool with my father-in-law watching me, how did this happen? I am in my bathing suit and once again failed to keep off all the weight I lost last summer. I am not going to let someone else dictate to me what I should look like. It is my house, my pool and my life. I am determined not to be ashamed of myself, or my body. That does not mean I do not feel intimidated, I simply refuse to show it.

I swim over to the steps to get out and find out who is on the phone. I look up as Steve pushes his head against the screen in the kitchen window next to the pool. His voice is low and controlled, not his normal tone at all. Without hearing the words, I know something is wrong. As he is saying the words, I am reaching for the steps and a towel.

I place my hand on the railing as he says, "Catie that was Cam, Bryant's girlfriend, on the phone..."

I place my foot on the first step, as he says,

"She said Ace called her..."

The second step is below my foot, as he says, "Bryant has been hurt..."

I take the third step, as he says, "and was taken to the hospital..."

I wrap the towel around me, as he says,

"Cam said, not to worry he would be O.K. Ace told her not to worry everything was fine."

He pauses then continues, "She only called us because she was shopping with her mother, and her mother told her to call."

I can tell from his voice there is more. I head through the gate and around the patio, running for the kitchen, dripping water across the pine floors of the laundry room and kitchen. I stand there dripping unable to function as I look into my husband's face. I feel my entire body involuntarily shiver. His voice is starting to crack and I can hear the tears he is choking down.

"Catie, I called all of the hospitals in the area around the Gorge. No one has a Bryant Hartsfield listed as a patient or in the emergency room," says Steve.

I am thinking, this is good, this could be a good sign, and maybe it's not that bad. He has been treated and released.

Steve continues, "One of the hospitals with a trauma center has a young man around Bryant's age being airlifted in from the Gorge. He is listed as "male gamma" and they do not know his name. I asked them how he was and she told me she could not tell me his condition; but she did say, we should get there as quickly as possible, it does not look good. She cannot confirm if he is alive, or not."

With that the tears start to fall.

"Catie it has to be him," Steve exclaims, while reaching for his keys. "We need to leave right now!"

"Steve, I have to get dressed, I cannot sit in an emergency room in a dripping wet bathing suit."

"O.K.," he says. "But hurry, or I am leaving without you."

I run up the stairs to our bathroom and start tearing off my suit; putting on a dry shirt and shorts. Without combing my hair, I grab my sandals and am down the stairs within minutes.

Somehow I knew, I just knew... is all I can think of as we run out the door.

Cam is waiting out in the driveway and she jumps into the backseat of the car. How that happened in the three minutes it took me to change I don't know. My head is spinning my emotions are running rampant. I find it hard to talk.

Little do I know I will find it hard to talk for the next year.

This is the phone call, the phone call no parent ever wants to receive. It is the phone call we are all so terrified will come. It is every parent's worst nightmare... my worst nightmare. All of those sleepless nights I spent with teenagers out driving; prom nights, Friday nights. I talk to them, ask to speak to the parents at the homes they are hanging out at, smell them when they come in from a night out with their friends, all of that and regardless my child, my baby is being airlifted to a trauma center. I sit in the car looking down at my hands—my hands that cannot fix this, that cannot help my child. All I can do is sit and wait.

Chapter 2
The Drive

"Courage is not the absence of fear.
It is the strength to overcome it."
– Captain Scheller, USMC

I ask Steve to repeat again what the girl on the phone had told him. It's not much, but I hang onto every word. It has to be Bryant, but what about James? Where is our youngest son, why hasn't he called us? Our children are so close, he wouldn't leave his brother's side. Nothing makes sense to me at this moment.

Holding back my tears, I tell myself I have to remain calm. Steve is driving fast. I have never been in a car going this fast. He has the pedal all the way to the floor as we zip down the interstate. He is driving in the fast lane and bobbing and weaving in and out of the other lanes as needed when someone, well everyone, is going slower than we are. I know if I lose it, Steve will lose it, too. I sit there thinking, *Where are the police? Shouldn't they be escorting us, why haven't they contacted us? Where are the police, shouldn't one have pulled us over by now?* The trauma center is a two-hour drive from our house.

Looking first at my husband and then the speedometer, which is hovering around the 120 mark, I say, "Steve, we cannot be of any help to our son if we end up in the hospital or dead. You must maintain control of the car. Please slow down a little bit, he needs us and we can't be there for him if we're injured as well."

Steve said, "Catie, our son may be dying; you did not hear her voice. She told us to hurry."

He had not said those words to me before. Our son may be dying!

"Steve, Ace had said he was O.K., that he will be all right!"

I am holding on to those words. I look expectantly into the backseat wanting Cam to back me up.

"That's what he told me," she replies.

"Catie, the woman on the phone did not sound as if he is all right. It has to be our son, coming out of the Gorge, and he is the right age. She could not even confirm that he is alive. She told us to hurry; the situation is critical. Our son could be dying, and I am going to get there as fast as I can," said Steve.

I know he is right, we are now out of the worst of the city traffic, and there are not as many cars on this part of the highway.

"Steve, please honk your horn when passing a car, and keep your flashers on so people will know it is an emergency. Can you do that for me?"

"I can do that," he replies, flipping on the flashers.

"What else can we do?"

"Pray Catie, all we can do is pray."

I am a little embarrassed; I did not think of it on my own. I look down at my hands and think: *Yes, I can pray.*

I have been learning how to pray again. I was so good at it when I was younger. Somewhere along the way I stopped praying. I now worry more, and am generally unhappy. I have been praying again, asking God to help my family and me. I even found myself praying this morning when I was looking at the family albums.

I ask God to save my son. I think of possible injuries, broken bones and internal bleeding. Oh my God, what if he is paralyzed?

God I will take him any way You give him to me. He is my baby, my son. I will take him in a wheelchair; I will take him in a bed, any way You give him to me.

I am making promises to God, making a deal.

Please don't take him yet, please let me keep him for a while longer, I plead.

I close my eyes and pray like I never prayed before,

Please dear God, I will dedicate my life to taking care of him, I will quit working, whatever You ask of me. Please do not take him yet. My thoughts go back to the day before when I had last seen the boys, right before the camping trip. The city had just put in a sewer line through one side of our property, the result of a very long battle I had been fighting with them. They won and got their sewer line, but I won as well; they had to allow us to hook into the sewer line. As a result they tore out a swath of trees forty feet wide all along the side of our property bordering a subdivision. The neighbors have been encroaching ever since, even mowing our area to keep it more yard-like. A creek runs through our property dividing our house from theirs and we keep that area wooded for our privacy. With the trees missing it has created some tension. We planted a dozen trees out there this winter and transplanted honeysuckles from the woods, trying to reforest it.

However, when we were out there yesterday morning with the boys, Steve discovered the dozen or so trees and bushes had been poisoned. Assuming it was the closest neighbor Steve went pounding on their door; but the daughter told him her parents were out of town and wouldn't be back until Monday. He took several silver metal shiny disposable pie pans and tied them to the trees and bushes. He wants them to look at the ugly shiny metal pans out of their kitchen window. He is really mad. This is unusual for him. I can't help thinking our last morning together was a little ugly because of all of it happening. I wish we had a do-over on yesterday.

I open my eyes, the scenery is flashing past us, Steve is driving so fast...I close my eyes again and think back to our last Holiday together. The traditions I loved so much will all be changing this year with Paul and Elizabeth both graduating and moving on. We recently spent another Mother's Day planting several new ornamental trees on the other side of the yard. Steve and the kids do that for me each year. Well, maybe not only trees, but a good long day of working in the yard. I always tell them, "I do not want them to spend their money on me, only their time." I cherish these days, all of us working outside together. My mind is searching for good memories, something for me to hold onto right now.

Our other neighbors told me after we had planted all of those new tender ornamental trees, that the Cicadas love to eat new trees. Well, maybe not eat the new trees but slit the bark open on the underside of the tender branches to lay their eggs. The eggs drop to the ground and disappear for another seventeen years.

This makes my mind wander to my baby, my seventeen year old, where is he?

"The Cicadas almost killed all of my new young trees seventeen years ago, I thought you knew that!" said our neighbor. At the time we were all still standing around with shovels and fresh dirt after a long day of planting.

Apparently the ground temperature has to reach seventy degrees before the Cicadas can emerge. We are starting to see the first of them. They are curiously ugly bugs with big fat bodies, clear wings, and red eyes.

I heard horror stories about them flying about and making a mess of everything. Mother Nature always has a plan and a reason for every creature. Cicadas have been around since the Cretaceous Period. Cicadas were found in caves, locked in amber, like in Jurassic Park. They have been making and remaking this circle of life for a very, very long time, surviving where others failed. They fascinate me.

A friend said the Cicadas get so thick that you can spin around and swat them with tennis racquets. They make a contest out of it to see who can swat the most in one spin. It all sounds pretty gruesome to me.

I am not looking forward to it at all. Recently I closed down my decorating store, and moved the business to the front part of our 150 year-old rambling farmhouse. I will not be keeping store hours and am looking forward to working in my yard this spring. I want balance in my life. It has been sorely missed for the past three years.

I drastically underestimated the amount of hours I would need to work to keep the business afloat. The store has taken off but it has not brought in enough money to pay all of the expenses and hire help. Our daughter Liz has worked with me for the past three years, and we have grown close. Paul and Bryant are off at school and they do not miss me much, but James has suffered the most. The past three years have been the hardest on him. James is the reason why I decided to close down the retail part and move the business back into our home. It's almost impossible for me to close the store down at four in the afternoon to attend all of his high school soccer games, and Steve is out of town for most of them. This is a choice I made, he is important to me. It's not as if I am totally shutting down the business, just allowing myself some flexibility.

"Will I be too late? Will I get time with my children, any of them?" My mind races, what wouldn't I give to have those three years back? Just yesterday Bryant and James, were throwing Cicadas in the pond, watching the fish jump up to eat them and now........

I keep my mind focused on the Cicadas. I hear they cannot fly for sometime after emerging out of their dark underground homes. They climb up the nearest tree, fence post, or anything tall, and sit there until they have the ability to fly. I don't know how long it takes, or why they cannot fly right away. I am guessing it has something to do with their wings developing or drying out or something like that. At this stage they are at the mercy of any bird, or young man with spring fever; completely vulnerable.

To emerge from the darkness after all that time with absolutely no way to fend for themselves seems cruel. Their reason for emerging into the light for a short time is to reproduce therefore ensuring future generations and to sing. Once they lay their eggs, it's all over for them.

Death doesn't seem far away right now, but my child hasn't had the chance to reproduce. I plead with God. Let him see the light of another day, let him sing again.

I know they are ugly bugs, but I begged my sons to stop throwing them into the pond for the fish to eat. The boys were laughing at me. They are so young and strong and good-looking. They have so much energy it makes me happy to think about them.

They laughed at me and said, "Oh Mom, you are going to change your mind when you see how many are coming!"

I understand the food chain and know Mother Nature has a plan for them. I know they will aerate the ground and feed lots of birds and fish, but the damage that will come with them is hard for me to reconcile.

I watched as Bryant plucked one off the tree, arching his arm over his head he completed a spin/jump and tossed the Cicada into the water. Landing firmly on the ground with his strong, muscular soccer legs he made it look so easy. The fish immediately jump up to eat the Cicada. It looks as if they will be good fish bait if nothing else.

Thinking of his soccer legs, my mind wanders to school. I was greatly relieved to hear Bryant would be staying in school another year to play soccer. I had concerns about him.

Choking back a sob, I pray once again for my son, pleading with God to keep him alive, to save him.

I don't know how long I keep my eyes closed, but when I open them we are approaching the city limits. I cannot speak. I cannot open my mouth for fear of losing control. All of my thoughts, all of my emotions are caught in my throat. Words are not here for me.

I hear Steve talking on the phone; calling Elizabeth and Paul.

Steve has an incredible sense of direction. If he has been to a location only once in his life, it is forever logged in his memory. He drives directly to the hospital. I look up and the hospital is right in front of us.

Chapter **3**

The Trauma Center

"You do not need to know precisely what is happening, or exactly where it is all going. What you need is to recognize the possibilities and challenges offered by the present moment, and to embrace them with courage, faith and hope."
– Thomas Merton

We pull up to the emergency entrance. Steve stops, and we jump out of the car, leaving it directly in front of the doors. We run into the waiting area filled with people, each one having his own drama. Perhaps it is the way we run in, or the urgency in our tones, but it feels as if all eyes are trained on us.

I am steps behind Steve. We run up to the desk, with Cam following right behind us.

"I called," Steve said with an authoritative tone to his voice. "I was told that you were expecting a young man in his twenties being airlifted from the Gorge. We believe he is our son."

"One moment," she says, turning away from us. She picks up the phone, talking softly into the receiver.

Within seconds a door opens, and a doctor ushers us inside to the emergency treatment room. I look back around the room; all of these people waiting here for who knows how long, and we are being taken back within seconds. I have never been to an emergency room where you do not wait for hours to be seen. I observe the sympathetic eyes of the other people watching us as we are escorted back immediately.

This cannot be good, I say to myself, and I feel as if their eyes are confirming my worst fears.

The doctor stops outside of a small conference room. He

explains to us that he would like to go over some things with us about our son before he lets us see him. He motions for us to sit down.

Walking into the area, I realize that probably all emergency rooms have special conference rooms in them, never noticing them before. How many other families sat in these rooms to receive bad news? How many other parents have been escorted into the back by a physician wanting to explain the special circumstances surrounding their child before allowing them access? How much pain has been delivered in this unnoticed space?

All I want is to see my son, if it is my son. I do not want to sit and talk. An eerie calm is starting to come over me. Steve seems to feel the same way as we both remain standing, unwilling to sit.

The doctor takes a seat. He looks at us, "Please sit down, we are running tests on your son. I would like to explain some things to you before you see him." So we sit, anything to move forward. Clearly he is not going to budge until we sit and listen.

I am still in denial, things like this do not happen to our family. We have four beautiful children, all healthy and strong. The words "running tests" gives me comfort. If they are running tests, he is alive! No one else is questioning if he is our son, why aren't they questioning it? Everyone knows our son had an accident, and he is within the right age, sex and ethnicity. It is beginning to sink in that it really is my son in there. I sit down in the chair feeling myself deflating as I sit. I don't think I've really believed it this whole time. Everyone else is so sure, but they could be wrong!

I look at the man sitting across from us, he is good-looking, kind, and seems to genuinely care. The concerned, serious look on his face as he explains the situation to us does little to comfort me.

"Your son was airlifted out of the Gorge. I need to explain we are a trauma center, and we deal with a lot of injuries…"

He stops for a moment to let us digest this information.

"The park ranger told the medics that he is familiar with the area, from which your son fell, and to his best estimate, your son fell a minimum of 150 feet off a cliff!"

He pauses again to let this sink in....

"We have never had anyone survive a fall like that," he says.

I am not comprehending what he is saying, it is not sinking in. Did he survive? I want answers. I want to see my son. I want him to shut up and give me access to my child. I am sitting on the edge of my seat, my hands grip the wooden arms of the chair.

I look up into his face and he has a look of awe on his face, and a hint of excitement seems to be edging into his eyes.

I hear him and yet my mind is unable to wrap around what is taking place. I hear once again the words he is speaking, but I am still not buying it's my child. Holding on to hope everyone is wrong.

"We x-rayed every part of his body at least once, if not several times."

I watch his face closely, his mouth turns up at the edges in a half smile and he chuckles in amazement, shaking his head for affect.

"Every bone in his body should be broken! We don't understand it. The absolute amazing part is we have not been able to find any broken bones. We did find a small fracture on a vertebra in his neck. He has a small puncture wound behind his right ear."

All I can hear is, his neck is broken. I can see his mouth moving and Steve is talking to him. I am thinking *"O.K. God, I told You I would take him any way You gave him to me. I can handle this."*

Then the doctor continues, "The broken vertebra is nothing really, we put a collar on his neck and with time it will heal. We are checking his internal organs, and they should be a mess, but so far we have not been able to locate any real damage. I am sure they are bruised and may bleed a little but the real trauma is to his head. I have been doing this for a long time and I am telling you I seldom see a head with as much brain damage as he has suffered."

This is too much information, why is he telling us all of this? I just want to see my son. I am thinking *brain damage, what is brain damage? Is it a concussion*?

I did not even pray about his brain; it did not enter my mind! I know nothing about brain damage. What an ugly word. Can't he say brain injury? I think he used the words traumatic brain damage.

This will be my introduction to the world of TBI, Traumatic Brain Injury as it is now called. At least this wording gives you hope. The ugly word *damage* leaves no hope of recovery.

You do not know my son. He will be up and out of here before long, I think.

I am in denial. Looking at the doctor, I cannot find my words. I am speechless. I am numb. I can feel the chair under my legs and my hands are on the armrest, but I don't really seem to be here.

He continues talking, "You need to understand your son may be a vegetable for the rest of his life. He may never come out of this."

He keeps looking at us for a reaction.

"His entire brain is damaged, and I believe he is paralyzed on his left side."

Steve and I exchange looks. These words are clear to me. There are moments in the life of a parent, words you will never forget. Neither Steve nor I will ever forget these words. Finally he has said something that penetrates the shock.

I am eerily calm as I look at him, as his words bounce off me. I finally find my voice.

"I just want to see my son. Can I see him?" I ask.

"Yes, you can. I will take you to him. If everyone will follow me," he says as he stands up.

Walking behind him I ask the words, the only words I care about right now, "Will he live?"

He turns around and looks directly at us, "I can't say. I simply don't know."

We follow him past several curtained-off areas. I feel like the sheep going to the slaughter. Just ahead, lying on a portable gurney, is our son Bryant. My heart lurches in my chest.

"Bryant, Bryant," his name spilling from my lips. I run the last few steps.

I run to his head. He has a blue and white collar around his neck and he is strapped down to the gurney, motionless. He is on life support with a ventilator tube going down his throat. I can see the rhythmic rising and falling of his chest as the air is forced into his lungs.

I see his blondish/brown hair and walk over to his left side. I look into his eye and do not see any movement or recognition. I walk around his head touching his hair and look into his right eye. He knows me! I see the recognition! I instinctively grab his hand, and his fingers tighten around mine. I bend over telling him how much I love him. I look into his one beautiful green eye and slowly, one tear and then another, falls from his eye.

A man walks into the room interrupting our moment. He picks up Bryant's left foot.

"We believe he is paralyzed on the left side. It is hard to know for sure, we cannot communicate with him."

He takes out a sharp object and sticks it into Bryant's foot, no reaction; he then moves it around his foot looking for reflexes. He continues up his body on his left side with no reactions. He then repeats the same movement on the right side and is able to get reactions consistently.

He is all business; not unkind, simply factual. He then leaves the room again.

Steve is standing beside me, moving around to the other side of Bryant. I watch as he encircles him, calling out his name.

I can hear Steve saying, "Bryant you are going to be O.K., you are a soccer player, you are tough you are going to pull through this."

His voice is very loud, as if saying it loudly will get our son motivated to get up and get well. I can hear the panic in his voice but I am unable to help him. He says it over and over again. Each time he says it with more force, and louder and louder.

I am having a moment with our son. I watch his fingers wrapped around my hand like he did when he was a newborn. I am thinking how much larger his hand is, yet how familiar. When was the last time he had held my hand? I continue to look into his eye he knows who I am. All I can think of is that he waited for me. I know I am being selfish but I do not let Steve have this side of him. I do not move. I watch the tears and tell him how much I love him over and over. *He waited for me, he is afraid and he wants his mother.*

"I love you Bryant. mom is here, it is going to be O.K.," I say.

My left hand is gently stroking his hair and his forehead. He then closes his eye and drifts off to sleep.

Steve runs to the top of his head and starts yelling,

"Wake up Bryant, come on Bryant, wake up! Wake up Bryant, don't go to sleep! Wake up Bryant! You are tough, you are a soccer player, you can beat this! Come on Bryant, wake up!"

Steve is using an old sports coaching method. He thinks he can bully him into being stronger and waking up.

No longer having his eye to focus on, I start telling him to wake up as well. Maybe Steve is right, this method of tough coaching has worked in the past.

"Please Bryant, wake up! Wake up, Bryant! Come on Bryant wake up, your tougher than this! Come on Bryant wake up," I yell.

They come over and shut the drapes around us. I am sure we are bothering the other patients with our yelling but we need our son to wake up.

It is suggested that perhaps we will be more comfortable waiting in the family waiting room. They must be referring to the room we were in before.

"Other family members are arriving and are waiting in there for you. Bryant will not be waking up for a while, he is in a coma," says the doctor.

The word "coma" rocks my world. Coma? I thought he fell asleep, comforted by his mother. I can feel myself becoming calmer and calmer. I can feel my world getting smaller and smaller. I am retreating into myself. This is how I operate. I am always very calm during times of stress. I can have my breakdown later. I say in a very calm, low voice

"You are saying he is in a coma?"

"Yes," he replies.

"Will he wake up from this coma?"

"We don't know. Given his massive brain damage I would say

the chances are not good. Your son could be a vegetable for the rest of his life, if he lives. He may have some limited abilities. With brain damage you simply don't know. He is young and healthy and strong, these are all good positive things, but if you have seen one brain damaged victim you have seen one damaged brain, they all respond differently."

"He is holding my hand, he knows I am here," I argue.

"No, I don't think he does. He is not holding your hand it is just instinct. It's a reflex," he states matter-of-factly.

I don't believe it. He is holding my hand! My world grows even smaller in that instant. I am holding onto him, and I believe he is holding onto me. I tell myself, *I am not able to help anyone else. I cannot help Steve, or any of our other three children. I do not have it in me. For this child to make it, I will need to give him everything I have. This child is in grave danger and I need to focus on what is best for him. I need to be calm for my son, and calm for me.* Instinct is beginning to take over.

"We will be quiet," I tell the doctor. "Please let me stay by my son's side. I do not want to leave him."

He looks at me as if measuring my ability to maintain my control.

"You can stay," he agrees. "I can't let you disrupt the other patients. Maybe one of you can go and speak to the other family members in the family waiting room."

"What about my other son," I ask. "Where is he?"

"I don't know anything about another son," he replies. "He was found by a group of hiking boy scouts. They called the ranger. I did not hear anything about another son."

"His brother and a friend were with him," I tell him. "Someone must know something about them!"

He disappears behind the curtain, leaving Steve and me alone with our son.

"James would not leave Bryant," I tell Steve. "I know that! If boy scouts found him, then where is James? You need to find James do you understand me? I need to know he is safe. I am hanging on to one child, I cannot lose another!"

My mind is racing. *If James had been with Bryant then why didn't they know Bryant's name? Why had they not found him as well? Oh my God, is he out there in the canyon injured and dying? Is he dead?*

My panic that morning had been for both of them. I am worried, James is not the type to not be there for his brother.

To take my mind off James, I survey the curtained off room for the first time, now that our "coaching session" has abated. Bryant lies on a gurney, naked except for a hospital gown. His legs stick out from under the gown and his toes are uncovered. His clothes are thrown in a heap on the floor, evidence of the trauma that has taken place in this room. Steve picks up his shorts and holds them close. I walk over by him. Bryant's khaki shorts and shirt are cut in two. Scissors sliced them off in an effort to save his life. A blue bandana lies there with his clothes. Picking up his shirt, and holding it to our noses we take a whiff. The remnants of vomit, sweat, dirt, and our child all mixed together. In times of tragedy, the smell of your child becomes very important.

Standing there we are as confident as we can be he will live. It does not matter to us what his capacity will be, we only want him to live. It does not occur to me this may be a selfish choice.

Steve looks at me. "I guess we can't save his clothes can we?"

I look down at the cut up pieces, "I guess it would not do much good."

Choking back the sobs threatening to surface I say, "What if he doesn't make it? I would want to be able to still smell him."

The thought of never being able to smell my child again is heart-wrenching.

Steve wraps his arms around me and I lay my head on his chest for the first time since our trauma has started. It feels good; I can hear his heart beating under his shirt, calming, and soothing me.

Pulling back from his chest I looked up at him. He reaches down and picks up the bandana, "How about if I take this, his shoes and his belt?"

I smile at him, "I didn't know Bryant wore bandanas."

We agree to leave the other clothes on the floor. It is good to have a moment alone with Steve.

"Catie, the doctor mentioned other family members have arrived, I think I am going to go see who is here."

"Check and see if you can find out where James is. I am really worried about him," I reply. "I don't care what they say about the boy scouts, I know James had something to do with his rescue, or he is hurt as well. Find him for me! I am going to stay here with Bryant."

I watch as Steve disappears behind the draperies.

My child and I are finally alone in this cloth-wrapped hospital room. I do exactly the same thing I did when we were first alone together after his birth; I examine his body to make sure everything is there. All his fingers and toes need to be counted and examined. We didn't live near family and moved every eighteen to twenty-four months, I never had friends or family surrounding me at the births of our four children. Steve was always there for the birth, but could only visit for a couple hours a day because he was watching our other children. I spent those first hours alone with my babies, exploring the uniqueness and similarities of each of them and bonding with them.

I have not been able to examine him physically like this since he was a young child. He is a twenty-one year old man, and I am careful not to lift the folded sheet placed over his groin area. I understand he still needs to be given the respect any young man deserves. He is lying there quietly "sleeping," the ventilator breathing for him; making the only movement. I start at his bruised and swollen toes and work my way up one side of him and down the other.

It is strange; his body is in unbelievably good shape for having survived a fall of that magnitude. He is still dirty with mud and dirt covering his body and hair. They have inserted an IV in his arm, a collar on his neck and a ventilator down his throat; otherwise he looks... like Bryant. Except for his hands, the skin is ripped off his hands and fingers, evidence he had tried to grab hold of anything and everything to stop his fall, proof he knew he was going down!

His hands are swollen and skinned. I look down at these hands and think about the emotions of my son as he tried to prevent his fall. Grabbing, clutching as he flew by rocks and trees.

I replay the grabbing and clutching scene in my mind once again, the falling nightmare of Bryant. What had been a nightmare for me a few weeks earlier has become a reality for him. The thought of this causes a shiver to run through my body. His fingers are covered with dirt; the dirt is embedded under his fingernails. Was the dirt on the way down, or did he find it at the bottom as he lie amidst the dirt and rock?

He has several puncture wounds on his wrist and arms. It looks as if IVs were placed here at some point, a stick made in the field by a medic or a "field stick." It is hard to know for sure as he is still covered in patches of dirt, blood and vomit. As I continue to move upwards on his body, I see a large patch of skin has come off his shoulder, and it looks like it might continue down his back. I cannot move him to know for sure. He has patches of skin off here and there. His right eye looks a little swollen and bruised.

I reach for Bryant's hand. Instinctively, he wraps his fingers around my hand. It is amazing, except for these injuries and the collar around his neck, he looks as if he is going to sit up and ask to go home at any moment. I am doing my best not to focus on the ventilator going up and down.

Standing beside his right ear, the one with the impact wound, I bend down to examine it closer. Just behind his ear is a small cut that has been stitched up. Some residual blood is still on his ear. I watch as a clear fluid leaks out of his ear; a slow but steady drip. I focus on that fluid, and continue to hold my son's hand. His fingers curl around mine.

Finding my voice, I bend over and talk to him, "Hang in there Bryant, we are here for you. We can get through this. We have faced tough times together before, we will get through this too. I love you Bryant, and Dad loves you, too."

When I was a child, my grandmother had "laid hands on me" once when I had the flu. She prayed over me, put her hands on me, and I immediately threw up, fell back asleep, and woke up feeling fine.

Our first son, Paul in his early years had a tendency to run really high fevers, I discovered the heart power with him. I discovered I could allow my heart to open up, and I would feel a heat come down my arms and into my hands. My hands would become really warm, and I would then place them on him. Of course, I always used traditional medicine as well. It somehow made me feel I was doing something to help. I imagined I was giving some of my energy to him to help him grow stronger.

When our babies were sick, I would hold them to my chest and let the energy flow. I open this energy up and feel the heat moving down my arm and into my hand, flowing into his body, an unseen umbilical cord sending life energy to him. I hold my other hand over his abdomen and feel the energy move out of my body and into his. It is all I can do for him. That, and pray. Maybe it's silly, but I look around to see if anyone is watching me, but it is all I can do. I have nothing else to give. I would gladly change places with him, if only I could.

They come in again, a quiet soft-spoken man, this time. He says, "We need to do some additional x-rays on Bryant, they will be coming in soon to take him."

"Can I go with him," I ask.

It is explained to me that I can go back with him, but I cannot go into the x-ray room. I will need to wait outside of the actual room. When I argue, I am told that no human being should be exposed to as much radiation as he has received today unless it is completely necessary.

I am grateful to be allowed to at least go back with him. He really is being as kind as possible given the dire situation. He has a lot to handle, given the vulnerability of our emotions and the dangerous precipice on which Bryant's life is balancing. I will forever be grateful for the training and abilities the staff of the ER exhibited. I am sure they are responsible for keeping him alive up to this point.

He must be a father, I think, *he knows these precious seconds are important to me and that my son may be leaving this earth at any moment.*

"All right, I can do that," I reply. "Can you answer something for me? What is this clear fluid leaking out of his ear?"

He becomes excited.

"Which ear are you talking about?"

"The right one, with the cut behind the ear."

Grabbing a Q-tip he runs over to the side I indicated. He swabs the fluid.

"Do you see this bone right here, the one with the wound, we hardly ever see it injured. This is the hardest bone in the body to damage. He hit his head really hard on a sharp point to create this injury. I am guessing this is spinal fluid leaking out of his ear. We were wondering how he survived all night with his brain swelling. When he hit his head on that rock, he drilled a hole in just the right spot to allow spinal fluid to leak out of his ear. It is as if a physician drilled a bur hole. This impact wound probably saved his life."

It has felt like an eternity to me since the phone call, but really Bryant has only been here a short time, given the time the airlift took. I am assuming they have not had a lot of one-on-one time with him, given all of the testing since his arrival. It appears to me they are clearly in awe of his survival.

I am speechless. This is the first I hear that my son had been injured and had to survive the night! My head is reeling with questions. He had not made it to the trauma center until around three in the afternoon. What happened the night before, and where is James with the answers?

He continues, "He also had a collapsed lung, which we had to re-inflate."

"I want to show you this, it confirms what we had suspected earlier. This is just amazing. He cut or dissected his carotid artery when he fell. Do you see this dark area here, pointing to a blob that I cannot make out on a recent image?"

"This is where he bled into his brain. He suffered a stroke, not unlike an older person who has a stroke or an aneurism. We suspected as much, but this proves it. It explains the paralysis."

The curtains part and someone comes in to take Bryant back for an x-ray. He gathers all of the equipment and starts to push the gurney out of the curtained area. I hold onto Bryant's hand.

"You will need to stay here, we will be right back," he says.

I look up at him, unwilling to release my son's hand. "I was told, I can go with him. Not into the room, but I can go back with him and wait outside of the room."

He looks over at the soft-spoken man for permission.

"Yes," he said. "We told her she can go back with him. This is his mother and she may not have much time left with him."

They continue to grant me precious moments with my child.

He shrugs his shoulders as if to say, you are the boss, not the way I would do it. He pushes the gurney carrying my son through the open curtain and into the middle of the sterile tiled, and fabric-encased hallway. As we walk down the center aisle, some of the rooms have their curtains closed, but many of them are open. Holding my son's hand and walking next to him I realize everyone here knows about our situation. The only privacy is the thin curtain; nothing is really private in this world. I can see their sympathetic eyes as we walk through to the double metal stainless steel doors at the end.

We exit through the doors, parking the gurney next to yet another door. We are now in an actual hallway.

"The room is occupied right now," the aide says. "Wait here, I will be right back."

Leaning over his body and looking down at him, he appears to be sleeping. I thought a coma would look different, somehow. His hand is still tightly wrapped around mine. I can hear the rhythmic sound of the ventilator as it pushes air into his lungs and then releases it. The doctor's words are sinking in.

"I may not have much time with you," I say softly. "Bryant, oh Bryant, what happened last night? How did you survive through the night, how did you get rescued, where is your brother? You beat the odds; you can't give up now. Hang in there Bryant, I am here for you, I love you."

No response, not even a twitch.

The doors open and they wheel out a young man who is thrashing around on his gurney. He is mumbling, ranting and is clearly not in his right mind. *And so young*, I think. What happened to him? His gown gets tangled with the thrashing, making him almost completely naked. The aide glares at me as she covers him up, and tells me that I should not be back here. It is not fair to the other patients. I look down at my son and ignore her. It would take a lot more than an embarrassing moment to get me to leave my sons' side.

They push Bryant's cart toward the door.

"You are to stay out here. We will be done in five to ten minutes."

I realize that I must let go of his hand. I can feel his hand gripping mine in a steady but strong grip. His hand slips out of mine and I lose my connection with him!

"What if he dies in there? What if he is still not alive in five to ten minutes?"

My voice is panicked, but then I remember to keep control.

"I don't care how much radiation you give me, let me have ten more minutes with my son, please."

They look at me with sympathy, "I am sorry that is simply not possible. It is against regulations. I am surprised that they let you come this far. Wait right here and we will be out with him in a few minutes."

I lean back against the cold block wall outside of the x-ray room. It offers support for my sagging body. I feel so alone and out of control. I hear them working away in the room, their words are muffled and not clear. I know I should be grateful for these extra minutes with him. Steve is not getting these extra minutes, I reason with myself. I will stay calm, it is the only way they will grant me these minutes here and there. Special privileges are not granted to those who make a scene.

I know I should share these moments. I have always been a good sharer; my whole life I shared with anyone who I thought was in need. My mother has always accused me of being too tender hearted, I am taken advantage of all the time. She has told me to toughen up.

I make my first decision. I cannot, no, I *will* not share these moments; they are too special. I am going to be by his side as much as is humanly possible. I need to be by his side, and he needs me here. I am not going anywhere. Other people can come and go, but I am not. I am going to hold his hand until he either gets better or dies. I am going to be nice, behave, not yell, and stay in control. I am going to win every second with my son that I can. It may be selfish, but I am going to fill my need. I am his mother and that is that. He needs me and I need him.

Finding a little control in an out-of-control event, I drop my head and pray.

"God I asked You to keep him alive and I would take him anyway You gave him to me. Here I am God. Thank You for keeping him alive. I will dedicate my life to his care if that is what You require. If this is a test of my courage and my strength God, please let me pass this test."

The door opens and they wheel him out. My eyes go immediately to the ventilator; I can see it going up and down.

"O.K., we made it through those ten minutes. Let's see how many more we have."

I reach for Bryant's hand. It is warm and it immediately wraps around mine. We walk back to his curtained room. They spend some time reorganizing the equipment. There are so many tubes and lines connected to my son. I stand holding his hand, another type of line, waiting for a moment alone with him. I look down at his eyes and he still appears to be sleeping; no recognition. I am confused; can people in a coma hold your hand?

They come over to Bryant after they get all of his lines organized. Loudly yelling at him, "Bryant, Bryant can you hear me?

Bryant, Bryant can you open your eyes for me? Bryant do you hear me? If you can hear me, lift one of your fingers up? Can you lift up one of your fingers Bryant?"

No response. He is still "sleeping."

Needing to quiet my mind I decide to hold my son's hand and send as much energy as I can. I feel my hand warming as I concentrate completely on my son and my heart. I do not notice what is going on around me.

I have never been the kind of person who likes to draw attention to myself. In fact I always liked to go unnoticed. It's an attribute left over from my childhood. Although my mother was a sweet woman when not drinking, I had learned at a young age to judge within thirty seconds of walking into a room if I wanted to be noticed or not. It was safer to go unnoticed. I liked to think of myself as blending into the wall. This does not seem to be a blending into the wall kind of thing to do.

Steve comes into the room, breaking my concentration, and holds Bryant's other hand. Suddenly he is talking to the doctor and our oldest son, Paul, who is there with his girlfriend Leigh. I look at him and know he must be in as much shock and pain as the rest of us. I am so glad Leigh is here for him. I know my other children need my love and support, but I don't have anything else to give right now. I feel myself closing down. My world is getting smaller and smaller.

Steve is talking to them, I hear him ask Paul to find James. I hear Paul say, "How am I supposed to find James?"

"You need to find him; he could be hurt out there as well. Your mom is worried about him and I need you to do this for me," said Steve.

"You have no idea how big that place is. It is going to be dark by the time I get there. Come on Dad, what do you want me to do?"

Steve thinks it through. Paul is right, going off on a wild goose chase is not a sound plan.

"The ranger told the medics boy scouts found your brother. I want you to call the ranger station, call the state police. I don't care how you do it but find your brother!"

It was not so much a request as it was an order.

"O.K., O.K. I will see what I can do," said Paul.

It is a tall order, but if anyone is competent enough to locate his brother, it is Paul. He is far more capable than he realizes. He has a strength and ability about him that few people his age exhibit, a natural born leader.

Listening to the conversation, I realize this is not a fair thing to put on his shoulders, however I am not capable of arguing. Maybe I am in shock, because I cannot intervene. All I am capable of is holding my other son's hand. None of this feels like reality.

Paul and Bryant have always been close. They are only eighteen months apart and are always hanging out together. I realize there have been arguments lately, something they never really did before. I attribute it to growing up. It is unusual that they are not together. This must be really hard on Paul.

"When did Paul get here?" I ask.

"Everyone is here in the family waiting room," answers Steve.

"Who is everyone?"

"Paul, Leigh, Mom, Dad and Elizabeth."

"How did they all get here so fast, it seems like we just got here ourselves?"

"I called them all when we were on our way here; they were right behind us."

Steve looks at me, "Don't you remember?"

"I guess so, I didn't think about it."

I tell Steve all about the carotid artery, the burr hole, the spinal fluid leaking out of Bryant's ear, and about the person letting me go back to x-ray, because he said we may not have much time left.

We both look down at our son and talk softly to him; holding his hand, simply being with him for the moment is a good thing.

Paul pops back in and says, "I spoke with the ranger's station and they say James was with Bryant. He's not hurt, he's fine."

Looking at me, Paul states matter-of-factly, "Mom, Bryant is going to be O.K. He's tough, he will be fine." As if he has had a little bump and will be well in no time at all.

I look at him, does he really believe that, or does he not understand the situation? I decide not to voice that question quite yet.

"You really found that out fast, how did you do it?" I ask.

"It wasn't really hard, I just called information and then the ranger's station."

"If James was with him, then why didn't he come in the helicopter with his brother?"

I am sure the information is wrong. It doesn't make sense.

"I don't know. All I know is that James was with Bryant earlier today. I'll try to call him and Ace."

Paul is able to take what seems like an impossible job and break it down with strategy and thought process. These are his strengths. He is not one to be emotional about too many things. He is matter-of-fact about everything.

"I know they say the boy scouts found him, but that confirms James was with him today. We need to remember we have two injured family members. James will be as injured as Bryant, only in a different way."

With that Paul backs out to the family waiting room, he hates it when I get philosophical. He is a great kid. He is a really good student, so smart. I don't think we really ever understood how smart he was. He was the first child of four, in five and a half years. He always had to mind me and I was a tough disciplinarian. I didn't have time to mess around. Steve had traveled a lot and when he was in town he worked long hours. Most nights they were in bed or going when Steve got home. His time at home was so short he wanted to be the "fun" parent, leaving all of the discipline to me.

Paul is clearly angry with us, and especially with me. High school had been tough years for our relationship. We fought constantly. He was grounded often in high school. What he did not understand, and maybe he will when he is a parent, is when you ground your children you also ground yourself. All of the time he had been grounded so had I. I could not leave the house either. I loved him so much, so much in fact that I thought he was worth the fight. It would have been so much easier to have given up on him and walked away. Just to have said "whatever." I was not that kind of person. I knew he was worth the trouble, I don't think he realized that...one day he will.

Steve moves back and forth from the waiting room and Bryant's room, letting others trade with him. I don't share with anyone. I need to be by Bryant's side. I am not leaving until he wakes up. I am so focused on sending energy that people come and go without me really paying attention.

The staff comes in every thirty minutes or so and attempts to wake up Bryant, he does not respond. No finger movements, no opening of his eyes. The lab confirms it is indeed spinal fluid, so the wound had allowed the fluid to leak out his ear. The nurse puts his head on a pillow to help facilitate the leaking fluid. They explain to me that you always want to keep a neck injury lying flat, but the spinal fluid leak takes precedent over the neck injury. It is important it be allowed to continue to leak out. Do not worry, they tell me, the body produces more fluid; he will not run out.

It's funny but that was the last thing on my mind. I wonder if the spinal fluid is like amniotic fluid. My daughter Elizabeth was born thirty hours after my water broke. They had told me not to worry the body continues to make amniotic fluid. There was really nothing to worry about there was no such thing as a dry birth. Is that only folklore? It all hurt like hell anyway. In this case I guess it is a good thing. We do not want his brain to hit his skull. If my high school biology memory is correct the spinal fluid encompasses the brain and cushions it, preventing it from hitting the inside of the skull.

The minutes turn into hours, and all I can think of is keeping my son alive one minute at a time.

Chapter **4**

Elizabeth

"What lies behind us and what lies before us are tiny matters compared to what lies within us."
– Ralph Waldo Emerson

Elizabeth wrote this essay down later, for an English class that wanted a descriptive essay. I had never thought about her reaction until I read it. I was amazed at her viewpoint, as compared to mine, and I am including her essay here, exactly as it was written, because I think it adds a good perspective:

Elizabeth's Essay:

Excitement pumps through my veins as I stop to think that I have exactly five days left of high school until I graduate. I am ready to be free from the jail of my high school and ready to start an exciting life out in sunny California. My overprotective parents aren't happy about their only daughter of four kids leaving home to live in California, where according to them, everyone is crazy or on drugs. Although I am anxious to get the summer started, I am not looking forward to the summer of the Cicadas, big black beetles with huge bulging red eyes. In our mid-western city, billions of Cicadas come out for six weeks every seventeen years and have no purpose in life except to crawl out of the thick soil and annoy people with their deafening mating songs. Of course, the Cicadas just so happened to come out of the ground exactly one week before my graduation and Paul's, my older brother's college graduation. It is starting to look like our outdoor graduation party is not going to happen. My summer seems to be starting out bad and it hasn't even officially started.

    My family is full of loud, sarcastic, perverted, and smelly but lovable boys. My mom is constantly cooking and endlessly cleaning up after my three brothers and my dad. My little brother James, who towers over all of us at the height of six feet, is a seventeen-year old eating machine whose sole purpose is to impress his two older brothers, Paul and Bryant. James is no genius, he struggles to pass his classes but he is a smooth talker and is able to woo his teachers with smiles and charm. My brother Bryant is twenty-one and is the sweetest brother out of all of them. However, he is also the most protective of me, his baby sister. When he brings friends over to the house, he makes sure they know not to even look in my direction. This protectiveness has made it really hard for me to date. Almost identical in looks to Bryant is my oldest brother Paul, who is twenty-two. Paul is graduating from the local university with his degree in accounting the same week I graduate from high school. He is unbelievably smart but trouble seems to always find its way to his doorstep. He is definitely the rebel child and is the only kid in the family that has the guts to challenge our drill sergeant, mom. My conservative parents are strict as can be, but they love us to death and would do anything for us.

    As my graduation is less than a week away, my crazy grandparents from Florida come in to help my mom prepare for the two graduation parties we are throwing. My Grandma Rose is seventy-five but has the spunk and energy of a young schoolgirl. She drags my eighty-two year old Grandpa Bernard, to aerobics every morning and feeds him a plethora of vitamins twice a day, every day.

    I desperately need to find a white dress, which is mandatory to wear underneath our white graduation gowns. I decide to go to the mall and take my Grandma Rose with me. After what seems like days of endless searching, but it's really only hours, we decide to just buy a white skirt and shirt instead because it seems that every white dress in the whole state is sold out. It takes us another ten exhausting minutes to find a white skirt that might work. As I begin to try it on in the dressing room, my cell phone starts ringing continuously. I am a little embarrassed because I am changing, and it just keeps ringing but finally I am able to dig through my purse and find my phone. I answer a little breathless and realize right away it is my dad. After a few seconds, I can easily sense that something is terribly wrong.

"Liz, listen to me carefully, Bryant had an accident while camping and he has been airlifted to the hospital. You need to get Grandma and come home immediately."

My dad tells me through held back tears. I am momentarily paralyzed and then I walk out of the dressing room and stand there in a daze. I feel as though I have stood like this for an hour, but it is probably only a minute. Finally, I snap out of it and go to find my Grandma. I take her by the arm and tell her Bryant has had an accident and that we have to leave the mall immediately. She seems childlike and confused. I can see her eyes start to fill with tears as she imagines the worst possible about her second grandson. It takes us a good five minutes to walk out to the car as calmly as we can. As I start to drive home, my mind is racing. I am retracing the events of this weekend over and over in my head. I remember that James, Bryant and Ace are camping for the weekend at the Gorge, a popular spot for camping and partying. I have never been there, but I know it is a big wooded area that is very secluded and filled with cliffs. I start to imagine the worse, but I am hoping for the best. I start to convince myself that Bryant just broke a leg or two and that he will be perfectly fine.

We finally arrive home but my parents are not there. I call their cell phones but, of course, my mom's cell phone is off. She never has it turned on or with her. Irritatingly the thought crosses my mind that they shouldn't even pay for phones if they aren't going to answer them. I go into the kitchen and see a note sitting on the counter from my dad. The note that he left is just a list of directions to the hospital. I figure that it will only be a thirty-minute drive or so. To my surprise it takes us two hours to arrive at the hospital. It is a really long drive without any information. I am thinking that I might have an anxiety attack because I have no idea what is going on and nobody seems to have any information to give me. I call my brother Paul, but he doesn't know anymore than I.

It has taken a frustrating ten minutes to find a spot to park at the hospital and then I frantically run into the emergency room. As soon as I step into the freezing cold reception room, I immediately see one of Bryant's friends, Mike, who tells me to go into a nearby room and I will find my parents. I am overcome by confusion. With my grandparents in tow we walk to the room as I scan the room and all the people in it. Inside the room are my teary-eyed father and my brother's frantic girlfriend. I don't even notice the doctor standing behind the door and as I shut it, he startles me. I offer my hand and my name and am expecting in return an explanation of some kind. Instead I am just stared at blankly by my dad and then led to another room.

My father takes me down the hall and tells me he is going to take me to see Bryant and to brace myself because he looks really bad. I walk down the endless white rectangle halls that have bare walls and cheap tile that makes a clanking noise as I shuffle my shoes on it. Following my dad I am then brought into a room that is filled with bodies hooked up to machines and the only thing that separates the bodies is thin jadite green sheets hanging from what looks like shower curtain rings to me. I have spent two years working at my mom's drapery store and I am trained to look at draperies, fabrics and accessories. I am amazed that this is what I focus on as I walk behind my dad, something familiar in an unfamiliar world.

I scan the room but do not see my brother and am relieved because I thought maybe he wasn't in this depressing room. The smell of antibiotics and rubber waft through the air and starts to make me nauseous as countless nurses in scrubs shuffle around the room yelling out orders to one another. We walk through another curtained off room and as the curtain is pulled back it reveals a horrifying image that will stick with me I am sure the rest of my life. There is no way that I am prepared for what I see in that hospital room at that moment. I take a sharp breath in, and my hand instinctively covers my mouth.

My mom urges me forward and tells me to say something to him, to talk to him, but I just stare and am unable to speak. My brother's naked body is totally unrecognizable to me except for the small patch of skin on his left breast that has the tattoo of a puma that he had just recently gotten. I scan his battered and bloody body several times trying to take it all in. He has endless tubes all over his body; an IV in his arm, a breathing tube down his throat, and various tubes up his nose. A blue and white neck brace encircles his neck. At this point he had not been cleaned off yet; so, he was covered from head to toe in dry mud and blood. He does not have any skin on his right shoulder and dirt and dried blood are still encrusted in his wound. He has an unshaven face with dried puke and blood still in his hair. His hands are all swollen and torn to shreds as if he was clawing at something and his toes are all broken and black and blue. After I take in his appearance, I realize that he is not conscious or moving at all.

My mom tells me that Bryant was airlifted to the hospital from the Gorge earlier this afternoon. They are unsure how the accident happened, but they were told that he fell off a cliff in the middle of the night sometime and was not found until later the next morning. It isn't until that moment that I realize that my little brother, James, is not in the room. I ask where he is. A worried look crosses over my mother's face as she explains she is unaware of where my 'little' brother is. They have not heard anything from him, and my mom is terrified that he is somewhere hurt as well.

It was not until ten in the evening that my little brother arrives at the hospital. Five hours after I had gotten there, six hours since my parents had been there. I am standing outside getting a breath of fresh air when I see Bryant's red Jetta pull up with Ace and James, looking like they just got off a battlefield. The boys are sweaty, dirty, and covered in puke and blood, which I assumed from the look of Bryant, was not theirs. The first thing they ask for is water and clean pairs of socks. I do what I can to find them some food and water from a gas station and give my little brother the socks I am wearing. They are not in a hurry to get inside and see our parents. I then take James and Ace upstairs to where our parents are.

Chapter **5**
James Returns

"You never really know someone
until you've stood in their shoes
and walked around in them."
– Scout in *To Kill A Mockingbird*

It is around ten that night when James and Ace finally walk into the drapery-covered ER room. When I look up, they are standing there, looking like they have been through hell and back.

Looking over at my youngest son, I feel a mixture of emotions. I am overwhelmed with joy that he is walking and uninjured, but then, where has he been? Why has it taken him so long to get here? Why hasn't he contacted us? I have so many questions. I want to throw my arms around James; however, to do that I would need to let go of Bryant's hand, and I can't.

The other part of me is confused, and irritated. I was wrong. He did leave his brother's side. I can't understand, it will not compute. I realize now we were all in shock, but at the time I cannot put the pieces together.

I remind myself, James is also a victim, and we have two injured sons. I need to give him some room to explain.

"James, where have you been?"

"Ace and I stopped to get a cheeseburger," said James, nonchalantly.

"A cheeseburger, you stopped to get a cheeseburger!"

"Yeah, once Bryant was on his way here, after we went to get the car, we stopped to get a cheeseburger. We were hungry."

My head is spinning; food is the last thing on my mind.

I then notice Ace is standing behind James. He also, looks as if he has gone through hell. He is standing back, looking down, avoiding my eyes.

Forgetting my own words about two victims, I feel my anger rising, how could they stop to get a cheeseburger? How could they act so casually about all of this? While my son, James's brother and Ace's best friend, is lying here fighting for his life. His life is hanging by a thread while they waste precious minutes eating a cheeseburger? This is too much for me to fathom.

"How could you, how could you let the boy scouts rescue your brother, while you stop, and get a cheeseburger? Explain this to me." I ask incredulously.

James's mouth drops open and he moves from side to side, clearly agitated. He's looking at me like I have five heads and clearly wanting to come across the room and strangle me.

"The boy scouts rescued him? The boy scouts, rescued him? How could I, how could I, eat a cheeseburger?"

James's hands are rigidly held out in front of him, he is clearly upset.

Ace then steps forward.

"Mrs. Hartsfield, James is the one who found Bryant. James is the one who rescued him. You're being way too hard on him. He saved Bryant's life. He got him to air care."

Gathering his confidence he continues, "They made us walk back through the woods, they wouldn't let us go with Bryant. You don't know what we've been through. We stopped for something to eat before we hiked back to the camp, packed up and headed here to the hospital. We hadn't eaten all day, we needed food."

I swallow hard; once again not following my own advice. "I am so sorry; we only know what they tell us. All they said was, the boy scouts found Bryant and rescued him. I knew you would not leave your brother, I couldn't believe it! I'm sorry. When you said you stopped to get cheeseburgers, I didn't understand."

James, shakes his head in disbelief, "The boy scouts huh, that's who they said rescued him? I can't believe it. That just figures."

Ace looks at me and then back down at the ground. "I am so sorry," he says. "I am so sorry about Bryant."

I survey the two of them, Ace and James's arms and hands are filthy, their jeans and tennis shoes are encrusted in mud. The once white T-shirts are streaked with mud, blood and unknown grime. Their faces are smeared with the combination of dirt and dried sweat. Surveying their faces, they somehow look, "older." They have changed in the past twenty-four hours. It is the appearance of a new maturity. But somehow they also look, I search again for the word, almost happy, no maybe proud! I can't get my mind or my hands wrapped around what is going on. I think about it again, they look... maybe the word is "relieved."

Looking down at Bryant laying in the ER on a gurney with the IV in his arm and the ventilator forcing air into his lungs, deep in a coma, how can they look so happy and relieved? I remind myself again, forcing the words into my head. I have two injured sons; give James some space and time to explain. I take a deep cleansing breath, and coach myself that if I became too loud or lose control I will be asked to wait in the waiting room. This time I listen to my own words, the calmness returns to me.

"Yuck" I said. "You guys are really dirty; I can't wait to hear how you got this dirty."

Smiles break out on both of their faces, as they exchange a knowing look.

"Really, because we put clean shirts on." James laughed.

If they cleaned up and they look like this it must be quite a story, I think.

"Yeah, you should have seen us before," said Ace.

Steve pipes in, "Hey we are going to go back to the family waiting room so the guys can tell us their story. Why don't you come with us?"

I look down at Bryant, who is still holding my hand.

"No," I say. "I can't leave."

They leave the curtained draped room and return to the family waiting room. I want to hear the story, but I am needed here.

I look down at my son; my heart feels like it will break in two with all of the emotions I am feeling for my sons right now. We had our share of problems but they stuck together, Paul found James, James found Bryant, and Bryant stayed alive. I knew our sons would not give up on each other.

I continue to hold Bryant's hand. His fingers still curl around mine. I look down at them, now so big they surround my whole hand. When he was a newborn they covered only one finger, yet the feeling is the same. This is still my baby and he needs me to be strong and to hold it together for him. Just like my strong sons holding it together, to do what they needed to do "what I expected of them," it is now my turn.

Bryant has been strong and waited to go into a coma until he saw me; my son has waited for me! This thought alone is overpowering to me. I put my head down and talk to my Heavenly Father. *"I told You Father, I would take him anyway You gave him to me. You kept him alive. I will accept him however You decide to give him to me. I will dedicate the rest of my life, if need be to his care, to help him to reach the highest level he can reach. I pledge this to You."* I relax my body and to the best of my ability open up my heart and let my love and energy flow down through my arm, hand and out into his body. I share my love and energy once again with him.

Then the curtain parts and it is time again for them to get Bryant to respond. "Bryant, Bryant, can you hear me?" She yells loudly as she leans over him.

Placing her hands into his, she continues "Bryant, can you open up your eyes for me? Bryant, Bryant, if you can hear me squeeze my hand. Bryant, can you hold up a finger for me?" She is getting louder with each request, virtually screaming in his ear at this time. No response. There is no response at all.

I inquire if he is sedated and they tell me no, and the less they sedate him the better his chances are of coming out of his coma. He is probably in a lot of pain I am told but it is really important he responds to their commands on a timely basis.

A white-coated man comes back into the room and repeats the

same procedure. Calling out loudly to get him to respond, asking for him to obey his commands. No response at all. I watch as he lifts his fist up over his head and brings it down quickly and firmly onto my son's upper left chest, right below his collarbone, right above his "puma" tattoo. Bryant jerks awake and opens his eyes, and just as quickly closes them again.

He smiles, "that's a good sign."

Pulling down Bryant's gown at the neck he shows me the device. A many sided metal prong has been inserted into his chest. Little droplets of blood appear around the sharp prongs. He has pierced his skin and used pain to force him to respond. They really are serious about getting him to respond every twenty minutes.

We are told they are waiting for an opening in the ICU and they will move him as soon as a room opens up.

As evening approaches, it quiets down a little in the ER. Someone comes in every twenty minutes to repeat this procedure, other than that nothing has happened.

James comes back into the "room," then looking around he see's Bryant's clothes tossed on the floor and asks.

"Why does Dad have that blue bandana?"

"It reminds him of Bryant," I reply.

Humph he mutters, "I would not want that thing, it is gross!"

It will be a while before I understand the significance of the blue bandana.

"What happened out there today?"

He sits carefully down in a chair in the corner. Clearly he does not want to repeat the day to me. He is thinking, carefully choosing his words. He nods his head toward Bryant and says: "He looks good. I knew if I could get him to the hospital he would be fine."

James's attitude is not making any sense to me. How can he possibly think he looks good? He is on a ventilator, in a coma, with a metal prong in his chest. I want to scream at James, that the doctors say he could die at any moment.

James sits there looking so cool, so calm.

The staff walks back into our small curtained off room; the

moment is lost. They tell me they are ready to move Bryant upstairs to the Neurological ICU and busy themselves with all of his life-lines. They suggest we take a break as it will be an hour or so before we will be able to see him again.

I must let go of Bryant's hand. I have not broken our bond since he went into the x-ray room, and to break it now is really, really hard. I bend down to give him a kiss good-bye on the cheek, whispering to him that I will be right back as soon as I can. It is agonizing to let him go off without me. I know he is in good hands, but they are not my hands. They gather all of their equipment and we are ushered out of the room.

I walk out into the hallway and meet Steve, our children and the rest of our small group. We walk out of the ER and into the outdoor entrance area. I lean back against the stonewall of the hospital, breathing in the warm spring air. The wall offers support to me, I feel weak. It is too much to bear, heart-breaking. I am not able to talk about it. Steve turns on his phone and calls my sister, the one who lives the closest to my mother. He asks her to pass the information on to the rest of the family; to inform them about the accident and the graduation parties are cancelled. I can't hear every-thing but, I can guess at her question. I hear Steve's voice crack and then he starts sobbing, he breaks down right there by the entrance while on the phone.

"No, I don't think he is going to be all right. He is on a ventila-tor and they do not give him much of a chance of surviving."

Steve has held it together, but having to voice the words we are both avoiding causes the dam of emotions to overflow. He hangs up the phone and we embrace. We hold each other and cry. This is our baby, our child and our lives as we have known them will never be the same.

Chapter **6**
The Camping Trip

"I will never quit. I persevere and thrive on adversity...If knocked down, I will get back up, every time"
– US Navy SEALS

(Narrative from Mom) I didn't know this part of the story until many years after the accident. James told me firmly that we would never speak of it again, he was only telling me this once so that I would understand the facts to write them down in this missive. It was important to him I know the facts and get them down straight. I was not there and have done my best to recreate the events that lead up to the accident.

The cherry red Jetta, flies down the road with three young men inside. They are headed to the Gorge, for a one night camping trip. Bryant, the driver of the car, is excited. He is finishing his third year in a two-year school and has just learned that a local university wants him on their soccer team, and they are awarding him a scholarship to play. Captain of his team, the team had an awesome year this year. This had earned him a spot as an all Mid-American soccer player, division one junior college.

Bryant's younger sister and older brother are graduating in a week or so. Grandparents, aunts and uncles are coming to his parents' house for a double party. Bryant is not such a great student and he knows that everyone will be asking him when he will be graduating. The truth is that school is hard for him, and he hates it. The only thing keeping him at school is soccer.

This camping trip is a great idea, just what I need before all of the people show up. Bryant's mind wanders over his life as he takes another drag from his cigarette.

He plans to work in the family business. Dad told him he needed to graduate college first, and arranged for him to work for a local company as an intern as well. He hates this job as much as school; they give him all of the shit jobs; filing and stuff. It's not working out and he needs a plan to change his life.

He has been sharing a house his parents own with his oldest brother Paul who will be moving on soon. Everything will change. Paul lives in the downstairs apartment; his girlfriend Leigh, is visiting right now. Her school is out for the year.

Cam, Bryant's girlfriend of five years, is really getting to be a drag. Her parents bought a small house for her to live in with her brother, and she is urging Bryant to move in with her. Anyway, she and her parents are urging him to make the move, a move he's not sure he wants to make. He has his priorities in line as he lovingly touches his steering wheel, he does have his car to pay for. If his parents are not willing to pay rent to Cam's parents, it would be hard to keep his car and pay the rent.

The last six months have been difficult, he's changing schools and not on track to graduate. He has plenty of credits but is missing some needed classes for his Associates degree. He hates his job, has girlfriend pressures and has been fighting off and on with his older brother Paul for the past few months. Life should not be so shitty. He knows he needs to make some changes.

Riding shotgun is Ace his good friend from high school. Ace knows things have been tough between Bryant and Cam lately. He is caught in the middle; he has gone to high school with both of them and considers them both friends.

Ace has been working with a lawn care company mowing lawns since high school. The owners are really good to him, and he likes being outside. He was even able to get Bryant a part-time job cutting grass. It has been fun working with Bryant. The company has talked about making Ace a year-round employee. Pulling a smoke out of his pocket he takes a long drag, yeah, life is good.

Sitting in the back seat of the car is James, Bryant's little brother, who, while looking at the backs of their heads, is simply happy to be along for the ride. He idolizes both Bryant and his older brother Paul. James goes to the same high school and is playing on the same soccer team both of his brothers played for. He has watched his brothers for years. He has copied their walk, their attitude, and he even dresses like them. He thinks they are the shit; he wants to be just like them.

James feels really accepted right now. He recently turned seventeen. Bryant had asked him to come along with him. He had never been camping alone with either of his brothers before. He has never been to the Gorge; he can't believe their mother approved of this camping trip she is usually so strict.

Dad is often out of town working in Florida a couple of weeks a month. Dad is pretty cool and fun compared to Mom. She is there; he cannot think of a soccer game either select or high school she has not attended cheering for her kids. He knows she will always be there and he can depend on her.

"Hey James, do you want this?" Ace asks, as he hands the smoke to James.

"Sure," says James as he reaches for it.

"Wow, I didn't know you were cool like that," says Ace. "This is the life, we should do this more often!"

The three of them laugh and agree; yeah life is good, flying on down the highway.

Arriving at their favorite parking spot, "It will be a long hike, only take the essentials," advises Bryant.

They laughingly load beer into their coolers from the trunk.

Walking in a light springtime drizzle, the ground is damp but not soaked. They walk for a while and stop to drink a beer. The dirt pathway winds through the woods, surrounded by trees and thick underbrush. Saturated leaves no longer offer cover from the rain. The young men are getting wetter as the light drizzle turns to a steady rain. Stopping along the way to visit with other campers;

but after a while continuing their trek hiking and drinking.

The now wet group set up camp but the rain is really picking up. It is putting a real damper on their fun.

"Come on," Bryant says. "I know where we can camp to get out of this rain."

Ace argues with him, having an idea where Bryant wants to go. He gives in without really putting up a fight. He agrees that the rain is really a drag.

Bryant is taking them up to the top of a ridge overlooking a canyon. The other two boys follow him. Bryant loves to camp, rock climb and hike. He and Ace have been here often in the past three years. The dirt is now wet and walking is more difficult. They hike for hours through the woods.

They climb up a steep incline to get to the last big hurdle. Bryant urges them on to go up and over steep, and now slippery sandstone boulders. Legend is that Cherokee Indians of old chiseled the hand and toe holds into this sandstone. The boys work hard to haul not only their tents but a cooler of beer up and over the Indian staircase as the rain continues to come down. It is a steep climb with straight drop offs on either side. The staircase consists of three huge boulders one on top of another. The glaciers of old set the boulders at intervals making a small area to regroup before climbing over the next boulder giving a giant staircase effect.

Finally getting to the top a mile long trail leads them to a wedge. This wedge is twelve feet tall at the cliff edge—tall enough for a man to stand—and then narrows as it goes into the mountain. The horseshoe-shaped mountain looks out over a huge valley. They can see the Indian Staircase on the other side of the horseshoe. They walk over to the deceiving edge. Small scrub trees, a couple of feet high and a few weeds block the fact that the face of the cliff is straight down. At the very bottom you can see a gradual slope of trees and rhododendrons are starting to bud and then nothing but forest as far as the eye can see. A stream runs through the middle of the valley floor, what a view. They are grateful they made it here before the sun set.

"This wedge will protect us from the rain," Bryant says.

Setting up camp is easy with only two tents. Inside the rock overhang is a rock shaped like a couch that Bryant quickly claims for himself.

They spend the rest of the night partying, laughing and telling stories. It gets dark, and James crawls into his sleeping bag early. Bryant and Ace sit out by the campfire talking. They hear James throwing up in his sleep. The older boys are telling war stories of their own puking experiences when they were younger. They both go over and try to wake James up; unable to wake him they pull him sleeping bag and all half out of the tent so he will throw up on the ground and not in the tent.

Bryant and Ace talk about friends, life and lawn mowing. Bryant loves the freedom of being outside with a lawnmower and has enjoyed his time working with Ace so much more than the internship or school.

"I'm going to make some changes in my life when I get back," Bryant tells Ace. "I think I am going to break up with Cam. Yeah, I need to make some changes in my life, it's not working. I'm not happy." He lies back on the couch.

The rain continues throughout the night blanketing the moon and stars with heavy clouds. The only light comes from the campfire. Bryant and Ace sit around talking until Ace finally says goodnight and curls up in his sleeping bag in the other vacant tent. Bryant had promised his mother to watch out for James, her parting words were:

"Take care of your brother, don't let him get hurt."

Bryant laughs to himself, Yeah, well she told me no alcohol either.

Lying back on the rock couch, he watches as the campfire slowly dies down. He falls asleep.

Ace gets up around two in the morning to take a pee. He looks over at Bryant asleep on the couch. He can hardly see him because the fire is burning down. James is still passed out, Ace crawls back into the sleeping bag and goes to sleep.

Bryant wakes up later, the campfire has burned out. Without the moon and stars it is completely dark. Remembering where he is, he stumbles off the rock couch. He is cold and heads over to the tent to go to bed. He needs to pee first. He walks over to the edge to go to the bathroom. His footing slips on the wet rocks, and he slides over the edge of the cliff.

He falls feet first. His back scrapes the rocks on his way down peeling away his skin. He grabs at anything and everything he can reach as he slides down trying to stop his descent.

He thinks to himself, Oh, fuck I have to stop myself. I really fucked up this time.

Down, down he goes. Slamming his head on a rock, he continues his descent in a free fall. One hundred and eighty feet in all, but he has no way to know that. He is limp like a rag doll, falling, falling, falling. He drops the equivalent of an eighteen-story building. He hits the bottom and then rolls for another fifty feet away from the cliff edge down a muddy, steep embankment.

Up above on the ledge both of the boys have passed out in their sleeping bags. They hear nothing at all, the rain softly falling around their campsite works as a sound machine, drowning out all other sounds.

Chapter 7
Jame's Own Words; The Rescue

*"The woods are lovely, dark and deep.
But I have miles to go before I sleep,
and miles to go before I sleep."*
– Robert Frost

Other than the fact that Bryant fell between the hours of three and four in the morning, we do not understand what transpired out there. James did not talk about it that night with us. However, Steve did give him a journal the next day and he wrote the entire story of the rescue down, leaving out the part about the partying from the night before.

It is great therapy for James to get it all out. He writes it while sitting in a chair in the corner of Bryant's hospital ICU room. What is amazing is that he was barely seventeen; his birthday had only been twenty-six days ago. James rarely speaks of the accident. I relate it to a veteran never talking about combat. As a matter of fact in the six years since, he only wrote about it in the journal that week in the hospital, and told me the story of the camping trip only once, four years ago.

At this point we only know Bryant fell, and James and Ace had some part in it; and they were late getting to the hospital because of cheeseburgers. This is a strong reminder that there are many sides to every story. He went three whole days without us understanding what he had been through. I think we still can't fathom the reality of the trauma these two young men experienced. These are his words as he wrote them....

Jame's Journal:

I will never in full detail be able to express what happened. Some of the things I can't put into words, others I simply don't want to.

My eyes opened at dawn on Sunday morning. I was allowed a beautiful view of the horizon as the first rays touched the chilled air.

I crawled from my sleeping bag and stretched my limbs. I found the stone sofa and passed out for the second time within 12 hours. (I was fucking exhausted!) The next time I woke up it was because Ace was walking around doing God knows what.

Ace was surprised to learn that I was not Bryant. I can't say I shared his amazement. He told me that Bryant had fallen asleep (passed out), in the same position and spot that I had. I was the first one to go to bed that night. Bryant would fall asleep on the stone sofa some hours later and Ace would be the last. Ace predicts (we had no real knowledge of time), he fell asleep around 4:00 a.m.

(I predict that when Bryant fell he was perhaps in the valley for a total of 3 – 4 hours by himself.) After I was fully awake, it was perhaps 7 or 8 a.m. I went to the bathroom and put my not so clean contact lenses in. When I returned to camp and Bryant had still not returned I became slightly worried.

Ace and I thought of where Bryant might have gone and why he would have left his pack behind. Ace was concerned but was able to convince himself otherwise. During our dumb ass brain storming as to where he could be, a loud and heart wrenching moan escaped from the valley. Our first reaction was that it was a camper (partier), with a terrible hangover. I yelled down for them to (shut-up). We dismissed the moaning for nothing more and that will haunt both of us forever.

To support the hangover theory I recalled Bryant telling me of an amazing camp site. The camp site as I recall was in the similar direction of the moaning. (I was also wrong about that.) So I thought it was simply campers suffering from the night before.

Maybe ten minutes later, perhaps longer, I decided to go look for my brother. I told Ace that I was simply going to ask around at other camp sites. I headed out and in the direction of the old site. The reason we had moved was because it had started raining at midday on Saturday. We then moved our camp to the cave. That was in the rock face on the complete other side of the valley. The mountain ridge was set up like a horseshoe. Our old camp was on one side of the shoe, the new one was on the complete opposite side, with the valley down below and between the two sides.

I hiked to our old camp site and was still able to hear the moaning. It echoed up the rock walls and was heard in every direction. Some will curse Ace and I for not heeding the moaning earlier. However, you the reader cannot comprehend that you never realize that this situation can happen to you. Not even once did I think Bryant could have fallen and that could be him moaning. I knew my brother to be a damn good climber, and never dreamed that he could fall. Never.

I decided to climb down the Indian staircase to search the valley. Why I decided to do this, I'm still not sure. But I did. But of course, I lost the trail and had to jump onto a tree and climb the rest of the way down into the valley via the tree. I finally came across a deer trail and simply followed it in the general direction of the moaning. Who would have thought, not me. It was as if I was being guided by some unseen hand. The closer I approached the moaning the more I realized that it sounded like Bryant. I quickened my pace and to my disappointment found no trail leading towards whoever it was.

I ran in a dead sprint up the incline that was totally covered in thick brush, trees, and rubbery plants. To clarify something, the terrain at the base of the cliff was at a steep incline. How far Bryant tumbled and rolled after he hit is not clear to me. But it was a very good distance! When I finally found Bryant I wasn't in total surprise. I think I had already come to that conclusion, but didn't want to accept it.

Bryant was without his shirt, he had on khaki shorts and his shoes were missing. He had on both socks, his belt buckle still in place. Behind his right ear he had a bad cut; it had spilt blood onto his face. His ear was clogged with dry blood and dry clogged blood was in his nostrils. Supporting him on the incline was a log that was keeping his body in place. I noticed later a branch in his groin and I believe that caused most of his discomfort.

When I first found him I covered his body with mine, as a mother would protect her young. Bryant had bleeding scratches on his back. I later learned that the first 10 or 20 feet of the fall was slanted rock. I believe Bryant slid on his back that first 10 or 20 feet down the rock face, ripping the skin off of his back.

The entire fall was estimated by the park ranger to be 150 feet. Later we learn that it was actually 180 feet. He free fell for at least 160 feet. I was told by the park ranger and later paramedics that the reason for his survival was the alcohol. He was so drunk from his alcohol intake that when he fell he fell like a rag doll. His body didn't have the time to react to instinctively react or stiffen. So when he hit the bottom he bounced like a rag doll and that is the key to his survival. (Not forgetting, God, his angels and me).

I believe Bryant was still falling mentally, reliving the fall again and again. He was whimpering and the moan was more of a scream when you were up close, his hand clenched the branches around him with a death grip. His left hand was limper than his right. When he looked at me, his eyes were extremely glazed over. I don't think he even knew who anyone was. I noticed that his left hand was terribly swollen, along with his left arm; this worried me.

I called up for Ace and told him, I had found Bryant.

"How is he," I think he asked.

"He's in bad shape; he's alive but broken. Get down here with help." I also noticed Bryant had all of his teeth still in place.

As Ace sprinted down the mountain, I was with my brother. We both predict it took Ace, forty minutes at a dead sprint.

It was hard to hold Bryant, and keep him stable because he leaned forward. He was bent forward with his right hand gripping a branch. His moaning will always echo in my ears. He had been throwing up and flies were everywhere.

I started to clear some of the brush. I had to be careful what I moved because some of the plants were holding him in place. Bryant never moved his legs while I was with him. He only moved his upper body and slightly in slow motion. I had to keep talking loudly so that Ace could follow the sound of my voice. His slow ass finally showed up, alone.

Our first reaction was to move Bryant and get him out of there. We had two problems, one, the brush and incline made it impossible to carry him by ourselves. Two, we had been told all of our lives to never move a victim for fear of making the injury worse. Three, (not two but three), Bryant would move away from our touch or start to sway back and forth. When I would try to hold his hand, he would remove it. He would then start to shake it as if to tell me something. I could not communicate with him. I caught catches and phrases as he mumbled all through the day. The most common were, please, help me, and swearing. I think I heard him mumble Mom and Dad once or twice.

Ace and I came to the conclusion that I would find help and he would stay with Bryant. I was in better running shape because of soccer. As I was getting up to leave, I remember Ace telling me that I was a good brother.

I left Bryant and Ace behind, and ran in what I thought was the direction of the Indian Staircase. But of course, it wasn't. I believe I ran for a total of an hour, maybe more. I had no judgment of time or direction. I literally did straight sprints up and down the mountain deer trails. I threw up once, and was lost about four times. I just kept running all the while hearing the voice of my soccer coach in my ears. He had coached all three of us brothers. I could hear him yelling at me in his Marine Captain voice. You're a pussy, get up and keep going. You can't stop now. You're sucking wind, you need to suck it up. It kept me going. Every time I thought I couldn't go on, his voice was in my head yelling at me and pushing me to do better, more than I thought I could. He kept me going.

(Narrative from Mom) James later explains to me that he was lost and climbed up to the top looking for a vantage point, to find help. When he looked out all he could see was miles and miles of forest, tree after tree and no path or person in sight. He was unable to find help for his dying brother. He felt that he had let his brother down and now couldn't find his way back to him. Desperate, he was now planning to carry him out in his arms, if only he could find him again. His brother was going to die out there, and he couldn't find him.

I never was able to find a living soul, and I was not even close to the ranger station. I was finally able to retrace my steps and found the right trail back to Bryant and Ace.

By the grace of God (no other explanation), I came across a scout leader of the boy scouts and three eighth grade scouts. I told them the situation and to my shock and great relief they already knew! They told me there was a large group of them that went to the creek to get water. They had a chemical that cleaned the water and made it safe to drink, but it still tasted terrible, I found out later. They were at the Gorge training for a wilderness adventure down in Mexico. They were in training and when one of the scouts took the lead they had gotten lost. The scout leader knew where they were, he later told me, but was waiting for the scout to figure out that he was lost. While getting water they heard Ace yelling for help! All of my running had been for nothing. It was Ace who found help.

I would later talk to Ace; he said that he wrapped his legs and arms around Bryant. His chest pressed against Bryant's back, in a great bear hug. He was scared, crying and vomiting and just started yelling, "Help" at the top of his lungs. The scout leader said they could barely hear him. That is how thick the woods are. I can't recall the names of the boy scouts, but if it were not for them, my brother would not have survived.

I told him that I had been looking for the ranger station, and I had no idea where it was. He told me he was already heading towards the station. He said the rest of the group was waiting with Bryant and Ace. He asked me if I would want to come along, but I rejected the idea. They obviously knew what they were doing and had things under control. I wanted to get back to Bryant and make sure he was O.K.

When I returned to Bryant, he was in the same condition I had originally found him. Ace was with him along with a scout leader, who stood somewhat apart. Ace was glad to see me, and I told him about the scouts on their way to the ranger station. I worked my way over to my brother and gently laid my body across his in a weak embrace.

Bryant was doubled over with his back to me. It was the first time I started to cry, but not uncontrollably. I was holding a breathing Bryant, and nothing else mattered.

I quickly pulled myself together and introduced myself to the scout leader nearest Bryant. I can't seem to remember his name, but his face I will not forget. He was kind and had a calming effect on me, knowing that I was not alone, was good.

(Narrative from Mom) Years later Steve and I attend a boy scout meeting, and we spoke with this scout leader. His praise of James was an eye opener to his father and me. He said that the scene was so horrific that he has trouble explaining it to us. The stench was overwhelming, the sounds, the flies, and the sheer horror was so overpowering that the three adult leaders had to take turns attending to the scene. They were all in awe of James's continued love and support of his brother. James did not leave his brothers' side again until Bryant was taken out of the Gorge, and only then because the medics refused to let him go with them. The mere presence of his younger brother had a quieting effect on the older brother. Bryant would fight and thrash uncontrollably when he was not right next to him to offer comfort and love. To this day they marvel at the strength and support that my young son exhibited on that day. They had positioned the scouts down the trail not only to mark the location, but to remove them from the horror of the scene. Years later, I could still witness the trauma on the faces of the scout leaders as they spoke about that day.

Ace asked me if he could leave to get all our belongings and put them in Bryant's tent. He said he wanted to prevent theft, of anything worth taking, that may have been the case, but I think he wanted to make sure there was nothing remaining of our party before the ranger got there. That was the last I saw of him, until hours later at the ambulance. He would tell me later that he was the runner to tell the paramedics where to find Bryant. He also talked to the police and medics about what had happened. I will always remember his help in getting me and Bryant out of there.

I predict I was with my brother for another two long hours before the paramedics showed up. The scout leader stayed with me the whole time. I was sweating badly from the earlier exertions. I had taken my shirt off and placed it under Bryant's head when I first found him. The scout leader was an angel with his kindness. He kept me in a brisk conversation as if we were sitting down to lunch. I was doing my best to stay calm and not break down in front of anyone. (It would be days later before I allowed myself to really cry). I even remember laughing with the scout leader and I will never forget his key role in keeping me company.

Bryant would go in and out of consciousness. He would alternate between sleeping and moaning every five to ten minutes. When he did wake up he would always bend forward as if to throw up. His grip would tighten considerably on the branches. He would occasionally moan "help me!" I heard "my ear" once or twice. When Bryant did get out of control me and the scout leader would calm him down by saying his name over and over to him.

By this time the horse flies were getting horribly bad. The whole time I sat with Bryant, I waved my hands just over his body to keep the flies away from him. Ace told me that he had done the same thing while he had waited for me. Both Ace and I later realized when we got to the car that we had horse fly bites covering us.

The worse part of all was the smell. Bryant had the distinct smell of alcohol on his breath. The mixture of that, the vomit, (including Ace's vomit), body odor, blood and I think Bryant had shit as well, anyway the smell was awful.

I borrowed a blue bandana handkerchief from the scout leader, and would wipe Bryant's chin every time he vomited. Still my brother had no real concept that I was there, or gave any real hint toward it. Whenever I held him, which was a difficult task because he moved so much, I held him to my chest. I was propped up against something, perhaps a log, and had Bryant's back to my chest. I wrapped my arms around the front of his body and held him in a stable position. This seemed to calm him some. I couldn't see his face real clear but could tell when he was slipping off because his grip on the branches would loosen ever so slowly. During those moments he would lay in my arms for a short while until he woke up again and started wailing and grabbing the branches. I only wanted to calm my brother down, but later the scout leader told my dad that I kept Bryant from going into shock. That was never my intention, it was all instinct, it just worked out that way, my intention was to calm him down. My body heat added to Bryant's, along with our somewhat stable position helped in more ways I guess than I can imagine.

The whole time I sat there I was nagged by a constant lack of water. After vomiting the night before, doing sprints in the mountains in the humidity, I was really thirsty. The only thing the scouts could offer was creek water with iodine in it for purification. But I drank it and was happy for it. Ace had tried earlier to wet a rag and hold it to Bryant's lips but the only reaction he got was Bryant "flipping out."

The scouts and scout leaders were coming and going. Every time someone came close enough for Bryant to hear them walking up the hill, Bryant would begin to yell for them to help him. I don't believe he had any idea that I was there! But that's O.K.; I don't want him to remember anything.

First the ranger came up to inspect the situation. With him was a volunteer, the camper I had met the night before. I don't remember his name, but the volunteer started removing brush from around Bryant. The ranger inspected Bryant. I believe that he placed a "collar" or neck brace around his neck. Then the ranger used his radio to explain the situation and what the paramedics needed to bring. The paramedics were waiting at the bottom of the hill.

I could hear two men yelling, one a paramedic, another a ranger. Both were carrying the stretcher. They were concerned because they couldn't find a path up to us. The brush is too thick to get the stretcher through. The ranger who was with me was in charge, he told them there was a creek, he told them to follow the creek up, and they did. I was so relieved when the paramedics showed up. To the best of my knowledge at least three hours had passed since I had found my brother and probably eight to ten since he had fallen!

A few more people began to show up and we soon had a good number of volunteers. They just appeared out of the woods; how they *got there I have no idea. The word had spread quickly. They worked efficiently and a path had been cleared from the creek to Bryant. The medics and ranger brought forth a stretcher, but they did not place Bryant in it right away. First a wooden plank was brought over to Bryant. The head ranger or sheriff told me I had to help place Bryant on the plank. I was at my brother's head, so I grabbed him under his armpits.*

He was begging the whole time for us not to move him. He begged, "please, please," over and over, asking us to leave him alone. He had no idea that we were trying to save him. He had a clear look of desperation in his eyes, one of pain and confusion. I can't describe it; it was awful! Like a wild animal with no comprehension. On the count of three we were able to move Bryant onto the plank. I had him by the armpits. Then from there we moved him into the stretcher, or what they called the basket. Bryant was crying out in pain the whole time.

Before I realized it we had a large group of men around the stretcher. I was by far the youngest but, who knew, we were all equals here. They strapped Bryant down into the stretcher with some difficulty. They placed an oxygen mask over his mouth. Bryant would later try to remove it. He also hated the neck brace and was constantly reaching for it and trying to get it off. Bryant was still fighting for his life, fighting them at every turn.

The terrain was uneven and mountainous. We were instructed to keep his body level at all times. It was difficult to keep the basket level. We were told to descend with his feet first, and we had to communicate. I was located in the back next to my brother's head, to keep him calm. As if I knew what to do if he got out of control! We had three men on each side, two in the front and two in the back. We would have to hike him out of the woods, mountains like this until we could get to a place where an ambulance could get him.

What I remember most is the way Bryant's voice sounded. His words were drawn out. He had heavy breathing and that also affected it. It was weak, but not in volume. You could hear the pain in his words. The word I would use to describe it is desperation. Desperation was in his voice, looks, and actions. He was desperate to live, to survive, and to understand.

Getting him out of the woods and onto a cleared path was the biggest challenge yet. I was literally in shin deep mud. We had to keep his body level while going down rough dangerous terrain, and on a slope. It was hard because if you fell, (and we all did) you had to keep the stretcher above your head and level with the group. If you were going down because of a drop off you would need to bend over to keep his head level with his feet. It was grueling.

One obstacle was a large pit we had to cross. One of the volunteers climbed down into it and propped his leg up. As we carried the stretcher we used his thigh as a stepping stone and were able to cross. The team work was outstanding. Any athletic coach would have been proud of that team. If not for every person there, my brother would not have lived. I realized we could have been carrying a coffin and not a stretcher and it kept me going.

Volunteers were rotating in and out giving each other breaks, every time I tried to be relieved Bryant would grow restless and start fighting even worse. I had to stay by his head the whole time. I was so thirsty, tired, hungry and bleeding from cuts and scratches, but I hardly noticed.

When we reached the bottom of the hill we found new paramedics. One was a female who took immediate control of the situation. We stopped for the medics to inspect Bryant. I was also greeted with more volunteers, some I had met the night before. My mouth was parched and I asked for water, only to get more creek water.

The next thing I remember was a wheel. It was a tire wheel but smaller. Its purpose was to latch onto the bottom of the stretcher. It hooked on at the middle and raised the stretcher waist high. It was easier to carry the stretcher with the wheel but we still had to keep it perfectly balanced and we still needed the same amount of people to carry it.

The problem was that the trail was now a deer trail. The stretcher was slightly smaller than the trails, leaving no room for three large men on each side. It didn't matter we still got him out. Every time one man fell another was there to take his place. It was a thing of beauty.

Bryant was trying to stop us the whole way. He was "asleep" some of the time. But three-fourths of the time he was awake and fighting. The medic finally just left the oxygen mask off him because he kept pulling it off. We fought with him to keep on the neck brace. We had to stop every time he pulled the thing off. Out of desperation we finally strapped his wrist to the stretcher.

I was so exhausted that I let a volunteer take my place. I needed to breathe. There was a woman with us, a mother of two sons. I don't know if they were among the volunteers or not. She asked me if I was his brother, and I told her yes. She had a small smile and asked "well how are you doing then?" I almost laughed. It was the first time in hours that someone asked me, how I was. I smiled and said I was fine. I noticed that she kept somewhat close to me, but not to close. She tapped me on the shoulder and told me that my heel was bleeding. I looked down and realized my shoes had rubbed my heel completely raw. Blood was visible and I then realized the pain. I laughed and told her that only "a mother would notice that!" I appreciated her presence.

Bryant had grown too restless and so I took my place again, back by his head. We had about a quarter of a mile left. We had to maneuver a terrible incline right before we got to the paths end. Completing our journey with my arms extended over my head to keep Bryant's head even with his feet, the men in the front climbing from a squatting position, always keeping him level. Finally we reached the ambulance that would eventually take Bryant to the helicopter and then to the hospital. They would not let me go in the ambulance with my brother. They took control, and then they were gone.

The first thing I saw was Ace waiting, and I called out to him, we embraced. A new bond had been formed between us. The ranger that I had first met came over and asked me a few questions, Bryant's name, my name and number, my parent's name, address, and phone number. He told us they would take him to the Hospital Trauma Center. He gave Ace directions to the hospital and then he was gone. I thought he would call my parents.

The mother who had befriended me came over and forced me to get my heel checked. They cleaned it with alcohol and bandaged it up.

She then wished me and Bryant good luck, and then she was gone. I will never forget her kindness. A few of the volunteers asked for my phone number so they could stay in touch. The group broke apart and then it was just Ace and I.

I then walked behind a tree and threw up every ounce of iodized river water. I swear it was a river of its own. Then Ace handed me bottled water and it was the best thing ever! We still had to hike back up the mountain to retrieve all of our stuff and break camp. But first we went to lunch and I had a wonderful cheeseburger and bought a milk carton full of water for the hike back.

The climb back up was a comic relief that both of us desperately needed. Ace managed to get us lost for a while, all we could do was laugh at the situation wondering what else could go wrong. I then dropped the jug of water and we started laughing uncontrollably. We finally reached the camp and we packed up. We had to leave our garbage and two coolers. We still had to carry Bryant's camping pack and supplies out along with our packs.

I glanced over the edge which Bryant had fallen from. I surveyed the enormous height, imagining my brother falling the first ten to twenty feet of stone, the free fall and then the steep hill and brush that he had rolled into. I had remained calm throughout the day and the reason was simple. I knew he would survive. I had witnessed the cliff from which he fell. I saw how far he had rolled. The fact that he was still alive, still breathing, and calling for help when I found him was enough for me! That he had survived out there for hours by himself, in the cool of the night, the rain and still he lived. Something told me he had already lived through the worse. He would hang on for a few more hours with me. Once he was with the paramedics and at the hospital he would be fine. We picked up our equipment and started the hike back to the parking lot, and then drove to the hospital.

When we got to the hospital everyone was so upset, to see Bryant with so many tubes. They just have no idea how lucky he is. When I sat with my brother out there and held him in my arms, I prayed and daydreamed of him in a hospital bed. My prayers have been answered. Seeing him hooked up to these tubes is the greatest relief and joy I have *ever experienced. Ace and I look at each other, we cannot help but to feel a great sense of pride and joy.*

(Narrative from Mom) No one called us, not the ranger, the police, the ambulance drivers, or the helicopter pilots. Somehow his name and all of his information had been lost. Luckily Ace called Cam, just to celebrate; he wanted to tell someone what a great job they had done. That was how we found out, that he had been injured and that he was fine!

For years I was in the dark about the role of partying and how it had played out in this drama. I never knew. Maybe the boys thought that I knew but I did not. I knew that Bryant had been drinking, but he was 21. What I didn't know was that James had been drinking with them. Maybe I did not want to know. The mother is often the last to know. Well, I now have a saying, if you want to know what your kids are doing, look at their friends. If their friends are doing it, so are they. They would not be friends otherwise. This is my advice, learned the hard way. I was unaware of James' partying at a young age. I was so caught up in policing my oldest son that I was blind to the vices and problems of my youngest son, and my middle son. Way too tough on one child, and way to permissive with the others. I was trying to control their lives, and I completely and totally missed the mark. I feel so foolish now, looking back at this.

James went home that night to his own bed, he and Ace drove Bryant's car home. I cannot imagine the emotions that were going through his head. He later told me that something wonderful happened when he arrived home. The phone rang, one call after another, telling James how sorry they were. People leaving messages on our answering machine, love was pouring out to James from the community. We, his parents were not able to be there for him, but somehow these messages of love and concern helped to comfort James. One small message of caring and love at a time, all added up. The mother of Bryant's and Paul's roommate called James that night. She talked to him for hours. What an angel she was to James that night. He only needed someone to listen to him. When you feel the urge to call someone, and you don't know what you will say, don't worry simply send the love. It's far more important that you say something, not what you say. You never know what all of those small pieces of love can do for someone who is in need.

Section Two
Miracles

Serenity Prayer

God grant me
The serenity to accept the things I cannot change;
The courage to change the things I can;
And the wisdom to know the difference.
Living one day at a time;
Enjoying one moment at a time;
Accepting hardships as the pathway to peace;
Taking as He did, this sinful world
as it is, not as I would have it;
Trusting that He will make all things right
if I surrender to His Will;
That I may be reasonably happy in this life
and supremely happy with Him
forever in the next.

- Reinhold Niebuhr

Chapter **8**
The Neurological ICU

"Life is a grindstone, it either grinds you down or polishes you up....
It depends on what you're made of."
– Josh Billings

This is an accounting of our personal experiences in the Neurological ICU. I cannot say how it is today, but at the time of the accident these were the conditions we found. Although the care given to the patients was excellent, the conditions and the lack of care given to the family members we felt were in stark contrast.

Because of the late hour the Neurological ICU waiting room is dimly lit when we arrive. Rows of chairs line both the center and outer walls of the room. I do not know it yet, but we have moved into a new and unfamiliar world. My education about the unique etiquette of the people in this room is about to begin.

Oddly most of the chairs are occupied by either "the savvy old timers," or filled with their pillows and blankets, with stacks of their personal belongings surrounding them. Our little group has to split up to find open seats.

The highly coveted chair/beds have been claimed long ago and are not shared with new people. A seniority of sorts is in play, with the most senior "residents" claiming the chair/beds out of the direct overhead florescent lights, making it easier to close their eyes to sleep. We quickly discover their personal items designate their area and these items are not to be moved or touched to allow access to two chairs together. They are like a group of homeless, desperate vagrants; the only thing missing is a shopping cart.

Should you be lucky enough to find two chairs together the wooden arms make it impossible to lie across them, forcing you to sit straight up with the chair supporting only the middle of your back, allowing your head to flop around.

Later that night when Steve tries to stretch out his back we discover that hospital policy prevents you from lying down on the floor. The rule, "you must be in the chair at all times unless standing," is policed and enforced.

Our names are called and we think it is to see our son, but instead we are given a briefing on the rules here in the ICU. HIPAA rules are only now starting to be enforced and are in effect during their morning and evening rounds. With these rules and barring any special circumstances, we will be allowed complete access twenty-four hours, but only two people at a time back in his room. A new person cannot come in until another one has checked out at the reception desk.

We are informed that young patients normally have a lot of visitors, and they do not want us filling up their waiting room. They suggest we make up a poster board and leave it out in the waiting room so anyone who does show up can write a message to Bryant and then leave.

The cleaning staff arrives at ten each morning and we must vacate the area. The area will be locked for an hour to an hour and a half with no access during that period. All personal items must be in your chair during that time, or they will be disposed of.

The hospital does not provide toothbrushes or personal items. They do offer a limited number of pillows and blankets but are currently out of them. They suggest that we go to a hotel and tell us they will call us if there is any change.

The biggest problem with this I will discover later is that the doctors do rounds between the hours of nine and eleven in the morning. They only come out to speak with the patient's loved ones if they are in the waiting room while they are doing rounds. Which is very frustrating and highly inefficient.

These rules may seem reasonable to the hospital administration and cleaning staff; however, when it is your child it seems intolerable. I cannot leave and go to a hotel room. I am afraid to leave, and I assume so are they. It could be the last moment on earth with your loved one, or it could be the moment they wake up. How could one not be there for that?

Now that everyone understands the rules, we find a few scattered empty chairs. Hours pass by, and we are still not allowed access to Bryant. Sitting in the straight back chair feeling so useless, I watch as Steve calls everyone. He is different than me; he can call out for help, for comfort. I did not bring my phone with me and there is no one I want to reach out to anyway. I am numb, holding on by pulling within myself.

Steve calls his friend Brad, who tells him, that he is on his way, which is uplifting to us. Brad has a real relationship with God. We feel comfort knowing he is coming. We need all the connection to God that we can get right now.

Word is getting out, and with all the phone talking and conversations between our family, and Bryant's friends are starting to show up. The noise level is picking up. The waiting room "residents" are either in bed or getting ready to go to bed. I ask everyone to keep it down. Some people go home then and the rest, a little later. Finally, the receptionist calls out our name. She presses the button and a loud buzzer unlocks the heavy doors, allowing us to enter into the confines of the Neurological ICU.

Chapter **9**
The Blessings

"For I know the plans I have for you,"
declares the LORD, "Plans to prosper you
and not to harm you, plans to give you
hope and a future."
– Jeremiah 29:11

Bryant is now in his new room. The ICU rooms are positioned along the outside wall, in a horseshoe around the nurses' station, or command center. There are several nurses at the command center as each patient requires at least one nurse. There are no doors on the rooms because quick access and constant contact must be obtained. This room has walls on three sides. The top-half of the sidewalls are glass, with a small window on the back wall.

Bryant is lying in his new bed with the ventilator still breathing for him. Tubes are still in his arms and down his nose. Wires are connected to his chest and hand. He has his gown on but no blankets. Fevers are common on this unit and they like to keep them as cool as possible. He still wears his neck brace and his head is resting on a pillow. He has a pad underneath his midsection, which I recognize as a "chuck pad." These pads are fairly large, blue and absorbent with a waterproof backing. I know their purpose is to absorb bodily fluids. I recognize the pads from the year in high school when I worked part-time in the central supply of our local hospital.

He is still, without movement, except for the ventilator. I notice he now has restraints on both of his wrists. My son is tied down to the bed. They encircled his midsection with a fabric strap, which is tied down as well. His toes are naked and his ankles are left unrestrained. It all seems so cold, and inhuman, and why all this when he is not moving.

Steve and I stand on either side of him and each take one of Bryant's hands, his hand immediately encircles my finger. We look over at each other. We do not know it yet, but this will be one of the few times we will be in the room alone with our son. Most of the time we take turns, having one of us with him at all times. We keep a constant around the clock vigil over him.

I look over at my husband of twenty-four years. I must admit we have grown apart over the past ten or twelve years. We had been so young and in love when we married at age twenty-two. The first ten years of our marriage had been difficult but wonderful with all of the moves and all of the babies coming so close together. We had loved each other with such passion. Every time I looked at him my heart would skip a beat. I am such a serious person, and he had the ability to make me laugh; I used to love that about him. Now, I am not sure what I love about him anymore.

He has been traveling every other week for the past two years to do a side job in Florida as a trainer and a consultant, along with running his own brokerage business in town. With the kids being at such a vulnerable age, I hate him being gone and really need him at home. Actually, I needed him around for years. I had approached him a year and a half ago, and told him I was unhappy. I needed him to stop travelling, or I wanted a divorce. He had promised me he would do what he could and to give him some time. Nine months later, not seeing any change, I approached him about it again. Steve looked at me incredulously and told me he had his first meeting that week with his business partner to discuss how he could "possibly...maybe" stop the out of town travel. They had set up another meeting to discuss it further. I had been disgusted. I had waited nine months for this? I realized then that he had no intention of ever changing. His entire self-image was defined by his job.

After a lot of soul searching, I decided to stay married. We were almost through the bulk of the tough years. James is a junior this year; Elizabeth is heading to San Diego; Paul is graduating and

Bryant, I thought, was at least moving forward toward graduation and a career.

Steve has been so focused on his own career that it has taken over everything in our lives. He has not been there for me for the past decade, and I have withdrawn from him as well. Oh, he has been here financially, supporting the kids and me, but not emotionally. He is completely about work, removed from our lives, and on his phone with work, all of the time. When he's home, he wants to drink a beer, relax and be friends with the kids and their friends. The problem is that everyone loves him, and I am always the bad guy.

I'm the person who does the dirty work, fights all of the battles for everyone, and enforces the rules. I've become an angry, bitter, lonely, overweight woman with an attitude. I was hoping to find a new peace. I have been unhappy for a long time. I started reading _The Purpose Driven Life_, by Rick Warren. It seemed to jump off the shelf at the store when I bought it for myself at Christmas. I have not finished it yet. It is one of those books you read a little bit each day. I do really well for a while and then I set it aside; pick it up later, and set it aside again. I would like to find out what my purpose is in life. Perhaps I will find it at the end of the book.

I am making changes in my life. I have chosen to stay married and move the business home, and I have been consistently losing weight and started praying again. I am using the principles and tips I learned in the book. I have prayed diligently for my life to change; for my purpose in life to be revealed to me.

I am grateful that I have rediscovered prayer right now. This is our first moment alone with our son since the initial ER visit. Neither of us knows what to say or do. I feel uncomfortable holding Bryant's hand and letting the energy flow while Steve is in the room, which is all so strange. Steve reaches across Bryant's body and we lock hands. Bowing our heads and shutting our eyes, we each silently pray in our own way, asking God to heal our son, to save his life and bring him back to us.

The nurse comes in and tries to wake Bryant up. "Hey, Buddy, can you hear me? Buddy, Buddy," she tries again louder this time. "Buddy," she virtually shouts into his ear, "can you open your eyes for me? Lift a finger if you hear me." She then raises her fist and comes down hard on the metal prong in his chest; Bryant's right eye flies open. "Good, good, we don't play around with them up here, like they do downstairs. We need a response or we need to get busy," she says! I don't know what "get busy" means and I don't think I want to know.

I look around the room, trying to find a place to focus my attention. Pieces of note paper are taped up in several places with the words "Dissected Carotid Artery" written on them. I assume it is there in case they go in through an artery to save his life. In an emergency they would not have time to look at the chart and they know the carotid artery will blow. It is all so serious, stark, and cold.

Steve's phone rings. It is his friend Brad, his wife, and another man from their church are calling from the waiting room. They would like to come back and do a blessing for Bryant. Steve leaves to bring them back. It is so wonderful of them to make the two-hour trip here in the middle of the night. We are not even members of their church or any church for that matter. I am overwhelmed by their love and caring. For the first time in many hours, I feel a real sense of peace knowing they are here.

Steve comes back into Bryant's room with his friend and the other man trailing behind him. Apparently church officials are not held to the only "two at a time" rule. Brad's wife remains out in the waiting room. I thank him for coming. He introduces us to his friend and then hugs me.

"Catie, I am so sorry," he says. "I need to explain to you how this works. Steve has given us permission to perform a blessing. We have been given the power by our church, to perform such blessings. Now, we do not know the outcome of this blessing, but when I am finished words will come out of my mouth. I do not know what I will say, it is what it is. Do you understand?"

I nod in agreement. I have no idea what will happen; I only know I am grateful to him. I feel an immediate and overwhelming peace come over me when he walks into the room.

The nurse comes in and pulls the drape to give us some semblance of privacy. He walks to one side of Bryant and the other man is across the bed on the other side. I am standing at Bryant's feet with Steve. This "room" is very small and not intended for a patient, all of the equipment and four adults. It is quite cozy.

I wish I could remember exactly what they said, but I don't. I know they held a bible and they prayed. They started at the top of his head and worked their way down. I held onto Bryant's feet the entire time he received the blessing. I did not know if it was allowed but I did it anyway. If there was a power and a blessing to be had, I wanted to see if I could feel the power coming out of his feet. I kept my eyes closed in prayer and concentrated on the energy in the room. It seemed to me that indeed I did feel energy and that is where I kept my focus. When the blessing ended, Brad opened his eyes and said "Bryant will heal himself; however, it is dependent on how the two of you perform."

"What does that mean?" we ask.

"I don't know," he says. "We believe these blessings come directly from God, and I cannot tell you what they mean," he shrugged his shoulders. "Trust me sometimes I say some really bizarre things."

It doesn't matter to me if I can understand it or not. It is the first time anyone has said that Bryant will live. He will heal himself. I am a little worried; apparently my performance is going to be held accountable as well as Steve's. We join hands, we cry, and we pray over Bryant.

The nurse comes in and tells us Bryant's new doctor has arrived, and would like to examine him now. Would we please wait out in the waiting room and he will meet with us when he is available. We go out to the waiting room to meet up with Brad's wife. We hug.

They call us back into the small conference room connected to the waiting room. We are introduced to our son's new doctor. He tells us he has examined Bryant and that he is a very lucky young man to still be alive. He feels that it is amazing that Bryant is still alive and confirms that he has suffered traumatic brain damage that is rather extensive, agreeing with all of the diagnoses made in the ER. His left side remains immobile, he is unable to open his left eye at all, cannot squeeze with his left hand and they cannot get any movement from the left side of his body. He also warns us that although our son is still alive he is still in grave danger.

They will continue to monitor him for swelling of the brain, if he does not respond at any time they will then do further testing and possible surgery. He explains to us that the spinal fluid not only goes throughout your spinal column but also surrounds your brain tissue. The brain is very sensitive and once the tissue is dead or damaged it does not grow back. It becomes gray matter. The spinal fluid in the skull cushions the brain preventing it from hitting the hard skull. When the brain starts to swell sometimes they remove a portion of the skull to prevent the brain from hitting the hard bone surface. Since our son made it through the night last night and today, he is starting to come out of the danger zone for swelling, but he will still need to be monitored closely. The spinal fluid leaking out of his ear is good. It is releasing the pressure on the brain. Once again, they explain how crucial this puncture is, perhaps saving his life during those first hours.

He hands us an inch thick binder with all kinds of information on brain damage. It goes into detail on the many different ways you can damage your brain and how each part performs certain functions and when damaged those functions are now altered.

"Read this and it will answer a lot of your questions," he says.

He continues on and explains that the biggest problem we are facing right now is secondary infections. They will monitor him and if his temperature starts to rise, they will culture him to discover exactly which bug has infected him. Apparently, they do not mess around with general antibiotics' they go after the specific bug on this unit. Each time we re-stick or re-tube him we open him up to danger. Pneumonia is also a possible big problem. Often patients who survive their accident do not survive infections. Your son is not out of the woods yet.

The nightmare is not ending and the words are simply not sinking in yet for me. This is the last straw. We are desperately looking for hope, something to grasp, they are not going to give it to us. I look at him parent-to-parent.

"Yes, but he is going to live?"

"I can't answer that," he says looking straight at me.

With that I crumble, I just crumble. Choking back the sobs that I can no longer hold in "that's my baby in there, that's my baby; you need to tell me that he is going to live," I cry out.

Steve puts his arms around me, half to hold me and the other half to restrain me. I do not want him to lie to me, but I need some hope. Can't he give me something on which to cling, anything, a little bit of hope?

With that the doctor stands up and thanks us for our understanding, motions to the book and advises that we read through it and says he will be in contact with us, and keeping a close eye on our child. As he is preparing to exit the room, he looks back at us and tells us "he is so sorry we are going through this." With that he leaves the room.

I go back in to stay with Bryant. I wrap his hand in mine. He is deep into his coma. He is no longer wrapping his fingers around my hand. These are very dark hours for us. He is still in the danger zone for swelling of his brain, and the non-responsiveness is scaring us greatly. The staff is keeping a very close watch on him, coming and going constantly. His chest is rising and falling with the ventilator, and his heart rate has dropped very low.

I look up as a man and woman come back in with my husband. He introduces them to me as family to one of Bryant's close friends. He has been to family functions Bryant has attended. He is a Baptist minister and knows Bryant well. Their love for him is clear. It is around two in the morning. The nurse closes the drape around Bryant and this time, a minister and his wife pray over our son. The minister does a formal prayer, calling on the Lord to heal Bryant, to give Bryant the strength to fight his way back from the depths of his coma. Then, the woman lays her hands all over my child's body asking for a healing for him. They are there for some time. The love they show to him and their confidence in his recovery helps to buoy our hopes for him. Hope is what we desperately need. We hold hands with them and cry and pray.

Everyone leaves eventually except for me, and Steve. Everyone went back home to sleep. We take turns staying with Bryant, never leaving him alone. I sleep fitfully off and on throughout the night for a few minutes at a time sitting straight up in the chair with the wooden arms. When I go back into the room, Steve comes out to sit in the chair and naps. We rotate off and on throughout the rest of the night, each of us lost in our own thoughts...our own world.

I continue to hold Bryant's hand and pray, I am starting to get the confidence to pray out loud. This is something I have never done in the presence of others. I pray many times a day, every day, quietly to myself. Praying out loud in a room without a door in the quiet of the night is new to me. I know other people can hear me. I am frightened, unsure, and desperate. I hold his hand, ask for a healing, sending my love and energy to him. I believe in angels, and I ask the angels to come and surround him with a healing white light. I call on ancestors or anyone I can think of who has passed over to surround him and give him strength. He is fighting for his life.

Sometime around three or four in the morning, Steve goes down to the vending area to get a cup of coffee, and then changes his mind. Instead he goes through the doors and outside. He needs fresh air, lots of it, and he needs to cry, and to cry out. He looks around and finds himself on the first floor of the parking garage. Locating the stairway he goes up, up to the top. He needs to see the sky, to get some fresh air. There on top of the parking garage, by himself he falls to his hands and knees, crying out for help from above. For the first time in his life he is humbled. On his knees, looking up at the sky, he calls out to God to help his son. He calls upon Jerry (his friend from college who has died from a broken neck in a car crash) to be with Bryant and to help him. He calls out to Chris (a long time friend who has also died of a broken neck from a rolled car) to stay with Bryant, to help him understand what is happening to him. He calls out to his beloved grandfather, whom Bryant has been named after to be with him, to bring our son back to us. He calls out to his grandmother. He sits there on his knees, crying with the tears streaming down his face, asking, no, begging for help from on high.

When Steve comes back into the ICU room, we spend the rest of the early morning, crying and praying. Crying and praying, hoping for a miracle. The dark hours continue with no response from Bryant, only opening his eyes for a second responding to the pounding on the metal prong in his chest. I cling to my son and send every ounce of healing energy I can to him.

One moment our world is what we know it to be, and then... it all changed. The reality of our new life is starting to emerge. Our entire world, our entire family is now evolving. We know this, but we do not fully understand the impact this will have on all of us. The ripple effect has already been put into play.

Steve calls one of our closest neighbors, Big Joe, to take down the ugly metal pie pans he hung on the branches of the dead trees and bushes to be spiteful. He feels that he needs to work on his "karma." Steve tells him God had told him to remove the negative energy out of his life, while he was up on high in the parking garage. Do onto others as you wish them to do onto you. Our wonderful neighbor got up in the middle of the night and went out with a flashlight, into the brush to take them all down. What can one say about a neighbor like that? I guess he heard the desperation in Steve's voice and he did it. Crazy, huh.

Neither of us really sleep. It is impossible to sleep sitting up in a chair that only hits you mid-back, and our emotions are too raw. I look around the room; it amazes me that all of these people who have slept here all night, never offered to let us lie down for even an hour or two. They too have been through this horrible ordeal, their own personal hell; yet, they turn their backs on us. I would think they would be the most sympathetic of all. Several of the people also snore, loudly. As they wake up, they carefully fold and arrange their personal items on their chairs and preserve their space, for one more day.

Chapter 10
Survival Mode
(Day two)

"In school, you're taught a lesson and then given a test; in life, you're given a test that teaches you a lesson.
– Tom Bodett

It occurs to me that I am going to be here for a while. I call home and ask Elizabeth to bring me some clean clothes and toiletries. I need to brush my teeth badly. I also ask for a small pillow and a blanket. The reality is starting to sink in. I am becoming one of the homeless people in the waiting room. I vow to myself that I will not become hardened like them!

It is the last week of school. James will be having finals this week. Elizabeth will be experiencing all of her last senior high school moments as well. She will not have finals. Paul will be doing all of his finals this week and next, and turning in his final projects as well. If he wants to graduate, he has to stay focused. It is a big week for all three of them.

Steve calls the high school and speaks to the principal for Liz and James. He explains the situation and tells her they will not be in today, and he's not sure about the rest of the week. She asked if there was anything she can do, and Steve asks her to pray, forgetting completely about the separation of church and state. There is nothing else to be done. Things are not looking good for Bryant. They are not giving us any hope.

Paul is left to fend for himself, except for Leigh who has become his rock. He is twenty-two and on his own. When we were twenty-two, we were already married with a newborn child. Leigh is wonderful with Paul. She keeps him focused on his projects and on studying throughout the week. I believe this is the beginning of their relationship solidifying. He shows up at the hospital that morning with his books and with Leigh. Looking back on this now, twenty-two no longer seems old to me, but it did then. Like I said earlier, I look at the whole thing now through a different set of eyes.

I can't help anyone. I can't even speak about the events. I am frozen, in survival mode. I am alone with my thoughts and prayers. Time seems to stand still. Someone brings in the suggested poster board, for Bryant's friends, and as they arrive throughout the day, they sign the poster board, meet with each other, hug and talk.

Sometime during the day, another poster board is made up featuring photos of Bryant, which we hang in his ICU room. I ask the kids during my morning phone call to bring in photos of Bryant. They do a wonderful job. I want the doctors and nurses to see the son we know. I want them to know of his life, his hobbies and his family. Doctors and nurses can get caught up in the everyday drudgery of work, especially with brain damaged patients. I want to remind them this is our child and that he has a family behind him, we have his back. It is not so much for Bryant to see but to remind his caregivers this is/was a young man with a life/future not just another unknown patient, a male gamma.

This is not unlike the strategy I used with teachers and principals, (I had discovered that with teachers and tutors, especially with LD students), it was good to remind them these are "my" children. I wanted them to know I was involved. I preferred they like me and I was prone to work in the classroom or on special PTA projects and often baked cookies for the staff and events.

Two of our children are high achievers scholastically and two have learning disorders. Bryant has a transference learning difference. We had worked really hard to teach him different strategies to learn. Even then, there were many times I had to stand up for my child and buck the system, and this did not always make me popular. I was always about the child, what was best for them, even if it wasn't my child. If I saw an injustice with another child, I had no problem speaking out.

I wanted my children to get out of school with their self-esteem intact; red lines through a paper were not going to tell them they were failures. There are many different ways to learn, some kids are better at learning the way a particular teacher/school teaches, and that's all as far as I am concerned. The old saying "There is more than one way to skin a cat," rang true to me. I had learned early the more educated and informed I was, the better prepared I was to help my children. I admit, I am lacking in tact. I am more like a "bull in a china shop," and my own self-esteem has been hurt in the process. Steve always came in at the last minute with all of the charm and grace to set things straight. If he could only have been there from the start, it would have helped tremendously!

When I am out in the waiting room, I read the information given to us by the doctor. It's good information, a little complex, but it does explain the different types of brain injuries and their effects. I am confused, not understanding, which type of brain injury our son has suffered. All of the information I am reading tells me this is not a race, but a marathon. It is best if we take care of ourselves, get lots of rest, food and be prepared for the trials ahead. We should keep our visits short and take care of ourselves first. I understand, I really do, but when you are on the "live-or-die-watch," it is hard to leave.

This is one of the hardest parts for Steve; he is a planner. He lives with his planner in his pocket. There is no planning or time-line with a brain injury. Steve is always asking questions, wanting a time-line on recovery. The only answer to: when will this stage happen, or if recovery might happen at what time is "wait and see." This is easier for me. My life since having children has been to adjust to my family's schedules, needs and wants. When Steve wanted to accept promotions and move four children, I adjusted. When a coach decided the team needed additional practices or an out-of-town tournament was a must; I drove. When plans were set for an evening, only to discover a big school project was due the next morning, I adapted. Yes, I had learned to go with the flow, to live a wait-and-see life.

We are told Bryant's recovery will be based on three criteria, pending no unforeseen setbacks: his age, physical fitness, and his will to fight to come back. All three are equally important and he seems to have all three on his side. They also think the alcohol intake possibly helped to pickle his brain, perhaps preventing further damage, along with keeping him limp when he fell.

When booted out for morning rounds, the nurses gave Bryant a sponge bath and washed his hair. He looks and smells so much better when we finally get back into the room. Steve and I both notice right away he has more color in his cheeks.

Steve shares with me he asked the Lord to help Bryant survive. He begged Him to help Bryant come out fighting like the *scrapper* we knew he was. When the nurse came in and did the "Buddy" check, Bryant opened his right eye; it fluttered open and then closed. We are thrilled. He is also squeezing our hands. Our hearts lift.

Steve's brothers arrive and he goes out to meet with them. I am in the room holding Bryant's hand when he sits straight up and quick as a flash, before I know what he had done, he doubles over and grabs the ventilator tube in his lashed down hand. Pulling his head back toward the pillow he starts to rip it out of his throat. I am not prepared for this, and I scream for help and the nurses come running. I am amazed at the sheer strength it takes from a number of us to subdue him. His fingers are pried from the tubing, and we pin Bryant down on the bed. Carefully, they reinsert the partially extracted tube back down his throat. He thrashes around wildly and kicks one of the nurses so hard she flies out of our room. Yes, he is wild, but thank God, he is alive and fighting. My heart soars.

Throughout the day, like clockwork, they continue to do the "Buddy" checks, and he opens his eyes each time. I finally ask why they keep calling him Buddy, when his name is Bryant. Laughingly, they explain they call everyone, Buddy. They even have a Buddy award. It is given out each year to the most deserving nurse.

At this point I am introduced to the Glasgow Coma Scale,

which is used to determine the severity of a brain injury during the first, crucial hours following an accident. They rate his responses assigning numbers to them, which apparently correspond with the numbers on the scale, it works so well it has a ninety-seven percent success rate. It does a pretty good job of determining if someone will live or die, but it cannot determine if a person will recover, live independently, or work competently. I am going to include it here, so you can understand what we did not understand that first night. The Buddy checks are designed to constantly rate Bryant's responses.

Eye Opening:
Spontaneously 4
To speech... 3
To pain... 2
None 1

Best Motor Response:
Obeys Commands 6
Moves within the general locale 5
Withdraws.. 4
Abnormal muscle bending and flexing 3
Involuntary muscle straightening and extending 2
None 1

Verbal Response:
Is Oriented 5
Confused Conversation 4
Inappropriate words.. 3
Incomprehensible sounds 2
None 1

They have been rating Bryant with this scale, since the ER. We did not understand the scale in the ER or last night. Maybe if we had, it would have been helpful. Maybe it wouldn't have been, perhaps we would have just been counting up the numbers each time they checked on him. Sometimes, ignorance is bliss. He was not scoring very well during those first dark hours when he was completely unresponsive, except to pain.

People arrive throughout the day but I stay in the room with my son. Steve comes in and asks me to go get something to eat. I have not eaten since yesterday and I also need to let someone else come back for a while. I know he is right, but I really don't care about anyone else. However, I am feeling better about Bryant coming around and this is a marathon not a foot race. I cannot let myself get too run down.

I am sitting at the square table in the dingy dining area with the vending machines; a small hot food area has opened up since last night. I survey my food options. I have been dieting like crazy for the past year and a half. First doing Atkins, and it had worked well, I had lost a lot of weight, but had gotten stuck. I then went to a local diet doctor and he had put me on seven hundred calories a day, along with laxatives. It was the earlier prescription form of what would eventually become a leading fat blocking drug. It was not a good diet for me the effects were bad. I had been able to lose around three pounds a week on the diet, as long as I exercised for two hours a day. I decided not to go back to the diet doctor. It was too much.

I was afraid for my health at the time. My blood pressure had been soaring for the past year. I knew I had to lose some weight but this very low calorie diet had seemed really unhealthy to me, so I quit. Since quitting, the weight is starting to come back on. I look around at the carb buffet. There is absolutely nothing here I can eat. I select a sandwich; the first sandwich in a year and a half. I would be lying if I did not tell you it tasted really good. The funny thing is, no matter how much weight I lose or gain, in my mind I am still drastically overweight. My body image doesn't adjust.

Steve's brothers are down in the café with me. They arrived as soon as they could from two states away to be by their brother's side. It is so supportive of them to be here. I turn around and some-one is standing there, someone who looks familiar, yet I cannot place him in this environment. It is my nephew. We embrace; it is so good to see him. He had spent several weeks a year with us as a child and he was close to his cousins. He had driven all night to be here for us. I had no idea he was coming. I like the fact he did not wait to be asked, he simply came to be by our side. It is wonderful, so much love.

When I go back upstairs I am surprised to find Jack and Jeff, friends of the boys from St. Louis. They were at our house constantly when they were children and feel like family. Their support is priceless, and we settle in for a long couple of days.

The Neurological ICU waiting room is an emotionally energized room, filled with many distraught people and their baggage. Steve's parents are back and bring James, Elizabeth, Paul and Leigh. Steve's brothers, my nephew, Ace, Cam and her mother and some of Bryant's other friends are also here. We are starting to fill up the ICU waiting room and no matter how quiet we ask everyone to be, we are still loud. Our growing family is invading the private spaces of the other "homeless" residents.

Paul and Leigh settle on the chairs in the back of the room to study when one of the other patient's family members yells at them to get out of their chairs. Emotions are running high in here, and with that we ask everyone to go down a connecting staircase to the main waiting room. We assign a contact person who will be responsible for relaying information and coordinating the rotation of visitors going back and forth to see Bryant. Being downstairs in the waiting room also allows them to recognize and waylay visitors before they come upstairs. This ends up being a great strategy and reduces the drama in the ICU waiting room.

I hardly ever leave Bryant's side to let others come back. Steve rotates in and out more often than I do. I am quite selfish. When I do let someone rotate in, it seems like hours before I am finally allowed to go back. I sit out in the waiting room during these times and visit with my other children or read everything I can about brain damage.

Chapter 11
Fighting For Life
(Day three)

"Do not let what you cannot do interfere with what you can do."
– John Wooden

James came into Bryant's room and tells me about the phone calls and messages at home that first night. He is so touched by all of the outpouring of love. He had to erase them to leave room on the machine for today's messages, and says he is sorry I did not get to hear them. It does not seem real to me; who are these people? I tend to be an isolator; my children, my house, my work, and my husband have been my life. I am personally glad I did not have to talk to them. What would I say? Thanks for your concern? In my grief and shock, I want to pull a shell around me and close myself off.

Throughout the day, things are really improving as they check Bryant for responsiveness. He can open up his eyes now, and can usually lift a finger when asked to do so. He has also tried several times to pull out his ventilator. He is still fighting for his life and wants the tube out and this is something we cannot allow to happen.

While I am back holding his hand, I notice a couple of nasty looking areas on his arm. The nurses tell me these are "field sticks," where the IVs were placed during his rescue in the woods. They are now infected and crusted over with a hard green scab, and the skin around the sticks looks angry and red. I am shown where to get hot water and how to hold hot compresses on these areas. The result we are looking for is a softening of the scabs and eventually the opening of the puncture. Once this happens it will allow the infection to ooze out. She also suggests I "milk" or rub the area around the opening to encourage anything to move out in the direction of the stick.

I fill my day working on these areas. I am making great progress. Several of these spots appear on his arms, inner elbow and wrist. I continue to hold the hot compress on his body. This gives me something to do, in addition to prayer and sending love and energy. I am discovering as I practice I am getting quite good at this energy thing. I am not trained and I am a complete novice but I believe in my heart I am helping.

The nurse comes in and once again does the "Buddy" check. Bryant does not respond and she repeats the check a couple more times with no response. She pounds him on the chest, digging the metal prong into his skin. His eyes fly open and he gives her an angry look. She looks him in the eye and says:

"Buddy, can you raise your finger for me? Just lift up one finger."

He looks at her, raises his middle finger, then closes his eyes.

I never thought I could be so happy my child has given someone "the bird." Yes, I am so very happy because this tells me he can move his finger and he can think. He cannot communicate with us because of the ventilator, but he can think. I could dance around the room.

Later that day, I am sitting alone with Bryant, holding his hand, and holding the hot compress on his arm with my other hand. Bryant quickly sits up again, and throws his head forward to remove the ventilator. I jump up and start screaming for help. I lay my body across Bryants', trying to hold him down so he cannot get to his ventilator tubing. I am screaming for help and this time no one comes. At that moment with super human strength, while tied to the bed, Bryant throws my body off his. He bends over and puts his mouth in his hand and pulls the ventilator completely out of his throat. This all happens so quickly I am still screaming for help.

Nurses rush in, the room explodes with people. Someone screams for me to be taken out of the room. I am angry it has taken them so long to respond and stand firm. The head nurse quickly takes control of the situation. She tells me I can stay if I can control myself. I assure her, I can.

She rushes up to Bryant's head; she explains to him they are going to need to re-tube him. In a loud, firm voice she explains to him that he has a broken neck and they must remove his neck brace in order to re-ventilate him. It is very important he doesn't move. Another nurse comes in behind him and places her hands on his head to try to immobilize him.

I grasp the severity of the situation and instinctively grab Bryant's hand. He wraps his hand very tightly around mine while they are working on his head. I can tell that he's frightened; he has had someone in here holding both of his hands throughout his time in the ICU. While I am on one side of his body, I can see his other hand opening and closing, searching for another hand to hold! While they are taking off his neck brace and trying to slide a new tube down his throat, I find a spot between all of the bodies around him and lay my body across his to reach for his other hand. It reminds me of a game of twister, trying to locate his other hand through the tangle of bodies. His hands and feet are tied to the bed, making it very difficult to grab his other hand. I feel his fingers tighten around my hand and this is something I will never forget, no matter how old I am. I knew then that he knew I was there. He had asked for me the only way he knew how, by the opening and closing of his hand. Both of his hands are now gripping mine.

Once the tube is inserted down his throat, Bryant relaxes and passes out again. I sit by his side and resume my duties.

They come in to ask me to leave; it is time for the evening rounds. They tell me it will probably be around an hour and a half before they let anyone come back in. I am feeling so much better as I head out to the waiting room, although a bit shaky after the past hour. My spirits are lifted by the thought that my son knows I'm here, he is holding my hand, he wants his hand held, somehow his brain is working, it is not only an automatic response.

Plans are made for us all to walk down the street to a pizza parlor; a cute little restaurant with outside seating. Walking outside the waiting room is beginning to feel surreal, being around people, hearing them talk and laugh about life doesn't seem to fit. I listen to stories of the "good old days," remembering childhood stories that include Bryant, Paul and James. We are laughing and reliving all of the crazy things they had done together.

Jack and Jeff then tell us they did not know Bryant was not in a hospital near our house. They drove straight to our house from St. Louis, and when no one was there, they started calling around and found out where we were. I laugh at them and apologize, it took them hours out of their way. In the confusion, the location had been left out. The love from those two wonderful young men, driving from city-to-city and state-to-state, to find their friend and never giving up is quite a testament to the kind of adults they have become.

"What are those crazy-ass bugs flying around your house," they ask.

We explain what we know about Cicadas and that they have been expected, but as of yet we really haven't seen many.

"Well, let me tell you, they are out in force," they say. "We could hardly get out of our truck, they are so thick at your house."

Sitting outside in the fresh air, eating, and telling stories with people I love, I am finally starting to relax. We spend the entire hour and a half sitting out there. I am feeling a little guilty, and I want to get back to the ICU.

When we get back, the waiting room is fairly empty. Most of the visitors are back with their loved ones. When Steve and I go back to be with our son, the receptionist tells us he cannot receive visitors yet. She tells us they could be running a test or a procedure, and we need to wait until they are finished. We do not like this feeling of absolutely no control at all, and we feel uneasy as the minutes turn into an hour.

Apparently Bryant has pulled his ventilator out again. This is getting to be a problem. My experience with his lightening quick reflexes, tells me they are not watching him close enough during rounds. I am also feeling guilty, I had been out eating and laughing while my child was going through God only knows what again. I know how frightened he had been the last time they had to re-ventilate him. I had not been there to hold his hand. I am frustrated but do not see many choices, they are going to make us leave every time they do rounds.

We spent the rest of the night sitting by his side, taking turns holding his hand and praying for his recovery. I isolate myself with Bryant and miss most of the visitors along with the love, trauma and pain that comes with them. I stay back in the room with my son. Later that night looking at the poster board, I am quite amazed at the number of people who have driven hours to be by our side. Most of them were turned away without visiting Bryant. Only family members and very special family-like people are allowed back.

Later as I head out to go to the waiting room, a nurse pulls me aside; she shows me a chair that folds down into a bed. She tells me she has been hiding it for me. I thank her; it is so thoughtful and I am overwhelmed with emotion. We carry it out to the waiting room, and I fold it down and make up my bed with my pillow and blanket. I pass out for a few hours amidst all of the snoring and coughing from the other "homeless" residents. It feels great. I am such a light sleeper that it is hard for me to believe I can sleep in a room with so many strangers and be so grateful.

Chapter

The Wakening **12**

"To be brave is to behave bravely when your heart is faint."
– Pat Henin

Clearly they underestimated how determined and stubborn Bryant is, and clearly they do not know me and how focused I can be. Years of taking control with learning disabled children taught me to depend on my own gut instinct. I researched different types of teaching, learning strategies, hired tutors and spent countless hours applying these skills to their strengths.

I form a plan and develop a strategy. The nursing staff only asks us to leave while the doctors do rounds. If I am really quiet, like in the ER they may ignore me. I will need to make sure I am back there before rounds begin, and be helpful, not a burden. I also need to be cautious about trading out with someone else. I want to be back there before they close the waiting room for cleaning in the morning, and then possibly be in the room when his doctor comes by. Our doctor came by yesterday morning while the waiting room was closed, and we missed him. I'm not planning on missing him two days in a row. It is a careful game of cat and mouse. It shouldn't be this way, but I don't make the rules.

While resting on my fold-out bed, I make some decisions. I am going to find a shower here at the hospital, and I am also going to eat. I need to take better care of myself. Bryant is starting to improve, and he is going to need us. Steve is right, neither of us will be of use to anyone if we get ill. Our son has needed us here for these past hours, but he is going to need us to be strong and healthy for the rest of his journey.

I am going to find a local hotel within walking distance of the hospital and rent one room that we can rotate in and out of for sleeping and showering. I need to take charge and get focused. I am not going to be a lost, desperate homeless person. I have money for a room, and I intend to spend it. I feel empowered by these decisions. After all, we are in a marathon.

Bryant is doing well this morning; he appears to be resting. When we are allowed into his room, the first thing I notice is that the "Dissected Carotid Artery" signs are down. I call to our nurse. She tells us a mistake must have been made in the ER. They did another scan and there is no sign of a dissected carotid artery, and for that matter there is no sign of a stroke either.

"How can that be," I ask, "I saw the blood in his brain on the scan myself. " She shrugs her shoulders as if to say "who knows."

Steve looks over at me and tells me:

"The power of prayer, Catie, what else could it be? We know he was paralyzed; he couldn't even open his one eye or squeeze our hands. Here is a phrase I have been repeating to myself for the past twenty-four hours; it is a phrase with seven very powerful words: *I believe in the power of Christ.*"

What we all have witnessed in the past few days has been truly a miracle. That's when I realized I was not the only one going through a transformation. I never heard those words come out of the mouth of my husband, not ever. I cannot help thinking, "*Who are you, and what have you done with my husband?*"

And yet, I know he is right, this is a miracle. I look over at him; we are on this journey together; yet, separate. I have not had much alone time with him at all.

We meet with the doctor that morning. He tells us that although it is looking positive, Bryant is not out of the woods yet, once again with the "out of the woods." They will continue to monitor him. The most crucial time for swelling of the brain is passing, and it looks like we have been lucky. He wants to know if we read the information he gave us last time.

I tell him I have read all of the information. I am confused about the different types of injuries that one can obtain. There is the impact, where the brain is hit by an object and the skull is fractured; there is contra-coup, where the brain is jarred on the inside and gets damaged by the impact of the brain against the skull; then you have the shaken-baby scenario, where the brain is shaken up and damaged by the jarring. You also have strokes, or aneurisms, that can damage the brain cells. I am looking at him as I explain what I have learned, and then it dawns on me: Oh my gosh! My son has them all; it's all rolled into one. I can hardly voice my concerns.

"Bryant has all of these different types of injuries doesn't he?"

Before he can answer I go on, "The impact came from the rock that shattered his skull and the side of his brain, the contra-coup damaged the front and the back of the brain from the force when he landed, he rolled over and over again once he hit the slope at the bottom, therefore the shaken-baby scenario, and the bleeding of the carotid artery into his brain caused additional damage. Is this true?"

"Yes, he has suffered all of these injuries," he says.

"His brain is damaged and the prognosis is not good. He does not appear to have damaged his brain stem, only the slight fracture on his vertebrae. It will heal in time. He is young, in good physical shape, and clearly he has the will to live or he would not have made it this far. However, like I stated before, secondary infections are the biggest fear at this time. What type of recovery he will have is unknown. Every brain injury is unique and different. An eight-foot fall, or a car crash with a bumped head can render someone useless, and then someone can fall 150 feet like your son and survive. We don't know as much as we would like to about the brain and its ability to recover. We will take it one day at a time, sometimes one hour at a time, we have no time-lines."

The grim reality is starting to sink in. I had read all of the information about what different types of damage can occur, but also how each of these injuries can hinder a person's ability to rationalize, think, respond, and impact everything they do. He has so many different types of injuries, I am unable to comprehend how different he will be. I am starting to get the concept of brain injury and brain damage.

Steve is talking to him about insurance, and rehab centers down the road, and at what point he would be moved to a hospital room and so on and so on. My head is spinning with the brain damage vs. brain injury. I will call it an injury from now on. I am not willing to accept damage; such an ugly word. I know that Steve, who is in the insurance business, will handle all of the necessary paperwork and use his connections to do whatever needs to be done. I am more than willing to hand that over to him and check out of that conversation completely.

That is when I look over at Steve; he has on a new collared T-shirt, one I had never seen before. It has "Medical Staff" embroidered on it. I don't know where he picked it up, but he is given a little more respect around the hospital that day and the next, while he wears it.

I watch carefully and sit quietly with Bryant when they close down the waiting room, and they do let me stay for a while, but kick me out when the teaching staff come through. I am frustrated but have gotten a few extra minutes with him. I do not trust them anymore; yesterday's de-tubing has scared me. It is important he be watched by a family member every possible minute to prevent any more episodes.

After they boot me out, I find a visitor's shower up on another floor. I cannot wait until I get a hotel to shower. The door does not lock but Elizabeth stands guard for me, and it feels wonderful. I brush my teeth and hair, and I put on the clean clothes she has brought me. This is the first time I have been clean in days.

When they open the waiting room again after the cleaning, the other visitors go back, but they do not allow us entry. We wait for what seems like a really long time. We know something is wrong, but we don't know what. I am afraid he has de-tubed himself again. He is really determined, and strong.

Finally, the receptionist calls us up and lets us go back. When we walk into his room we are in shock. The ventilator is no longer down his throat and he is breathing on his own.

The nurse walks in and smiles at us.

"He was able to get his ventilator out again this morning during rounds, as well as last night. He also had that incident while you were in the room."

She looks knowingly at me, she is the same nurse who has rescued him both times he has de-tubed himself.

"Every time we have to re-stick or re-tube him we open him up to the germs. Plus the longer he is on a ventilator, the higher his risk of pneumonia. When someone is that determined to get the ventilator out, it is best if we can take it out. I called the doctor and spoke to him. He had been breathing for hours down in the Gorge, clearly he was able to breathe. We are taking a chance, but I think it is one worth taking. We will monitor him closely and if he has trouble breathing, we will need to re-tube him. He still has a tube going in through his nose and into his stomach for food. We need him to keep that tube. He will be able to talk though, with that tube."

We are elated; this is great news. He can breathe on his own, he has come so far. I am also feeling a combination of guilt, irritation and fear over his four de-tubings. I stopped him once, and would have the second time if help had come faster. The fact he had gotten the best of them both times we were not back here, upsets me. I cannot trust them to watch him closely. The threat of infection has me frightened, and yet, the ventilator is out, and this is good. Bryant is continuing to fight.

We are encouraged by our child's advances. We decide Elizabeth and James will go back to school the next day, and try to finish out the week. We talk to them about it and decide if at any point it is too much, to just go home. Thankfully, their grandparents, Rose and Bernard, will be staying at the house with them, while Steve and I are here at the hospital.

We will rotate between the hotel and the hospital. We have not made any plans to return home; we are living one moment at a time.

Chapter 13
The Other Side

"For He shall give His angels charge over you, to keep you in all your ways."
– Psalm 91:11

They continue with the "Buddy" checks, but this time Bryant is able to make sounds. The sounds quickly turn into words, and sentences. He is able to cough, which is good. The more he coughs the more he will clear out his lungs and lessen the chance of pneumonia. During one of the "Buddy" checks, the nurse asks him if he recognizes me or his dad. He does not seem to know who we are. I tell him it is all right because he will. He is also able to blow his nose now. He really appreciates tissues, and he filled four of them. It has been a wild afternoon. Bryant is now using complete sentences... only some of them are a bit inappropriate with random comments like:

"Fat F***ing cow, I hate you. Get me out of here. F#*#k off. I have to go to the bathroom, and we'll all go one, two, three... you didn't go, wanting the nurses to leave when he counted to three."

Later that night, the minister's wife stops by again to pray over Bryant. He opens his eyes and looks at her while she prays over him, and then he relaxes and falls back asleep.

Shortly after she leaves I am sitting there holding his hand when he opens his eyes and says:

"She is powerful. Are you praying?"

"Yes, Bryant," I said. "I am praying."

"They say you must pray louder," he tells me. "They say it's not decided yet."

And with that he falls back to sleep or back into a lighter form of his coma, I can't tell the difference. He has been drifting in and out all evening.

I look around the room, I am the only person in here, and no one else has heard him. I know this message is directed at me.

If they say it, then it shall be done, I think to myself.

I start to pray loudly this time. I can no longer worry about what other people may or may not think about me. The little girl in me that wants to hide in the wallpaper will have to be noticed and heard. No more "wallflower prayers" worrying about other people. I want it to be decided, and decided in our favor. I want Bryant to return to us.

He opens his eyes the next time I am alone in the room with him. He looks at me, and says:

"Who is the man in the corner?"

I look over at the corner.

"There isn't anyone in the corner, Bryant," I say, thinking that perhaps he is hallucinating.

"He is there, in that corner," he says with certainty.

He drifts back into his "coma."

A while later he opens his eyes again. I am still sending love and energy down my arm to him, and praying softly out loud.

"That man, he is still in the corner. He says he knows you."

He closes his eyes and disappears once again.

I look over at the corner, a feeling of uneasiness coming over me. I am unsure what to think. Who could it be, and who knows me?

Bryant wakes again.

"That man in the corner, he was with me when I fell, he stayed with me in the Gorge."

Bryant starts to drift away again and I call out to him:

"Wake up! Wait, there's no one there!"

He opens his eyes slightly.

"Yes he is, right there in the corner, I can see him. He never leaves."

This has exhausted him and he drifts away. I don't know what to think anymore, I don't know where my son is going when he closes his eyes, I don't know with whom he's talking; I don't know anything anymore.

I look around the room.

What is going on, I think. *Is there someone here in the room with us?*

The hair on my arms stands straight up. Who could it be? He says he knows me, and it's not decided yet and that I have to pray out loud. I realize that I am having the most horrendous moments of my life. Yet, I am having the most spiritual moments of my life at the same time.

So many people have wanted to know who the man in the corner is when they hear this story. I do not have the answer. He is whoever you believe he is. I can only tell you this story is the truth and report it to you the way it happened. I am looking forward to someday finding out who he is.

Bryant drifts in and out of consciousness throughout the rest of the day and evening. He is becoming agitated. Somewhere down deep in his mind he knows that it is wrong to go to the bathroom on himself. The pad they have under him to catch his own bodily secretions is not acceptable to him.

He is growing restless, and they inform me if he continues to get agitated they will have to sedate him. The more often they have to sedate him, the harder it will be for his mind to recover. It is important that he comes around as quickly as possible.

He is yelling that he has to "piss," and thrashing about and pulling at his restraints. If my son has a kernel of recognition in his mind that knows it's wrong to urinate on himself, I want to encourage this sense of being treated normal. Going to the bathroom on himself is not a normal thing to do. They bring a urinal over, but he seems unable to release it while lying down. He grows more and more agitated as time goes by. I ask the nurse if we can try to stand him up to urinate.

Much to my surprise she agrees. His neck brace is on and he seems to be no longer paralyzed on his left side. We sit him up slowly and let him sit there for a couple of minutes, but he is growing restless. We seek the help of another staff member to help balance him. I stand in front of him, with both of his hands on my shoulders to help steady him. The three of us slowly help him to stand, and I am not prepared for how weak my son is as he starts shaking uncontrollably. I am holding the urinal for him and he suddenly starts to go, the problem is that he empties his bowels at the same time.

The staff member we asked to help us is disgusted, "He's incontinent; he is going everywhere, what a mess. He is incontinent. Why did we do this?"

I know why, it is because I had insisted. He is weak and shaking so terribly we have to lay him back down on the soiled bed. We roll him onto his side like a child and clean him and the bed. The efforts have exhausted him; once he is cleaned up, they tie him back down to the bed and he passes out.

I sit by his side and resume my work of applying hot water compresses and milking the greenish colored ooze out of his arms, it is really starting to come out now. I sit throughout the rest of the evening in that capacity, holding his hand, praying, and working on his arms, sending all of my love and energy out to him. He is very calm and relaxed for the rest of the night.

They continue with the hourly "Buddy" checks. Around two o'clock Thursday morning, the nurse wants him to open his eyes, but he refuses. She asks him to hold up a finger for her and he refuses to do that as well. She pinches continuously, not wanting to slam her fist down on his metal prong. He gets angry and gives her the finger; we all get a laugh out of this.

I don't share my experiences about the man in the corner, or the incontinence with anyone. I stay in the room most of the night as people come and go. Steve and I like the nights best when no one else is around. He encourages me to go out and lie down in the waiting room. He is concerned about my blood pressure. I know he is right, it is not a foot race but a marathon and if I stroke out, who will be here to help my son.

I rest for a couple of hours in the waiting room, but can't go over to the hotel, so much has happened and I need to be close. I encourage Steve to go to the hotel instead. I sit with Bryant. He is quiet. Wrapping his hand in mine, I notice his field sticks have closed back up, so I continue my duties: love, energy and hot water, grateful to have something to do.

While I'm alone with him, I watch his heart monitor. Sometimes his heart rate picks up when I come into the room, but mostly it slows down. I think maybe he feels safe when I am here and he can let go. His heart rate mainly stays in the fifties with occasional ups and downs.

As I sit here with him, I watch as his heart rate goes down into the low thirties. I am not a nurse but that seems low to me. I call the nurse over. Looking at the monitor she quickly calls the doctor. I can hear her on the phone saying that he is "bradying." I don't know what it means but I don't think it's good. I watch as she gets what looks to me as a very large syringe, fills it and stands over him. My heart is pounding fast enough for both of us. She calls out to him, hitting the metal prong on his chest. He responds by opening his eyes, and his heart rate goes back up. She tapes the syringe to the end of his bed.

We lock eyes and she tells me she does not want me to spend the rest of the time he is in the hospital watching the monitor, afraid. It is going to be all right, but just in case, she pulls up a chair next to mine, and that is how we spend what is left of the night.

Chapter
Self-Prophecy
and a Red Eyed Wolf

14

"Now faith is the substance of things hoped for, the evidence of things not seen."
– Hebrews 11:1

The next morning Bryant's heart rate is looking good. I am so happy, it has been staying around fifty-five to fifty-six, it even went up to eighty-three when I took his hand in mine. Regardless of what the nurse said, I watch the monitor constantly. I now have a fear that his heart will simply stop.

I hold his hand in mine and do my duties: prayers, energy, and field stick cleansing. Yesterday they had red streaks emulating out from them, but today the hard crusty areas open up a little easier and the red is almost gone.

The nurse steps back into our little room. I am beginning to feel at home here. During his next buddy check they are unable to get a response from him. She tries everything from yelling, pinching to pounding on his chest. She works on him for quite some time. Returning to the nurse's station she calls the doctor. My blood pressure must be soaring; I can hear my heart pounding in my ears. We have come so far we can't lose him now.

He will not squeeze my hand back, when I squeeze his. He will not open his eyes or lift a finger. He is out cold.

The nurse swabs alcohol soaked cotton all over Bryant's face, calling out, "Hey Buddy can you hear me, can you give me a sign, can you hear me?"

Bryant lifts his middle finger. We are so relieved.

Bryant opens his eyes and looks at me, "I want to go home."
He does not call me by name, but he knows that I am about
home. My heart is soaring.

I sat in the room with Bryant most of the day, holding his
hand, working on his field sticks, and sending love and energy
to him. He is calm this morning and he is responding to most
of his Buddy checks. Sometimes they have to work harder than
others, but he is responding by opening his eyes, moving a finger, or
answering them with a word here or there. They are starting to get
more complex and they want him to do all three. It is like an Apgar
test done on babies to test their ability to respond. They rate him
after each check.

He is assigned physical and occupational therapists to work
with him. While they are moving his arms and legs around, Bryant
is yelling "ouch." His muscles must be really stiff and sore; they have
taken quite a beating from the fall.

He has been talking to me, but has not used my name, or the
word "Mom," but he continues to know what I represent, home. I
am good with that for now.

Bryant opens his eyes when we are alone. He asks me again,
"Who is the man in the corner?"

I am starting to get more comfortable with this conversation.
I tell Bryant that he is his guardian angel; this seems as likely as
anything else to me.

He looks at me strangely and says, "Oh," like he doesn't really
believe me, but accepts it. I don't know what else to say.

Later that day when we are alone he looks at me and says
"Won't we have a jubilation when I come home?"

A few minutes later he opens his eyes again,

"Won't we all rejoice when I can swim in the pool again?"

I feel the hairs on my arms and the back of my neck rise again.
I look around the room. I know that someone is talking to me
through my son.

My hard drinking twenty-one year old son does not know the
word "jubilation" and he is not anyone to talk about "rejoicing." He

is not a big reader and has not been in Sunday school since he was a small child. I am starting to have a small freak out. I know that I am witnessing something unbelievable but I really don't know why me, or what to think about it. It only seems to be happening when we are alone together. I look around the room and I cannot help but wonder who else is in here with us. *Who is reaching out to me from the other side? Who is going to believe me?*

The list of miracles is starting to get lengthy. He lived through a fall of 150 feet without being broken into pieces. He survived around ten hours without even a shirt in the rain before getting medical aide. A burr hole was drilled into his skull by a rock preventing death as his brain swelled. Then the miraculous rescue, the disappearing dissected carotid artery, the blood mass in his head vanishing, and the complete reversal of paralysis, come on. Now the man in the corner and the conversations with "the other side." This is a lot to digest.

Once again Bryant is growing agitated. To my knowledge he has not eliminated his body waste since yesterday. He is yelling once again that he has to "piss." He is getting loud and thrashing around trying to get out of his bonds. I know that if he continues to act this way, they are going to sedate him.

I talk softly to him, telling him that it is all right, to go to the bathroom on himself. He can't do it. Now that he has been labeled as incontinent, no one wants to help me with this problem anymore. I don't know what to do. This goes on for a couple of hours. I feel so useless. I try getting a urinal for him but to no avail. Why don't they just put a catheter in him? I feel that they do not treat brain injury patients with the dignity that they should be treated with. I am desperate. I have not heard anyone use the word brain injured, only brain damaged. I am taking it as if a brain "damaged" person is to be sedated and left to urinate and defecate on themselves. This does not sit well with me.

I know by instinct that my son is in there and he wants to be treated with dignity, like a man. How can they expect him to recover if they do not treat him like a man? If there is a seed of dignity in there, it should be nourished and embraced. All day long I sat here and heard people calling out for help. Some of these calls are ignored as the ravings of a mad person; I am so frustrated with the entire situation. All I can do is pray.

I vow that my son will have a family member with him at all times throughout his recovery. No matter where the recovery stops. He will not be treated like this, a raving mad man without respect.

Bryant quiets down for a couple of minutes, and drifts off.

I look over at the corner and speak softly to the man in the corner,

"O.K., I can't see you, but Bryant tells me that you are here, I need your help. You want me to know you're here and I need you to help me. Bryant needs to go to the bathroom; you understand what is going on here. I need you to help him go. Please help us."

Within seconds Bryant opens up his eyes, "Mom that man in the corner, he's there again."

"Yes, Bryant he is your guardian angel," I tell him.

"No, I don't think so." he exclaims, "His eyes are red. They're scary. Oh no!"

He claws the air with his securely lashed down hands and kicks his feet, trying to protect himself from his attacker. He screams again and again.

Several health care workers come running. He is clawing the air trying to ward off his attacker, letting out the most heart wrenching screams and sobs I have ever heard in my whole life.

At that moment I am wondering, *what red-eyed demon have I unleashed on my son?* My heart is breaking.

Then he looks over at me and says:

"Did you see that? Did you see that? That thing just turned into a wolf. It was a wolf, and it jumped on me and it shit and pissed all over me."

It is true. He had been so frightened that he released his bladder and his bowels all over himself. He doesn't think he is responsible for this unacceptable act. It was the "wolf" that had done this to him.

We clean him up and then he falls peacefully back to sleep. No sedation needed, crisis adverted.

I sit down in shock, thinking through the events that have transpired. I am so out of my realm here. I look over at the corner then back at my son. What have I invited in? What have I done to my son? That thing in the corner has helped me and provided exactly what was needed, within seconds of my asking. It was the perfect scenario: Bryant was able to keep his manhood intact, yet go to the bathroom. It was not a fluke. The man in the corner is clearly powerful beyond my imagination. My son is clearly seeing things that I cannot, but what about me? What am I witnessing here? My heart is pounding. I should seek clerical help at this point, but I am afraid. I can't talk about this to anyone at all. I decide to keep it to myself. My throat and voice are getting tighter and smaller.

Chapter

Facing the Unknown 15

"Challenges are what make life
interesting; Overcoming them is
what makes life meaningful."
– Joshua Marine

The doctor has prepared us that there are several stages of recovery, and we are now entering into them. Bryant could skip some of the stages or get stuck on one and never progress. He is now venturing into the agitation stage. This is to be expected they tell us. He is now using complete sentences, and many of them are quite improper.

He is really agitated with the buddy checks, and is responding with "I hate you," "Get me out of here," "F__ off," or when asked who someone is he say's "Pamela Anderson." They prepared us that being sexually inappropriate will probably come next.

Brain injuries are very tricky, your strengths will possibly still be your strengths although watered down and whatever skills were weakest will probably be even weaker or nonexistent. Bryant has depended on his social skills to make it through school. His social skills still seem to be here, although primitive.

We are also entering into another phase of recovery as well, a phase of financial pre-recovery. Nine months earlier we purchased a new house for my mother in Florida, near one of my sisters. Steve and I own the house my mother lived in prior to that for 16 years. My parents had chained smoked in the house the entire time. It looks and smells like a smoke bomb has gone off in it. We are close to having it ready to put on the market, but not quite. Steve makes an odd request of a nephew in the process of jumping in his car to come visit us. In exchange for the long drive here would he consider emptying out the garage and the basement for us? He agrees, and it is a great help. With everything else on our plate, Steve realizes that we are now going to need to pick up our efforts and get it sold, soon.

He is worried about our finances and knows that the bills from the accident are going to add up quickly. Many people lose their homes or go bankrupt over accidents such as this. He is preparing for the financial onslaught coming our way.

While I am in the back with Bryant, Steve is doing what he does best: negotiating with insurance companies, talking to people at the hospital and making financial decisions. He knows that this is going to be a really complicated and expensive bill, and we need to get every dollar paid for that we can. We will not qualify for any financial help.

He is also talking to professionals with connections on the best type of care and recovery options available for our son. They convince him not to put Bryant into a hospital room upstairs, but to move him directly into a rehab setting. The faster he starts rehab the better for his brain, the better his chances for recovery, time is of the essence.

They tell him Bryant may be in the rehab center for up to four months. Steve decides that it will be better for all of us to move him to a highly recommended rehab center closer to home.

The hospital insists that he must be transferred by ambulance in keeping with hospital procedure. Steve arranges for an ambulance to transfer him when he is ready to leave the ICU. I go along with his plans, it all sounds good to me.

Steve is with Bryant, and I come out to sit with our family in the waiting room. I am rather awe struck. I have been praying non-stop for days now. I have experienced real spiritual moments back in the room with Bryant. I am not comfortable talking about my experiences. Stress, unhealthy food, and lack of sleep have definitely taken a toll on me; yet, the spiritual experience is still amazing. It has me buzzing on the inside. I want to hold it inside of me for now. I really don't know what to make about it all, until I understand what is happening. I feel really silly trying to explain this to anyone, and I don't want to take a chance that someone may pooh-pooh me about it all. I am in need of both spiritual and emotional recovery as well. I am so confused.

Who is the man in the room? He was with Bryant when he fell. He had been in the Gorge with Bryant. He stayed by his side when Bryant was alone, crying out for help. I believe that he was instrumental in keeping Bryant conscious to call for help. Maybe he had been the spirit that had guided James down into the canyon, when he had no idea where he was going. Something or someone had guided his feet that fateful morning. He is with him now in the ICU. He is letting me know he is there. He acted upon my request.

I don't know what to think anymore. What if he is not good? What if he is really evil? Those red eyes and Bryant's insistence that he doesn't think he is a good guardian angel have me unnerved. What if I have invited something really evil to interact with my son? One thing I know, if there is a light, there is also a dark. Have I invited a good spirit or an evil spirit into my son? I am so confused; I don't know where to turn anymore.

Who is telling Bryant that it had not been decided yet and that I need to pray harder, louder? Why was it important that I pray out loud? Who is speaking to me through my son? Who is using the words jubilation and rejoicing? Is it Bryant? Is it a deceased family member? Is it a good spirit or a demon? Where has my son been? What is going on here? I am so out of my league. I sift through the facts, trying to make sense out of it all.

How can I tell anyone else about my experiences in that room? I can hardly believe it myself? I do not want to be judged harshly, made fun of, or looked at like I have lost my mind. Who am I to be witnessing these things? I have not been a true "Christian," as I would term the word. And yet, my son is moving his body, his carotid artery is no longer torn. He is speaking to me, breathing and he is alive. He fell 150 feet and the only bone broken in his body is a slight fracture in his neck. He should be crushed; his body should be broken into pieces. His internal organs should be mush.

Praise God. I want to shout hallelujah, but I don't have the self-confidence to do that right now. So I sit here quietly, thinking everything through. I move back and forth from Bryant's side to the waiting room, taking part in the conversations but not really engaging. My head is swimming with these unanswered questions throughout the day.

Chapter 16
Family is a
Relative Term

*"Holding on to anger is like grasping
a hot coal with the intent of throwing
it at someone else; you are the one
who gets burned."*
– Buddha

I have just read James' account of the rescue, it adds to my amazement and to my confusion. I realize I don't really know anything, and that I have no control over anything. I had no idea how big a role James had played in getting his brother out. How would I? He has not talked about it with me. Clearly I am not the only one unable to talk. Ace has become like an instant family member, being at the hospital as much as possible. It was the outpouring of love, fear, and emotion that had forced Ace to cradle his friend's body and scream out for help. I will forever be indebted to him. It was his mournful calls echoing off the walls of the canyon that summoned the help that was so desperately needed.

James has adored his two older brothers his entire life. He has been drinking with them since the cruise last Christmas, when his brothers slipped him alcohol. This gave him a new admittance into their lives that, until then, he had been excluded. He does not want to rat out his brothers. Deep down his world is now upside down. He knows that the alcohol is the catalyst, but he does not know what to do with this newly-found understanding. He does not feel that he can confront us with this information. To not admit it and stuff it down seems the only option at this time.

Paul immediately understands that alcohol is the main cause. I also know that alcohol is involved but not to what extent. I can only imagine what Paul is feeling after all of the grief that I have given him over drinking. The punishments and close eye I have kept on him, the judgments. Here I am, only loving on my other two sons when they mess up. He has always been so close to Bryant. It was always he and Bryant on the same high school soccer team, Paul sweeping and Bryant as the full back at his side. The two brothers, side by side were hard to beat. The same friends, the same parties, and now this is all about Bryant and James. I imagine that he feels somewhat excluded. I do not know, I can only speculate. He draws closer to Leigh, and I pull away from everyone and withdraw into myself.

That evening the soccer coach that James imagined was spurring him on during his sprints up and down the mountain drops in for a visit. It is so good of him. He no longer works at our high school, and I am surprised that he has heard about Bryant and able to locate us. It is above and beyond, and a true act of care for the kids he coaches and their families. It's not a short drive for him, and it is taking time away from his family.

He keeps our spirits up by talking about our family and the different antics he had experienced with our three sons. It is loving and good, and a much needed pep talk. Always the consummate coach, he is coaching us by telling us how strong and driven Bryant is. He tells us, "Bryant will make it, he will come back." He reminds me that one cannot have strong sons without a strong mother; "Boys with drive come from a strong mother." It is good for me to hear; I need it.

That evening my niece arrives with her four children. We think that Bryant has come so far and is looking so good. We are all laughing, Bryant with his head injury, recognizes her, but Paul does not. She has changed quite a bit over the years. She is no longer the teenage girl that they spent their summers with. We are taken off guard when she is unnerved by Bryant's condition. We have become hardened, just like James in his first moments in the ER.

Steve books several rooms at a nearby hotel that is within walking distance. We rotate in and out of it throughout the day, catching a few hours of sleep and then coming back. We make sure that a family member is constantly with Bryant. Other family members also come and go out of the room. It is getting late and Steve books a couple of extra rooms for my niece and the boys from St. Louis.

I am so fixated on my blood-line family, I fail to realize there are families of the heart. I have "family" all around me. The poster boards are filled up with notes from friends and cousins visiting and sending their love out to us. Almost all of these names evoke a memory, a face, and a story for me. I am so grateful and over-whelmed by the outpouring of love by these young adults. The love I have showered on my nieces, nephews and the friends of my children over the years has been showered back on our family during our time of need. This makes me feel warm and fuzzy on the inside.

For me, it has always been about the children, about the next generation. Vacations always included extra kids, soccer trips, soccer sleep-overs with the entire team at our house, cooking for and feeding the friends of our children. I made chocolate chip cookies and milkshakes by the dozens and hosted instantaneous pool parties after an extra hot soccer practice. The years have been filled with children, children and more children for Steve and me. I get real warmth from all of these kids. My husband is the biggest kid of all. He is the life of the party, standing at his Jadite green antique triple milkshake maker.

I have always wanted to make a difference in the new generation. I wanted to break the cycle that appeared to be generations deep in my family. Although I have four sisters, a brother, and a mother they are not here. I have not spoken to them, except for a short conversation this morning when a sister called the ICU room to tell me that one of her colleagues also has a son who suffered a brain injury and that maybe my sister could be of professional help and give me her colleagues number. She told me his son is really doing well and is even able to dress himself. She asked if she should come, I couldn't bring myself to ask.

I need to hear something more positive than this, is that the best for which we can hope? I need to believe that he will recover more than being able to dress himself one day. Am I reaching for something that is impossible? I cannot listen to this. It would be selling out hope for my son's recovery. I cut the conversation short.

The family dynamics have suffered for the past few years, but we have reached an impasse, as hurtful judgments and condemnations delivered to me by my family are still too fresh. Things have been said and done on both sides. I am unable to ask them to come, and they are unwilling to come unless I ask. I take the sadness of this in stride. I have not heard from anyone else. Clearly, they know about the situation because many of my nieces and nephews are here or checking in with us. I have learned to accept this behavior as normal. Our family dynamics are really complicated.

My relationship with my family took a terrible turn eight months prior when a cousin passed away. The year before he passed, my cousin and I had renewed our friendship. When we were kids we only saw each other once or twice a year. He was my protector from his two aggressive brothers. I was shy, quiet and quite uncoordinated. He always came to my rescue and watched over me at all family events. He was like a big brother to me, but we grew up and apart.

We had lost contact with each other for over twenty years. He had been married and divorced several times and was currently married with a son. When he became sick, I had gone to see him. We spent four hours talking in his back yard. Sitting across from each other, knee to knee we filled each other in on our lives since we were sixteen and fourteen. All of the years between us had just vanished, and we were once again, good friends, brother and sister like.

I understood better than most, what it was like to be home alone, with little contact with the outside world. He was unable to work, did not have a driver's license and lived in a small one-horse town. We traded letters and talked on the phone once a week for at least an hour. His wife and my siblings did not understand our relationship, but I told myself it did not matter. He was in need of a friend, and I was going to be counted when the counting needed to be done. I felt that God was asking me to be there to support him. We talked a great deal about life, death and repenting past sins. During one of these conversations, he gave me some great advice. He told me that he had been looking back on his life. He told me he was not a great thinker, but one thing he did know was this; he had been married several times and eventually all of his marriages ended just the same. Somehow, he had created the same marriage time and time again with different women. The problem was with him, not them. He kept looking for and creating the same problems over and over. He gave me great advice and suggested if I divorced my husband, I would probably only create the same problems with a new man. He said that I needed to work on my own problems. He said my husband was a good man; to work on myself, then on my marriage. These were his last words to me.

After he passed, I called to say I wanted to contribute some money for his casket, a very expensive casket that he had shown me in a photo. I was distraught when I called and my tone was flippant. I take responsibility for my casual arrogant attitude. I asked them to call me because I wanted to talk about "the gaudy or God-awful casket." You would need to understand my relationship with my cousin, he was a Navy man and we often cussed, spoke roughly to each other and teased each other frequently. That was our relationship, and I should have toned it down when I made that call offering to purchase the casket. My heart had been in the right place, even if my mouth was not. A recording was made of my voice message, and our family told me not to come to the funeral.

I had become so upset about all of this that we took a cruise over Christmas as a distraction; the cruise on which my oldest son, Paul met Leigh. This was one good thing that had come of all of this. The question that keeps bothering me is, how can they still be shunning me, with my child's life hanging in the balance. It is a constant in the back of my mind. I want to feel loved.

What have I learned from this experience; when someone you love is in pain, do not believe them if they tell you they are fine and you do not need to come. Go and see them anyway. They are probably completely unaware of what they need. They are in shock. Even if you only sit quietly in the background and all you do is give them a hug, go and be there for them anyway. The key here is to be there for them, not to judge them. If you can't do that, then send a card or flowers. No one needs to be judged at a time like this.

Chapter 17
Different Types of Fathers

"The greater danger for most of us lies not in setting our aim too high and falling short; but in setting our aim to low and achieving our mark."
– Michelangelo

My own father had abandoned us when I was fifteen months old. No phone calls, visits or even birthday cards, no support payments. It was my mother's second marriage. She had four children with her first husband whom she had left, and then had three more children with my father.

My father took off one morning right after my mother had given birth to my youngest sister and simply never came back. He simply walked away and left everything behind, including us. We had not known for many years if he was dead or alive. I went to his funeral when I was thirty-two, only because my sister had seen his obituary in her local paper. I wanted to see his face at least one time.

I left the babies with Steve and drove all night through an ice storm to see his face one time before the casket closed on him for eternity. Somehow I felt that it was important for me to have closure. Imagine my shock when I discovered at his funeral that he had been married before my mother and had six children before us with his childhood sweetheart. I don't know what happened, but somehow he ended up with my mother, well sort of, long enough to produce us.

It was not an easy life for my mother with all of those children to raise on her own. My grandmother took one of my sisters and my brother went to live with an uncle. I had not found out that I had a brother until I was twelve. Our family had many secrets.

That left the four of us girls. My mother was overwhelmed by the disappearance of my father. I think that she really loved him. I never heard her say a bad word about him. I think she was depressed and I assume she found comfort in a bottle, I don't know for sure. I always remember her drinking. My oldest sister became a second mother to me. She married when I was seven, which left me feeling alone. I grew up fast then, and learned to be responsible for dishes, laundry and many household tasks.

The good thing that came from this situation was that we had a Baptist Church across the street from us. My mother sent us to Sunday school, which was the highlight in our week. We also went to Vacation Bible School every summer. My mother usually attended as well, until the Minister admonished her in front of the entire congregation for hanging out her wash on Sundays. She stopped going after that but continued to send us.

One Sunday my Sunday school teacher told us that we all had two fathers, our Heavenly Father and our earthly father. Well, this opened up a whole new world to me. I had a father, maybe not two like everyone else but I had one. I had a very special relationship with my Heavenly Father. I could take Him anywhere with me. I talked with Him all the time, asking Him if I should do this or that. Which would be the best decision for me. He was included in everything I did. I was a very lonely and shy child.

I was born in 1958 and to not have a father was a bad thing. Times were different and divorce was an unheard of thing. My mother invented a story that our father had died in a car crash. I was taught that I needed to lie and be ashamed from the time I can first remember. We were very poor and lived on welfare, until my mother got a job in a potato chip factory when I was in second grade. Then, we moved up the ladder from welfare recipients to just plain poor....bad housing and rummage sale clothing were a way of life.

I knew when I was at school that I was poor, and different, but at home I was unaware that our life was different than anyone else's.

It was all that I knew, and I enjoyed my sisters. A yearly highlight was when my mother scraped together the money to get us each a new Easter dress and a pair of shoes. School was difficult because I was very pigeon toed and at that time it was acceptable to laugh and point at people who were "different." I tripped over my own feet quite often, making me always the last one to be picked when it came to gym time. I also had a speech defect. I had seven years of school speech therapy to correct it. It made me very self-conscious and shy. Other kids would ask me to say words so they could laugh at me. My youngest sister always wanted to fight people who were picking on me. I always talked her down and told her that it did not matter. I always admired her spirit and her ability to fight back at the world. I preferred to retreat to my world of books and stories. I could always escape to another world in a book, and my reading skills made me a good student.

I had never been able to come to grips with being a beautiful person physically. I think all of the components were there, great eyes, curly hair, straight white teeth. I was essentially what we socially accept as pretty once I got through that awkward prepubescent stretch. However, I still cannot see it in myself. If you do not think of yourself as beautiful, slowly the outside of you will catch up to the inside belief. I gained weight to prevent myself from being too pretty, I did not wear make-up and paid little to no attention to how I dressed. I loved <u>Little House on the Prarie</u>, <u>Pride and Prejudice</u>, and <u>Little Women</u>. I wanted to be a good person, someone who did good works and lived a life that mattered. No matter how hard I tried, I was always different, always on the outside of society.

My low self-esteem and inability to be accepted into society became a blockade for me. In the beginning I really wanted a relationship with my in-laws. I hoped that they would fill the void, that hole in my heart, but they put so much value on being good looking and dressing nice. I had been a disappointment to them. I was stubborn enough to go in the opposite direction; I wanted to be more than a good-looking arm piece. I needed to know after my father's death that I was loved for whom I was and not how I looked. When I looked down at my father in the casket, I realized how strong the physical resemblance was between us. His good looks had taken him places and had allowed him to be someone I did not admire. As I looked around the funeral parlor at the family that did not know me as family, the dark skinned good looks of their faces were not wasted on me. I wanted to be more than a pretty face.

My heart hurts. Where is my family and why doesn't anyone want to be here for me? I have done so many kind things for people in my life, bought houses for them, ran to their side when they were in need, watched their children, sent money when they needed it. Why aren't they here for me?

Later that night my in-laws, Rose and Bernard, are in the stairwell that leads down to the main waiting room of the hospital. I give them a hug good-bye thanking them for everything they have done over the past few days. They watched over the three kids for us, transporting them to and from the hospital when needed. They have been there in the evenings for Elizabeth, James, Paul and Leigh.

Rose heads on down the staircase.

Bernard stops, turns and looks right at me points his finger and says:

"This happened to Bryant because of you. You do not have the right relationship with God and this is why He did this to your son. This is your fault."

I cannot believe my ears, how can he stand here and say this to me while my son is in there fighting for his life. Something inside of me cracks wide open. I have had my fill. My mother, my sisters, my in-laws, a lifetime of harsh judgments, standing there in the stairwell of the hospital, I find my voice.

"How dare you," I say, raising my voice. "How dare you! You have known me for twenty-four years; yet, you never wanted to get to know me. You don't know anything about me. I pray every day, several times a day. I have more spirituality in the tip of my little finger than you have in your whole body. Get out of here, and don't you ever come back, do you understand me. Get out of here!"

Rose hearing the commotion runs back up the stairs, grabs Bernard and takes him down the stairs, disappearing with him around the corner. This encounter with my father-in-law cuts me deeply. I had hoped when I had married into the family that he would be the father I had never had. It started off so well, and now here we are, our relationship even more broken and shattered than before, by our hurtful raw words... his and mine.

I always thought somehow my in-laws would see past the outside of me and see me for the wonderful person I am on the inside. It did not matter who was right or who was wrong anymore; this was one more hurt on a pile of hurts...the last straw. I am done. Done with wanting them to see me, to really see me, see the person inside. The rub here is I wanted them to be something they were not, and they wanted me to be something I was not.

Thinking back on this moment I realize that there are always at least two sides to every story. I will never know where this belief of his originated. Why he thought God would be a punishing God. He was not nice to me during this crisis, but he did spend the last five years of his life telling me repeatedly—with tears in his eyes—that he loved me. It was the closest he would come to an apology.

I hold it together until I get to the hotel room. There in the darkness of the room, with no one around, I finally cry. I cry and cry, curled up in a little ball on the hotel bed, wrapping myself in the sheets so I can hold onto something. I bawl, for my son, for my marriage, for my other children, for me; I am beyond desperate. My world is crashing in around me as I watch a really corny religious program on TV. Some man dressed up in a crazy outfit, speaks words that ring true to me:

"All you have to do is touch the hem of His garment and ask to be healed, so I do. I ask God to heal my son that night and to heal me. I sob and sob, alone in my rented hotel room. Finally spent and exhausted, face wet, nose pouring, I fall asleep for a few hours.

Chapter **18**
Early Morning Rush

"Life moves pretty fast. If you don't stop and look around once in a while, you could miss it."
– Ferris in <u>Ferris Bueller's Day Off</u>

I wake in the dark after only a few hours of sleep, at first not remembering where I am. Then it all comes back, rushing in like a tidal wave. I walk back to the hospital in the rain, unable to relax or sleep anymore. The weather matches my mood; I hardly notice the raindrops hitting me. I climb up the back staircase to the Neurological ICU, shuddering as I pass the battleground of last night's encounter. I walk through the doorway and am greeted by the loud snoring of the waiting room residents passed out on their beds. I make my way back to Bryant's room. I am emotionally spent and drained.

Steve is there with him. We sit on each side of him, each of us holding onto his hand. He appears to be sleeping, or maybe this is a light coma. His forays into and out of consciousness are becoming the norm. This is one of the few moments that we have had alone together with our son since the accident happened. Our life together is no longer measured in days but in sparse, and precious moments.

I tell him about the encounter with his father in the stairwell. He listens and tells me that he will deal with it. He loves his parents, and I am sorry to put more on his shoulders. I need him to take a stand for me, for us. He is sorry that his father has said this to me.

"Sometimes" he says, "I just do not understand him." He tells me that he will call his brother and have him deal with their parents. He will make sure that they are not around me. He thinks about it for a while and then asks, "Do you care if they stay at our house?"

I appreciate their help with Elizabeth and James. It is a good thing that they are there with them; they need their grandparents right now. All of the kids love and adore them, but I don't want them here with me. I cannot deal with anything more. I need all my energy to help our son recover. It would be really mean to ask them to leave. Bryant is their grandson, and I know that they love him, and it wouldn't be right to make them leave town. It is also not right to ask them to stay away from the hospital—but I can't take anymore of the nastiness. I need them to stay away for now.

"No, I don't mind if they stay there as long as I am not there. I don't want to see them," I reply.

We are sitting and listening to the rain and wind outside. Both of us caught up in our own thoughts, each of us holding onto our son's hands, and he the catalyst holding us together. Suddenly sirens go off and we can hear the nurses' station radio. The volume is turned up. A tornado has been spotted and it is close. I look around the room. How can they possibly move these patients to a place of safety? What else can go wrong?

Steve and I walk over and look out the window. The trees are bending over and the wind is really intense. No effort is made to move the patients and apparently we are going to ride it out. Being mid-westerners we have grown complacent with tornado warnings. We have several each year and so far a tornado has never hit us directly, certainly around us, but not us. After recent events we should be aware that catastrophes can and do happen, yet it seems absurd that no move is made to move the patients. Where would one move them? It was a reminder of how vulnerable we all are each and every day. We are not in control of our lives. Life's storms are always there, only a storm cloud away.

Steve and I sit down again in our chairs holding Bryant's hands, and each other's hands. We hold onto each other this way, connecting and grounding ourselves as best we can in the wake of the storm. The wind blows and the sirens howl outside. We sit there and fill each other in on our day. I leave out the spiritual stuff. I am not comfortable talking about it with him. What if I unleashed something horrible on our son? The red eyes and the wolf frighten me. The tornado warning passes, but the thunderstorm still rages outside. We sit like this for a few hours. Bryant has been quiet, only waking when they do a "Buddy" check. Steve encourages me to go out to the waiting room and lie down before the morning rush starts.

We are going to have a busy day. Today, we are transferring Bryant to a rehab center near our home. I think it is a good idea to rest some, and I go back out to the waiting area. I actually don't know when or if Steve is sleeping. I believe he has visited the hotel room a few times during the day. He gets his energy from people, I find people to be a drain. It amazes me how little sleep he really requires. Neither of us can sleep more than a couple of hours at a time.

My bed and items are here, just like we had left them. It looks like Steve must have been resting here at some point. I get the pillow and blanket and doze for about an hour. My mind is racing and I wake up too wired to lie there. I look over at a woman sitting upright in a chair trying to sleep. I recognize her as a new "recruit" to our little family. She came in late last night, right before my blow up with Bernard. I have not spoken with her.

I ask her if she would like to lie down on my bed.

She looks at me gratefully,

"Yes, thank you," she says, "It is impossible to sleep sitting up in these chairs, and people around here don't share."

I laugh a little and hand her my pillow and blanket. I realize I am no longer the newbie; I have graduated. Bryant has regained consciousness so much faster than the other patients. His recovery so far has been miraculous. I know I have much for which to be grateful. The least I can do is share my bed. I explain to her that we are hoping to move to a rehabilitation facility today, and hopefully

I will not need the bed anymore. I make the transfer to her and head back to Bryant's room.

When I walk into his curtained off room, I cannot believe my eyes. Bryant is in the bed with his eyes open talking to his dad in complete sentences, telling him that he remembers falling. He thinks that he was planning to go to the bathroom when he slipped off the edge. He knew that he had really messed up, and he was trying to get back up to the top of the mountain before anyone woke up and found out that he had fallen. He was really embarrassed.

He knows who we are. He recognizes us and seems to have his mind about him. This is amazing!

I turn around and the ER doctor is standing there, smiling. He introduces himself to Bryant. He says that the nurses had called him up. He had to see this. He didn't want to stay long and impose on our reunion. He looks softly at me and says,

"You guys seem like really nice people, I am glad that you got your son back. We do a lot of trauma here and we do not get to see this very often."

Tears are running down our faces, we have our son back; we really have our son back. We sit there for a while and talk with him. He tires quickly and falls back asleep.

I look over at Steve and ask,

"I would have missed this if I had continued to sleep, why didn't you come and get me?"

"Catie, I didn't know how long it would last and I could not leave him to come and get you."

I understand, but what if I had missed this moment? I am also jealous that Steve had him longer than I did. Our son had been awake for a while. He had opened up his eyes and had started talking. It is unbelievable. At the same time I am so grateful. Something woke my mind up and didn't let me sleep. What a gift this is. What an early morning rush. From tornados, to talking, it has been quite a morning.

Steve goes back out to the waiting area, and I sit quietly with

Bryant. Once again I apply the hot towels to his arms, and hold his hand, sending prayer, love and healing energy to him. I am really getting good at this energy thing.

My mind wanders over Bryant's story. The courage and strength of this young man just amazes me. He was at the bottom of the cliff after falling all of that distance, beaten and broken. He remembered trying to get back up to the top before anyone realized that he had fallen. He was still trying to stand up when James found him. With one side paralyzed he was trying to stand and climb back up to the top of the mountain. He never quit, so focused that even in his beaten state he kept trying to stand up and climb to the top again and again. Calling out for help continually until his swollen brain made the words unintelligible; but continuing with the moans, until he was located. He would have never been found had it not been for his grit, his tenacity. He would not have survived if it had not been for his undeniable will to get up and go at it time and again. His fight, his never give up attitude is what saved him, and is still in play. He is not going to accept defeat.

I sit here quietly lost in meditation with him sleeping. I look up and realize that the residents are standing in our room. My plan has finally worked. I had been so quiet that the doctors went on their rounds and didn't notice me. I apologize but they tell me it is fine and that I can stay. Ha, I think to myself, I'm going to make it through a morning without him taking out another tube. He has continued throughout his stay to try to pull his feeding tube out of his nose. He is a determined young man and wants to be tube free.

We spend the morning with PT, OT, and doctors checking him out and approving his transfer. They are upset that we are not sending him upstairs or to the local rehab center. We want our son close to home. If this is going to be a four-month recovery we need to be close to our other children. Steve has done his research and has been assured that we are sending him to a top-notch facility, very state of the art.

Chapter
The Ambulance Ride 19

*"Face your fears with
ridiculous faith and experience
the ride of your life."*
– Shook

The morning passes quickly and the ambulance arrives around
one o'clock to take our son back to our city. He continues to be
alert and sharp. He has not gone to the bathroom at all today and if
history repeats itself we are in for a rough time. He is never going to
accept being treated as less than a man. He has stayed in a somewhat
mellow mood all day; answering his "Buddy" checks and responding appropriately when required.

All visitors are called off for today. This day is for us, and our
son. Only one parent is allowed to ride in the ambulance, and Steve
offers to let me be with Bryant while he drives on his own. It is really
sweet of him, but it also gives him the chance to make a lot of phone
calls.

They transfer him onto a gurney, which he does without too
much agitation, and they tie him down. I must admit I am a little
nervous, but I am confident that we are making the right decision.
He is doing so well and this is another necessary step in his journey.

They roll him down the halls of the hospital and we come out
into the daylight. I watch as Bryant looks around. We are both
outside people, and we spent his childhood together swimming,
riding bikes, riding horses, walking through the woods, camping,
canoeing, and gardening. I hate the canned smell of air conditioning and usually kept the windows open all summer. I needed to

feel connected with the outside, inside air conditioning feels like a prison to me.

I know that Bryant is thinking the same thing as he looks around and sniffs the air. I hate the thought of having to close him in for the rest of the summer. I know that it is going to be difficult for both of us. I assume that the rehab center is not going to let us have an open window. I look around, no Cicadas here. I have been hearing from family members how thick the air is with them, but so far I have not seen them in mass.

We climb into the back of the ambulance. Bryant's gurney is secured down on the left side of the ambulance. I sit on a metal bench on the right side. The ambulance is stark and hard. Above Bryant's body are rows of metal doors, all filled with different items. They hang up his IVs, and hook monitors up to him as well. They place a small pillow under his head as spinal fluid is still leaking out of his ear.

There are two attendants. The driver is a young man, the other is a young woman and she rides in the back with me. The ambulance lurches forward and that is when I realize we are in for quite a ride. The ambulance bounces hard over the speed bumps as we leave the hospital behind.

I reach across the aisle. It is hard for me to reach Bryant's hand. I am on the hard metal bench and he is on the other side of the ambulance. I do not have a seat belt and slide around. I must work to stay in place. The ambulance is like a ride at an amusement park; it is the bounciest, hardest ride I have ever experienced.

I watch Bryant's face, it is changing right before my eyes. He has gone from being coherent and able to talk to me, to being agitated and rambling. He is cursing and not making any sense at all. He is screaming that he has to pee. I ask the attendant for a urinal, she does not have one. They only have catheters. I ask her to put one in and she tells me that she does not have doctor's orders.

There are no windows in the back of the ambulance and I am not wearing a watch. Minutes feel like hours. Suddenly the ambulance pulls to a stop and I say a prayer of thanksgiving. Then I realize that we are only half-way, and the ambulance driver has stopped to use the bathroom. I am in shock at the irony of this. My son is screaming because he has to use the bathroom, yet the ambulance driver can stop to use the bathroom, and take precious time.

It had taken us only an hour for Steve to get us to the trauma center, on our crazy fast drive to the hospital. It took over two hours for the bouncy ambulance to complete our journey. Only this morning I had my son back, and now I don't know who this is in the back of this bouncy torture wagon. Bryant's eyes are glazed over; he is no longer talking or responding to me.

I realize we made a grave mistake. Why didn't someone tell us, warn us that this bouncy ride would be the undoing of our son? I sit back here and watch as my son disappears; he might even be dying right before my eyes. I am distraught and feel like I want to throw up right there in the back of the ambulance.

The driver says that we have arrived and I breathe a sigh of relief. As we arrive he drives over five huge speed bumps, each one bouncing Bryant's head up and down. I ask the attendant if we can get him out of here and physically push the gurney up to the door. These bumps are not good for him. I am begging at this point. She looks at me with sympathy and says no.

To my horror, we arrive at the wrong entrance and now must turn around and go back over the same speed bumps! Bryant's entire body, especially his head is bouncing up and down over each agonizing bump. He is no longer conscious and has drool coming out of his mouth. I am feeling so foolish, so stupid. I was given a miracle once, and the chance of getting another one is not good. My son is gone again. I want to blame the ambulance crew. I want to attack them for this awful ride. I am choking down tears, vomit and rage.

We pull up to the correct doors this time. They unlatch his gurney and take him into the back entrance of the rehab center.

Section Three
Recovery

Lyrics to:
White Flag by Dido

"I will go down with this ship,
and I won't put my hands up and surrender,
there will be no white flag above my door.
I'm in love, and always will be."

(Catie's fight song)

Chapter **20**
The Rehab Center

"When you get into a tight place and everything goes against you until it seems that you cannot hold on a minute longer, never give up then, for that is just the place and time that the tide will turn."
– Harriet Beecher Stowe

The rehab center is beautifully decorated. It is very sleek, clean and modern. It is not what I expect. We are met at the door by a team of orderlies that take over. This is their facility and they know what they are doing. They quickly wheel Bryant down the clean, modern, wide hallways. The ambulance drivers are following us and commenting on how nice this facility is. They have never transported anyone here before.

"No doubt," I say under my breath. "You never should either."

I will be so glad when they are gone. The incompetence shown during the transport is unequalled in my mind.

Steve joins us. He is pushing a cart with flowers and assorted items that had been delivered to Bryant's ICU room, the poster boards and all of our personal items. He is really organized, and in such a great mood. He has probably been on the phone for the past two hours, telling all of Steve's well-wishers that Bryant is almost back to normal; he has no idea what has taken place in the ambulance. As far as he knows Bryant is simply resting.

I want to grab him and tell him about the drive. I think perhaps what I really want is for him to help me pummel the driver into unconsciousness. I know now that it is not their fault, but somehow it should have been brought to our attention that the bouncing drive could cause a major setback. I want to blame someone other than us. The last two hours have not only been Bryant's undoing, but mine as well. I do not have much left to give.

The orderlies take us back to the Neurological or Brain Injury section. It is locked behind beautiful wooden double doors. We are buzzed back and taken to Bryant's new room. They waste no time in getting Bryant settled into his new bed. He does not wake up or respond during this process. He is limp and lifeless.

An efficient nurse comes in and informs us that because it is late Friday afternoon, and a holiday weekend they are working on a skeleton crew and the normal routine will not start until Tuesday, Monday is a holiday. They start their days early here. Bryant will need to be up and ready to go by eight on Tuesday morning. He will be meeting with his doctor, PT, OT, speech therapist and several other professionals on his team. They will evaluate him and come up with a plan for rehabilitation at that time.

She checks Bryant's vitals and hooks him up to monitors. After checking him over, she looks at us.

"This boy is sick, he should not be here. I am going to call the local hospital. He needs to be admitted. He is too sick to be at a rehab center. Who released this sick boy?" she exclaims.

I look over at Steve he is confused. When he last saw Bryant he was sitting up, talking and alert, now he is back in a coma, unable to respond. Steve explains all of this to her, and then I tell her and Steve all about the treacherous ambulance ride. I plead with her not to put him back into another ambulance. I must look pitiful.

Mm....mm....mm, she says. "This young man is really sick. He is running a temperature. I will call the doctor and ask him to order antibiotics. We will watch him closely this weekend. He has this weekend to come around. If he is not better by Monday we will send him back to the hospital," she looks us both directly in the eye to emphasize how serious she is.

This wonderful nurse is giving him a chance to come around. I am willing to take that chance and thank her. Neither of us can take another ambulance ride. I am devastated, looking over at my child. He is not responding. He is lifeless.

She asks me a lot of questions about how he had been, before the ride here. His heart rate is so low, I tell her about the "brady-ing" episode. She leaves the room to call the doctor. She just keeps shaking her head and saying, mm....mm....mmm....

My heart and mind are in shock, unable to accept this new turn of events. I thought that once we left the ICU and arrived at the rehab center that we were on our way to recovery. I had not been prepared for this back slide. God, why would You give me a glimpse of my son, only to take him away again? It feels so unfair.

She continues working on Bryant, bringing in clean restraints, although at this time we do not need them. I help her take the old ones off him. As I remove the wrist restraint I see a field stick that I missed.

"Oh my gosh," I say. "I missed one."

It is streaked an angry red, crusted hard and green where the opening should be. I immediately ask her where I can get a wash-cloth and hot water. I explain that I had done that to the other areas and that somehow I had missed this one.

She looks at me and says, "You say that you worked on these other areas? You did?"

"Yes, I worked on all of these others," pointing to the now healing marks still on his arms. I'm sorry, somehow I missed the one under his restraint. My heart is wrenching out of my chest for my son. I had taken on this responsibility and somehow I had missed one and let him down. I feel like a complete failure after the relapse.

Her face softens, "First of all," she says, "you shouldn't have been the one to do this, it should have been a nurse. You probably saved his life, just one of these could kill him, if they were all this bad, look at how many you healed."

I am speechless. She is giving me a lifeline and I am going to take it. I need one. I need someone to give me some credit, some-thing positive to hold onto. She brings me the supplies I need and I sit down by Bryant's side and get to work.

Bryant is listless. I watch his heart monitor, the only visible sign that he is still here. What had happened? Was it the fever or the bouncy ride that took our son away? Was his brain jarred, causing it to swell, forcing our son to disappear, once again? What had we been thinking? Why had we been allowed to do this horrible thing to our son? This has to have happened before; why weren't we warned? I sit here, desolate, lonely, and dejected. Once again nothing to do but hold my son's hand, to send love, energy and prayers asking God to bring him back, once again.

The Buddy checks are not as frequent as they were in the ICU, they prepared us for that before we left. I had been told that his nursing care would not be as intense. However, when not operating on a skeleton shift the rehab center has a ratio of two patients per nurse.

The nurse comes in again to see if she can get him to respond. She calls out to him, and he opens his eyes this time.

"Can you tell me your name," she asks.

He looks at her with an unsure, confused, and absent look in his eyes, and then in a soft childlike voice says:

"Buddy. My name is Buddy."

I am trying to keep my cool as I explain to the nurse about the "Buddy" checks. He has grabbed at the first name coming to his mind. He thinks that he is Buddy. Bryant does not know his name. He does not know who he is. What has happened to my son?

I sit in the chair doing the best that I can to remain calm, fighting back the bile rising in my throat. I remind myself that I need to keep calm, keep it together or I may not be allowed to stay with my child.

Professionals are invaluable and dedicate a lot of time educating themselves and give a lot; however their caseloads are usually so large and their own personal and professional lives are busy. Therefore based on my experiences as a mother, I believe that the most important advocate a patient can have is a family member. I believe it to my core. It is especially true with a brain injury patient, or a child with special needs.

My child is unable to do the most rudimentary of things for himself. I believe that it is important that a family member be right here in the room with him at all times, not only because he is help-less and vulnerable, but also because of his explosive strength and, with his inability to reason, he is actually a danger to himself.

Sitting here this afternoon, with my son unresponsive and very child-like, something inside of me continues to break open, just another crack in my facade.

Steve busies himself with getting all of Bryant's items stowed away. Bringing in the rest of the flowers from the car. He has a huge basket of cookies on sticks with an enormous yellow smiley face balloon attached to it.

My eyes wander around his private room. It has a private bath-room and is nicely decorated. The bed is in the middle of the small room, with a TV that can swivel over his bed. One side of the room is all windows overlooking a green courtyard and the bed is positioned so that you can look out into it. The courtyard is in the center of the U shaped building with an opening in the back. The back section is fenced off to prevent residents from walking off, I later learn.

Steve places the flowers around the room, and hangs up the posters that all of Bryant's friends have written to him, messages of love and hope for his speedy recovery. Looking at these tokens of love and encouragement, once again the message is clear: Children and young adults get it, they don't wait to be invited, to think it through. The distance, obstacles or trouble are unimportant. They show up and give their love to the best of their ability. Even if it is only a note on a poster board, it's fine. They do not think about it, they just do it.

In contrast as adults a lot of us lose that spontaneity that springs forth from having an open heart. We get into our heads and reason it out with thoughts such as, I don't want to be in the way, or they will have too many people there and we talk ourselves out of showing up. I have been guilty of the same thing. I didn't get it until now, how nice the showing up is.

The outpouring of love from adults has been comforting on a different level. People that we do not know well or at all, respond with prayer chains. We are in awe of how many different prayer chains have been started for Bryant from all different denominations, and locations, even a church over in England. I am sure that there are many more. As someone has said to me, "We have started so many prayer chains that the good Lord can't help but hear, and I know those prayers are being answered."

I sit in the chair, thinking about these prayer chains. We gave up going to church when we had to choose between church, or soccer on Sundays. With four children all playing competitive soccer and traveling, weekends were crazy at our house. Most weekends were spent out of town traveling to tournaments with at least one of our kids, with the other parent staying home to cover the regular at home soccer schedule. Many weekends Steve would head to one state with one or two of the kids, and I would head to another state with the others.

A direct result of this is that we now do not have a pastor or a church to call upon for help when we need it most. We are relying on the relationships of people we know still connected with their own churches. I am grateful for these relationships, and the nourishment that we are now receiving from them.

This schedule and lifestyle has not only affected our religious affiliation but has had a direct impact on our marriage. We became two different people, married and living together, still in love, but both of us going our separate ways during the week and separated with our children on the weekends. Working to raise our children, not fighting, just existing. Our main connection is the kids, but even on that we do not see eye to eye. We don't share experiences anymore. I am missing the emotional intimacy that we once had.

Bryant's angry red wrist is responding well to both the antibiotics and the warm compresses. I continue to hold the hot washcloth over the hard green opening as it starts to soften. I continue with my labors, it gives me a focus. When it opens up, I am able to milk the green infection out of his wrist and wash it away with clean water.

Later that afternoon he eliminates all over himself, not even aware of it. The implication of this is not wasted on me; it saddens me. The seed that had been planted in my son to be treated like a man is gone. It no longer matters to him. Only yesterday this was a monumental occasion and today it is a non-event. We have digressed, he has disappeared right before my eyes, and I was help-less to stop it.

Steve sits with Bryant for a while so that I can check out the new facility. The brain injury unit is one long narrow hallway with eight rooms on each side. Most of the rooms are private rooms, with a few capable of holding two people at a time. Half of the beds are empty and most of the patients are in their beds, lying quietly.

I continue down the hall. At the far end is an entire apartment. I find out later that once patients progress to a certain point they live for a few days in the apartment to practice independent living skills. I have no idea how much Bryant will need to relearn. Before the ambulance ride, I thought he would get up and go home one day.

As I wander around the unit I discover a kitchen in the front across from the nurses station. This is where we will later learn to mix up special milk shakes for him. The physical therapy room is a huge room with lots of mirrors and strange looking break-away beds, harnesses and lots of equipment. Everything is clean, sleek and modern, and sterile. It's not a bad place, just not warm and loving.

I go back to Bryant's room, and Steve and I work out a new plan. We are both in shock at the change in our child. Neither of us wants to leave him. We decide that it will be best to take shifts. I will be there from six or seven in the morning and he will relieve me around seven or eight at night. Steve will spend nights here, and work some in the daytime. I will spend the day with Bryant and be there for Elizabeth and James in the evening. Steve decides with my high blood pressure that I should sleep in our bed at night. It is the best plan that we can devise. I am grateful that I won't need to be here twenty-four hours around the clock. It is becoming clear to me that our son is going to be reborn, as the literature I had read had told me. He will be different after this experience; we will all be different. If he is going to be reborn, I want him to be reborn into a family and not a cold sterile hospital.

I can't help but to think of all of the seconds, minutes, hours, days, weeks, months and years that I had been beside him, helping him to grow up feeling loved and special. I never wanted him to be ostracized because of his learning differences. It has been so important to me to let my children know that they are not alone and that they are loved.

It appears that all of those seconds, minutes, hours, days, weeks and years are all washed away. He might not know who we are or who he is, but he will know that he is loved and special. He thinks his name is Buddy. If my child is going to be reborn, then O.K., I accept that. He is going to be surrounded by love and family throughout it all. I will not have it any other way. If I must stay here day and night then that is how it is going to be. Fortunately, Steve is here for me, for our family and I will not need to do it alone.

Steve knows how determined I am. We have always made an unbelievable team. If we want something accomplished, we pull together and do it. We started out with nothing, a couple of twenty-one year old kids, no college degrees, living on high school diplomas and a lot of love. We had planned all four of the kids. Maybe four kids in five and a half years is not good family planning, but they were all planned.

Steve moved up the corporate ladder quickly, while I stayed home with the kids. We could not afford for me to work; childcare was too expensive. I had never planned to be a stay-at-home mother. I grew up in a home where the mother was expected to be both mother and father. I always intended to work and pull my own weight financially.

When I finally realized that I was not going to be able to have a career even after they were all in school, I was crushed. I did not have a lot of respect for my own mother so how could I respect myself for my decision to dedicate myself to motherhood. It was tough to keep everything at home in order, help two children with learning issues, be a mother to four and do all of the sports while my husband traveled. If motherhood was to be my only calling in life, I was going to go about it as dedicated as I could. I threw myself into it.

That may sound funny now but that was during the 80's when women were all about careers, breaking the glass ceiling and stay at home mothers were considered lazy. Once again, I was ostracized by my peers. People would humph me when I said I did not work. My own mother commented to me on what hard workers all of her children were except for me.

I had found the time to start my decorating business from home while the kids were at school. It offered me the flexibility to have a career and yet be there for them. I did not work many hours in the beginning. Computers were pretty much nonexistent back then, and home based jobs simply weren't there.

Steve's corporate jobs had moved us around a great deal. The company for which he had been working had been bought out four years ago. Instead of us moving our family again, he had started his own insurance brokerage business. We had gotten a small buy out from the company when it was sold. We had lived on that money and started his business with the rest. He was doing well, but still found he needed to do consulting on the side to financially keep our heads above water. His current consulting engagement took him to Florida two weeks out of every month. Juggling both jobs kept him working long hours.

To be honest, I knew it was more than the money. The job in Florida was good for his ego. He was struggling not being in the corporate world, and being told that he was a rising star. He loved to do his training and then collect evaluations. He could not wait to read the comments and have people tell him how wonderful he was. It was very addicting. I could not compete with this kind of attention. I was just bitter and angry with him for not being home.

He had been on the phone a great deal with Florida this week. I had overheard snippets of conversations. I knew that one of his co-workers in Florida had a husband who had suffered a brain injury. She had been a storehouse of information for Steve, advising him on the ins and outs of hospitals and rehab units.

Everyone sooo loves Steve. He is the kind of person that everyone wants to be around. I love to be around him too. That is the central point of our trouble. I want him around, and he doesn't or cannot make it happen.

All of this background is in this room with us, whether we know it or not. His childhood, my childhood, our married life, it is the ugly, two-ton elephant, lying heavily in the air between us. What are we going to do? How do we move forward? This is all uncharted water, unknown to us. It isn't only us in this space but all of our baggage as well. Baggage comes to the forefront in times of stress. We will later learn that a very high percentage of marriages do not survive a tragedy. A wobbly marriage like ours would not be given much of a chance.

It is already after eight in the evening, and Steve wants me to head home. I am not quite ready to leave. Neither of us has eaten anything, and we start munching on the cookie basket. I don't remember a cookie ever tasting better.

James comes up to stay with Bryant and his dad. Elizabeth calls and asks if she can go to a graduation party with her friend and spend the night with her. This is something I would not have agreed to before, but she is leaving for San Diego at the end of this summer, and I need to give her some space.

Chapter **21**
Comfort

"When one door of happiness closes, another opens; but often we look back so long at the closed door that we do not see the one that has been opened for us."
– Helen Keller

Steve talks me into heading home to get some sleep. The thought of no children at home, my own house, my own bed, it sounds so good. No one there for which to care for, only quiet and solitude. Looking over at Bryant, he is out and there is not much I can do for him. Hopefully the antibiotics and a good night's sleep will help to heal him. James is sitting in a chair with his journal, ready to continue with his account of the rescue. I kiss everyone good-bye and head outside to my car.

It is early dusk, and the air is thick with Cicadas. Their rhythmic vibrations fill the air, throughout the drive home. I race down the highway with my windows open, sucking in the air. It is the first normal moment I have had in a while. It is a forty-five minute drive from the rehab center to our house. I love the feeling of the breeze blowing my hair.

I look around me and consider that only a few hours ago I was in the back of an ambulance going down these very roads. One tear after another escapes. I wipe them away with the back of my hand. I am going to stay strong, I tell myself. A song I recognize as Dido's "White Flag" comes on the radio, all about not surrendering, it reassures me and lifts me up. I belt out the words singing it over and over. I find comfort from this song.

Unbeknownst to me, Steve and his brother agree to not have

their parents come up to the rehab center today, and they are still at our house. Steve calls them the minute I leave the rehab center and asks them to leave and to give me some space. I'm sure it was a hard conversation, and he had not often taken my side over his parents; this is a really big deal. Now that I am older and wiser, I cannot imagine what it would be like to be turned away from your son, and grandson during a life or death crisis. I did not have the presence of mind to think about their emotions, I was in too much pain.

Exiting the highway and taking the twisty-turny tree lined street to our driveway relaxes me. Our street is one of the original old farm roads for the area. It is narrower than roads of today. It does not have sewers on the side of the road, but instead has deep trenches for the water to collect and go steadily downhill to the river. Huge mature trees, now a haven for Cicadas, line both sides of the road.

I love our old rambling farmhouse. I am sure it started off as a saltbox some time back in the first half of the 1800's. Being added onto several times over, it has a collection of huge old rooms. I worked for the better part of ten years rehabbing this old house. Spending every spare moment pulling off wallpaper, putting up trim, painting walls, pulling down plaster, rehabbing bathrooms and the kitchen, you name it. It says home to me. This is my place of comfort, my creative outlet.

Both sides of the long narrow drive are flanked by five foot tall stone pillars that curve outward toward the street with three foot tall flower boxes on the ends; a leftover from another time, another era. They were designed for a horse and buggy, and my car struggles to fit through them.

The front part of the property had been sold off sometime in the past. Two mid century houses now border the front of our house, allowing an occasional peek of this historic landmark from the road. Our pond is located in our front yard and is a buffer between these houses and us. The long narrow drive is actually shared by us, and one of the houses in the front. That is the house that "Big Joe" lives in with his wife and three daughters. He is a gentle giant of a man; the females in his house have tempered him.

As I inch through the pillars and straighten out the car, Big Joe is outside in his driveway talking with a friend. They are waiting for me right before the entrance into my yard. I slow down and wave at them, but they are not having it. They want to talk, and I have my windows down.

I put the car in park. Big Joe looking at me with such kindness, motions for me to get out of the car. He shows me the "pie plates" that he had taken off of the dead bushes. Batting the Cicadas away from my face, I listen as he explains how Steve had called him. I did not know that Steve had called him. I wonder what else Steve has done that I know nothing at all about. I had not been able to call anyone, let alone to think about calling the neighbor. I am amazed at his ability to reach out and touch people when he is in need.

The man standing there with Big Joe is someone that I recognize. Both are big men, oversized from birth and their years of working outside. I recognize him immediately as a co-worker at a company James had worked for the previous year. He approaches me and says, "I am so sorry to hear about your boy, you guys are really good people, and I am so sorry. How is he?"

I just look at him, how do I answer that? What can I say? I open my mouth to answer him. No words will come out. A sob escapes out of my throat, first one sob, then another and another. Tears start pouring out of my eyes and down my face. My whole body starts to shake. I sob uncontrollably. How can I tell anyone how he is.

Big Joe and this nameless man embrace me. They both encircle me with their arms and bodies. I can't stop crying, sobbing. The damn has broken and I can't stop. I am slobbering all over someone's shirt. My nose is running uncontrollably. They hold me like this for what is probably only five minutes but it seems like an eternity. What an act of love. There in the middle of that circle I am finally surrounded by love. I am finally able to admit that I am not so strong, releasing all of the emotions that I had been bottling up throughout the day. How is my son, how do I answer that? I don't know how he is. I don't know anything anymore.

They are standing there holding me when a loud beep pierces the air, followed by a series of beeps, one after the other. I peek through the circle of their arms. I see my father-in-law's car. I shake my head inside the center of love. I bring a hand up and wipe my eyes and nose onto my shirt.

I look up at Big Joe and say "that's my father-in-law. He wants me to move my car so he can get out. My car is blocking the drive-way preventing his exit."

"You must be kidding me, let him wait."

He continues to beep. It is clear to all of us; he is only a few feet away. There is no doubt that he can judge the situation and that he does not care. He wants to leave my house and he wants out now.

I wipe my face off again with my shirt. "No, I want him to leave," I say, "so let me move my car."

The two men break their circle and let me out.

I walk over to my car; neither of my in-laws get out of their car to offer comfort to me. There is no way they do not see what is transpiring here. I back into Big Joe's drive-way to let them access the road.

I watch as they pull past me and out into the road. They do not even look my way, only straight ahead.

I stay in my car thanking both of the men profusely. Big Joe tells me to give them a call if I need anything at all. I drive my car out and down the driveway. I park the car in the same drive that days before Steve, Cam, and I had pulled out of to head to the hospital. The same drive where just days ago Bryant had been spinning around throwing Cicadas into the pond to feed the fish. So much had changed since that day; nothing will ever be the same.

I walk in through the side porch door. The room is still set up for "the party that will never be." It is surreal. I go into the kitchen to look for something to eat. I look around in amazement. The kitchen counter is full of food. I have no idea where it came from as there are no notes, only food everywhere.

Little do I know that this is the beginning of a downward slide for me. It will be years before I make the actual connection between stress, food and addictions. Being overweight with health issues can kill you quicker than a bottle of booze. Some people in my position would have had a drink, a smoke, a joint, popped a sleeping pill or whatever, food was my drug of choice. I make a plate for myself and heat it up in the micro. The all-carb casserole is really tasty. Like a drunk who has been off booze for awhile, I have a carb fest. I eat bread, casserole, cookies and whatever else I think will give me comfort. After I am satisfied, I wrap up the overabundance of food and put it away in the refrigerator.

I listen to a couple of messages on the answering machine. I see that James has been trying to keep track of the messages that have been left, there are too many calls for the overburdened answering machine. There are words of comfort, some of the people are just mere acquaintances, people I worked on committees with. People are asking me to call them if I need anything at all, leaving their numbers for me. I don't recognize most of the names. I wouldn't know how to ask anyway. How do you call someone up and say, I need..... I don't know how to ask for anything. I learned from a young age to not ask, my role has been to give and not receive.

I am spent, almost zombie-like walking up the stairs to bed. I try to sleep but I can't. Tossing and turning I finally turn the television on. As a light sleeper I have never been able to sleep if I hear any noise at all, but now I find the quiet disconcerting. I cannot relax.

I walk downstairs to find Rose standing on the staircase. She walks up the stairs and wraps her arms around me. She hugs me and asks me if I want them to stay or to leave. I don't know what to say. I think about it for a minute and tell her that it's fifty-fifty. With that she decides that they should go. I agree that it is the best thing to do. I return back upstairs to my bedroom. I do not know how to sleep anymore. I leave the television on and sleep fitfully throughout the rest of the night.

Chapter **22**
Re-booting

"Each success only buys an admission ticket to a more difficult problem."
– Henry Kissinger

I sleep on and off for six hours, and it feels like an eternity. Taking a shower in my own shower is great but it is also mixed with feelings of guilt. I have been gone too long from Bryant's side.

I check in on James; he is asleep in his bed. He must have come in sometime in the early morning hours and chose to not wake me. I decide to let him rest and do not wake him either.

I head out to my car. The Cicadas are still sleeping in the pre-dawn. I can feel some of their dead bodies crunching under my feet as I walk over the oversized drive to climb in the car. I fire up the engine and roll my window down. I am anxious to breathe as much fresh air as I can before I head back into the canned air. As I drive the forty-five minutes back to the rehab center, I turn on the radio. My fight song comes on again. I am laughing to myself; sometimes a song really speaks to you. I turn off the radio and sing this verse over and over to myself as I approach the luminous building in the early light of dawn.

I am buzzed through the wooden doors of the rehab center, the same controlled access as the ICU but much more stylish. Missing are the groups of people waiting out front for a chance, a word, a small sign. The visitors here all go home at night; perhaps they are more conditioned and accepting of the situation. Most of them have jobs and families, and life continues. For me, right now, this is my life.

It has not yet dawned on me that we are no longer hanging onto life and death, here the goal is functions of daily living. It still feels like life and death to me. The lines between the different stages of recovery blur into each other, twisting and turning like a rollercoaster. Bryant's recovery has been anything but textbook. All I know is that my child needs me, and I need to be here.

Steve and I visit for a while in the quiet of the still sleeping rehab center. He has not slept and is anxious to get home and get some sleep. He tells me that Bryant has been incoherent most of the night. He has responded to his checks but his ramblings are not making any sense.

Our talk turns to our finances. It has been on Steve's mind a great deal. We took a pay cut with Steve starting his own business, and money has been tight. We also have tuition for two kids in college, and a third on her way. Four car payments; two jet ski payments and oh, yeah, three mortgage payments, and living expenses for us and my mother and lots of insurance for homes, cars, utilities, two businesses and the list goes on and on. We are now facing unknown medical bills. Steve has been trying to keep our heads above water financially for a long time.

He has kept the specifics of the financials from me, much like his father had not divulged those details with his mother. He does not share the numbers with me now, only that he is worried and is going to sell some items to cut down on our payments. I have been so involved with the finances of my own business and the household budget, that I gave him free reign with our personal finances. I trusted him with this responsibility; he wanted to give us everything and kept our pending financial disaster to himself. We will not be the first family to face financial ruin over unexpected medical expenses coupled with excessive spending.

This is why he is traveling and working so much. It is easier to leave and get accolades at work and collect the money we need to stay afloat than to face what is going on at home, and an angry, disappointed wife who doesn't understand why he is never there.

He sees an opening with the mounting medical expenses to start discussions about our possible impending financial meltdown. Steve explains to me that he does not have his hands around how much the medical bills are going to cost; he knows it will be large. It seems in the small print of our policy he discovered that only a small amount is available for "ambulance" charges, around three hundred dollars. The charge for the airlift out of the Gorge alone will be around ten thousand dollars, in addition the ambulance ride from the Gorge to the airlift and the ill-fated ambulance ride to the rehab center.

We talk for a short time but are interrupted by Bryant's doctor. He explains that he is on call all weekend and will return full-time on Tuesday. He has been reviewing Bryant's chart and will be ordering some additional tests that they will be able to perform here, no need to move him to the hospital at this time.

He is, however, concerned about Bryant's inability to eat, because the brain needs an enormous amount of calories to heal. It appears that the tube in Bryant's nose is supplying him with much needed nutrition, however, it seems to be lacking in calories. He tells us, our son needs to start eating as quickly as possible; it is a priority. He explains that they need to make sure he can swallow and not let the liquid go down the windpipe and into his lungs. If the speech therapist determines that he has the ability to swallow then they will know it is his frontal lobe that is preventing him from eating. They will start off feeding him with a thickened liquid diet and progress from there.

They will also continue with his anti-seizure medication. Bryant has been receiving daily injections into his abdomen to prevent seizures and blood clots. Seizures apparently can be common with brain injury patients. It is hard to say if he will have seizures for the rest of his life or not, or how intense the seizures may be. That is something that we will only know with time. For now, they plan to continue with the injections.

The doctor continues to explain how things will work here at this facility. It looks as if the mornings at the rehab center start early. He wants his patients on a strict schedule, and he would like to see Bryant sleeping at night and awakening early in the morning for breakfast and therapy. He explains to us that they will prescribe sleeping pills for Bryant at night to make that happen, stressing that a restful night's sleep is important.

We look at each other. Since infancy, Bryant has never been one to take naps, or to go to sleep early. His natural tendency is to stay up late and sleep late. Even as a small child we struggled with this. It was far worse as a twenty-one year old. This would be a struggle, brain injury or not.

Catching our look, he assures us that they know how to get their patients on a schedule.

He wants to know if we have any questions.

I ask about the change in Bryant since the ambulance ride. He does not seem to be that concerned. He thinks that Bryant is responding to the antibiotics, and is in an acceptable range for rehab. I can only think about the range he was in before the ambulance ride, I am having trouble moving beyond that.

He explains to us that all brain injuries are different and all patients respond differently. The brain is very complex and while they know much about it, they continue to learn more all the time. There are different stages during recovery. Bryant may go through each stage or he may skip over some; we need to wait and see.

Shortly after our talk with Bryant's doctor, a young woman evaluates him and determines that he can indeed swallow. She tries to get him to drink a thickened liquid, but he is unable to swallow it. He looks at her and tells her "No more alcohol." She continues on unfazed and states that she will be back at twelve-thirty to try again. She explains to us that if they cannot get him to eat they will need to put a tube down his throat and pour the fluid directly into his stomach. My stomach lurches at that idea. I realize that these people are serious. They are here to rehab him, and to work with him. The thought of another tube is enough to make me ill.

As the young woman leaves, a young man comes in to measure Bryant for his wheelchair. He explains that Bryant will need a back that reclines since he cannot hold his own back upright. He explains to me again that by eight on Tuesday morning they expect him to be out of his bed and dressed, ready for the day. He hands me a list of things to purchase before then. On the list are high top tennis shoes to support his ankles, the kind he used when he first started walking, gym shorts and T-shirts.

Reality is starting to sink in, they do not expect Bryant to wake up and be the person he was before. They expect a long, slow, measurable recovery. The glimpse of our son in the ICU made us think he would simply wake up and be himself, and that he would walk out of here. Perhaps it was just a brief interlude and we're in for a long fight back.

Steve finally heads out the door our short window of opportunity to talk about finances and our future has now closed. I think that he is going home for a long-deserved sleep. He later tells me that nothing has ever felt as good as his own bed, but he couldn't relax for long. After a few hours he was up and at it once again. Steve runs errands including going shopping for high-topped Nike shoes for Bryant. He returns his new jet-skis to the dealer, who is sympathetic but unable to take them back. He offers to put them on his lot and see if there are any takers. Steve is unable to shut down and relax.

Back at the rehab center, I start looking my son over, my child. He is lying there lifeless, curling up in as much of a fetal position as he can with all four limbs tied to the bed. He has been so docile since we arrived that we loosened his bonds. I learned the hard way that when the urge hits him, he has superhuman strength; so for his own safety, and mine, it is best to not totally untie his restraints.

I continued to hold his hand, send energy to him, and work on his wrist. I feel silly but I truly believe that I am making a difference. I believe that he is able to tap into my strength. That somehow the love, heat and energy flowing from my heart through my arm and hand are helping him to heal. I pray again to my heavenly Father, for Him to give strength to Bryant, that He heals his damaged brain and body. I tell Him once again that I will take him any way that

He gives him to me. I will accept him and care for him all the days of my life if this is what He is calling for.

I feel deflated and somewhat defeated by the ambulance ride. To have had a glimpse of my son and then watch him disappear has played hard on my emotions. I hold onto that memory in the ICU, those fleeting moments of clarity; but now looking at my child, my baby, and yes he is in an infantile stage right now it all seems to be an insurmountable challenge.

He does not know his name, or who we are. He is clueless as to what is transpiring. He babbles on occasion, but it is gibberish. Occasionally I hear him say, "It is all wrong, so wrong." I am inclined to agree with him, it is all so wrong, so wrong. This is not how it is supposed to be.

Three of my friends have disabled children. Maybe it is easier to adjust when your child is born that way. Somehow, I don't think so. There was a moment in their lives as well, that moment when they realized that their child, their baby would never be "normal." Will I always compare the before and after, will I ever be able to accept his new limits? Am I strong enough to do this? It is beginning to sink in: my child will never be the same. He may need constant care for the rest of his life. I read the material on brain injuries and none of it is promising. It tells me that best case will be that my child can learn to live independently, eventually. Just like a senior citizen that can no longer care for himself; it is talking about different degrees of daily living skills. The long-term damage might make living independently impossible.

The young woman comes back, trying once again to get Bryant to drink the thickened liquid. He will not drink it. He acts like he wants to but he cannot. She explains to me that the frontal lobe injury is preventing him from eating. It is not that uncommon. Their hope is that he will eventually get hungry enough and survival instinct will kick in. We just need to keep him going that long, he is starting to look very thin.

We tighten his wrist and ankle bands to the bed. They are going to insert a tube down his throat and ask for my help. They want this tube to stay in until he can start to eat. Another tube; my heart lurches. I understand, but this is so hard.

Another person comes in to hold his head steady as I hold onto Bryant's hands, once again trying to give him comfort through yet another ordeal. His fingers wrap around mine as they slowly snake the tube down his nose and into his throat. I imagine that this tube is larger than the one he had before because once they get it down they use a funnel to pour the thickened fluid directly into his stomach.

He is not very happy about this, or with me either, and fights me to get free. Sometimes a mother has to be hard. Some things need to be done; you don't want to do them, but they are for the best. It's not easy being a mother. It's not for the faint of heart. Once this ordeal is over they hook the tube back up to the fluid that he had before.

The soft lighting and quietness of the unit are soothing compared to the ICU, and I can see how Bryant will be able to concentrate more readily here. I feel hopeful in this new setting.

Later that afternoon Bryant comes up with a new game called remove the feeding tube. His concentration has certainly improved; on the feeding tube, he is intense about it. State law prohibits restraining his chest only his waist and limbs can be tied down. The ability to bend at his waist, allows him to get his head down to his hand and pull the feeding tube out, just like before with the ventilator. I am not fast enough to stop him while sitting, I now must stand over him with a half bend in my back, hands open and at the ready, poised for action. I hover over him, only inches away, our eyes locked on each other. He is testing my reserve and I his.

While I am in this position, he lies still. If I divert even my eyes to look in another direction, in a split second he pops his head down to his restrained hand and grabs the tube. He has managed to get it out once already today before I knew what he was doing. He makes other attempts, but I am able to get the better of him several times today. As long as I catch him as he goes to move his head, I can hold his shoulders down until the urge passes or help arrives. He is not going to get it out again, not on my watch. I stay alert, locked in this position for the next five hours.

The babbling and gibberish are starting to make sense to me. He is talking about events that I recognize, his early years, about getting a new puppy, then I hear something like, "come on Paul let's go down to the creek." This isn't babbling at all, these are memories of his childhood. His brain is rebooting, much like a computer reboots, searching and trying to put all of this information into chronological order. He is living through his life at warp speed. I pay closer attention and realize that there is a sequence. I watch him go from an infant, early this morning, into his early childhood years. I recognize the events—I was there for all of them—I am fascinated. For the first time today, I actually feel hopeful. My brain takes off and I start to think about all of the conversations, replaying them in my mind. I am certain about this. His brain is actually rebooting. Maybe he will come through this. His brain is working hard and it is taking every bit of energy he has.

I am excited and relax for a moment by straightening my back out and rubbing the lower part of my spine. The moment I straighten up, he tightens his stomach muscles and throws his head forward so that it is now down near his hands. This all happens within a few seconds. I react as quickly as I can, grabbing his shoulders and using all of my strength I try to push him back down onto his pillow, but I am unable to push him backwards. He is too far forward and I have lost the opportunity to get him back down on the pillow. He has his hands on the tube and will not let go. I wrap my fingers around his and try to pry them off the tube. Turning his head to the side he blocks me from access. He threads and works the feeding tube through his fingers, pulling the feeding tube out through his nose.

Frantically I push the button for the nurse and scream out loud for help. He is fighting me with everything he has. Every muscle in his body is tense and he is fighting for what he believes is his life. By the time help arrives he has been successful and once again we need to go through the re-tubing. This is painful to be a part of, painful to watch, painful for him, painful for me. I feel so guilty and vow to myself, that no matter what, I am not letting this happen again. I feel like a failure.

Chapter **23** *"Men are what their mother's make them."*
Glimpses of the Future — Ralph Waldo Emerson

Paul stops by later that afternoon. He wants to talk. I cannot risk getting out of position to turn and talk to him. I dare not take my eyes off Bryant's for even a second. I do not want to take the chance that Bryant will de-tube himself once again. I know the chances of infection are too great. I have been warned that they can only tube him so many times before it's impossible and then they will need to do surgery to put a feeding tube directly into his stomach.

Paul is standing behind me talking to me. He is graduating with his Bachelors in Accounting.

He tells me, "I do not know what I want to be, but I am certain that I don't want to be an accountant. I feel like you and Dad talked me into doing accounting. I agree that I did not know what I wanted to do, and Dad told me that Grandpa had gotten his accounting degree, and it opened up lots of possibilities including the FBI for him. It had sounded like a good idea at the time, but now that I have worked in accounting, I hate accounting jobs."

"Leigh and I were talking, and I have decided to move to the east coast with her right after graduation. I think that I may join the Marines. If you remember, I wanted to join the Marines right out of high school, and you talked me out of it. You told me to get my degree and I did; now I can go in as a commissioned officer. It's pretty tough to get in, but I want to give it a try."

This is a serious conversation, one that should be done over a table, eye to eye. Paul deserves my undivided attention, something that I cannot give him right now. I feel like he is sticking a knife right into my back and through my heart. Doesn't he understand how much pain I have right now? How much I love him? I cannot lose another son! We are in the middle of a war. Each word is just another knife blade piercing me, or maybe a sledgehammer. What is left of my broken heart feels as if it is being shattered into smaller and yet smaller pieces.

"Do you understand that the number one injury in the war right now is brain injury," I ask. "The body armor is so state of the art, that they are now surviving blasts that would have killed people in previous wars. Their brains are being shaken badly, leaving permanent brain injuries. The walking wounded. Not to mention PTSD. How much can you ask of me? Do you want me to pull another bed up next to Bryant's so I can take care of both of you?"

This is not how I imagined our conversation about his future would go down. I cannot even meet his eyes, let alone encourage him. I want him to stay, and I cannot tell him that either. I cannot turn around and hold him, and I cannot stop him. The whole time I am asking these questions I am bent over in position, eyes locked on Bryant's ready to move in a split second to grab his chest and push him back down.

"Paul, my nest is emptying out. Elizabeth is leaving and I cannot stand to lose you, too."

I realize he wants to shake the dust from this town and family off and go. What is there really to say? Sons have been striking out on their own since the beginning of time. Is the timing ever really right? I know that he loves me; I know that I love him; we just do not show it to each other. Each of us in our own way brings out the hardness in the other, neither one of us wanting to show vulnerability or weakness. I love him so much I assume he knows that. I think the way to show my love is to be tough on him and to keep him on the right path. It must be the way I was raised, the tough neighborhoods, I don't know. I never want to appear needy, or soft. I want to hold him right now, to have him hold me; instead I stay where I am.

One of his best buddies, a friend from high school, was recently arrested. It doesn't look good for him. Paul has a great deal lying heavy on his heart right now. I imagine that with everything happening at once, the thought of leaving town and starting over sounds really good.

We talk about his friend for a while, and then he tells me his friend's dad had told his son that he was lucky to only face a few years in prison, rather than to be Bryant. Bryant has a life sentence.

Paul's voice rises, "Can you believe he would say that?"

Part of me does not know what to say. I know that Bryant is facing a tough sentence. I want to believe in the possibilities, but the literature I am reading is not preparing me for anything good. Who knows, maybe his friend's father is right, maybe he is wrong. We are in uncharted territory here, no way to know what the future will hold for Bryant.

Paul believes in his heart and soul that Bryant is going to be fine. He is shocked by the comment of his friend's father. He does not believe that Bryant is in any real danger. He does not get the gravity of the situation. I don't know if that is because he has not been here in the room with Bryant hourly, or he simply has a positive faith in his brother's ability to fight his way back.

The whole time we talk, I am bent over prepared to catch Bryant should he lurch for the tube. We talk about all of the changes in our family. I tell him that I will quit working, and donate my time to Bryant's recovery. He is my son. I am here for him.

His only comment is:

"Yeah, but how unfair for Bryant to lose a whole year. You know, Mom, this did not happen to you; it happened to Bryant. You are acting like it happened to you."

I know that he is right, but somehow it feels like it is happening to me. I cannot separate that anymore. My life has completely changed in a blink of an eye. I am already leap frogging ahead in my mind. I know that I am going to possibly close down my business and care for Bryant the rest of his life, or probably the rest of my life. It is happening to me. Paul can go on with his life and his dreams but I cannot, I will not. I know this is my choice, but I always place my children first. That's who I am.

After he leaves, I am in shock. He just doesn't get it. How can he leave and join the Marines? I choke back the sobs. I want to support him, but I do not want any more worry right now. I know that I am being selfish, but I do not want him to go. I want him safe.

I have never been a fearful mother; well not until now. Fear has found its way into my heart, and I know true fear for the first time. I have had no real fear for myself, rough neighborhoods and seedy schools have made me tough, but this is different, I have no control over any of this.

I know that I cannot transfer this fear to Paul. He has the same determination that I have, and I know that he is going. He is more like me than he thinks. So strong, so determined, so fearless, able to look anyone in the eye and stand his ground; yet, so tender underneath it all. I am his mother; I know he has a heart of a poet and a warrior. There is nothing that I can say or do too change his mind. I feel like my world is out of control and crashing down around me.

I spend the rest of the evening bent over in my awkward position. I am listening to Bryant as he mumbles and talks about people and events. I know exactly where he is in his life at this time. He is still in grade school. His brain is retrieving memories for him. I imagine little nerves reconnecting, synapses reaching out for a connection. His brain is working overtime, sapping all of his energy as it tries to put the jumbled jig-sawed pieces of itself back together.

Bryant has wet and messed all over himself. We clean him up and then they come in with a Texas catheter. This is an external catheter; it allows the urine to flow into a bag at the side of the bed. This is simply something else for him too be angry at, something else for him too spend time trying to remove. It seems a much more humane answer to our problem, but it quickly becomes another reason for me to stay on guard bent over his bed. No need to worry about him wanting to stand and go to the bathroom anymore; he has no separate control over his bladder and intestines, both eliminate simultaneously. His ear has started leaking fluid at a steady pace, telling us that once again there is pressure on his brain. He is a baby, in every sense of the word. He cannot take care of himself, cannot survive without constant care.

Bryant would have pulled out his feeding tube many times over that afternoon had I not been there to catch him. I'm not sure how people survive without families watching over them. I don't know how our family will survive this constant stress. I am watching our entire family life get changed dramatically right before my eyes, and I am helpless to stop it. I do not want any of these changes.

I think back to the "homeless" families in the ICU waiting room. Many of the patients were victims of automobile accidents. I think to myself: *I don't even have a drunk driver with whom to be angry. I could be angry with Bryant but that seems pointless. I have no one to take my anger out on, and no one to give me comfort. I, too, am a victim.* I am beginning to understand what happens to a person who is under extreme stress. Will I become like those people? Will I become a selfish person unable to give up my chair to someone else? A nasty, mean, un-showered woman with frizzled hair, puffy eyes and angry at the world? I see the person I could become, and it is just wrong, so wrong. I agree with you Bryant, it's all messed up, it's just not right.

Steve is going to Florida to work soon because we need the money, and as a consultant—no work, no money. Paul is going to the east coast to join the Marines; Elizabeth is going to the west coast to begin college, out in the land of freedom and opportunity; Bryant is somewhere I cannot identify and James is home, for now, struggling with his own problems. How am I going to do this? I will need help in the next few weeks, months. Once Steve starts traveling again, how will I cope? Emotionally I am going to keep it together. I have been through tough times before while Steve traveled. Physically, there are not enough hours or enough of me. I am needed at home, here and what about my health? These are the questions that swirl through my mind when I have a chance to think. Luckily, I am so busy caring for Bryant I do not have much thinking time.

Chapter **24**
The Pit Bulls

"Do what you can, with what you have, where you are."
– Theodore Roosevelt

Bryant has a pit bull named Ali. Bryant rescued him from a homeless situation when he was eighteen. It was another one of those times when he did not listen to me but followed his heart. I thought at the time that it was hard enough for an eighteen-year-old college student to make it on his own and that the dog could complicate things. Now that complication is staring me in the face. Ali has been crated in Bryant's apartment for the past week. Both Paul and a boy renting out the top floor apartment had been letting him out, but it is painfully apparent that Bryant will not be coming back soon to his apartment, if at all. The current situation had to be addressed, and I was forced to make a decision on what to do with the dog. I know how much Ali means to Bryant. With that in mind there is only one decision I can make: I give approval for James to bring Ali to our house to live. James picked him up and brought him there today.

Although Ali has been at our house on occasion, I am nervous around him. Pit bulls do not have the best track record; they are said to be unpredictable. There are countless stories in the news over the past few years about unreliable pit bulls attacking children and such. He seems to be a sweet dog when I visit Bryant, but I have never had him at my house without Bryant around. We had dogs in the past, but only outside dogs and Ali is an inside dog. After the assortment of pets that the kids had during their childhood, I am enjoying not having the complications of pets at this phase of my life. An indoor dog will be an adjustment, and our yard is not fenced. No matter how I argue it out, it all comes down to the fact that Bryant loves this dog, and I cannot give him away to another home. Besides, no one would take a pit bull anyway, not even a shelter. Pit bulls are illegal to own in our city luckily, we are in suburbia.

I am only able to sleep for a couple of hours. My mind is constantly on, searching for answers about things to do, or how I can help. I catch a few hours at a time as long as the TV plays. The quiet is more than I can take and deep sleep is evasive.

I am not a list maker, not in the normal pen and paper style, but I make lots of lists in my head. I mentally start one now. I am going over the steps that will be needed to help Bryant begin his rehab in a few days. He needs to be dressed and ready to go... those words are swimming around in my mind. I am watching the upcoming events as if they are a movie. I go over them again and again, thinking how can I make this work smoothly, what are the obstacles at hand? Step one will be to get him dressed. If I cannot take his neck brace off, how will I get a T-shirt over his head with his neck brace?

I toss and turn unable to turn off the replay button to my own personal mental list making. I finally give up on sleep and climb out of bed after thinking of a way to help. Stumbling down the stairs I find some old T-shirts in the downstairs closet. I get out my sewing scissors, Velcro and the sewing machine. I cut a slit in the neckband of the T-shirt at the shoulder seam. I extend the cut from the neckband all along the shoulder seam to the beginning of the arm, forcing an opening. I then sew Velcro onto both sides of the opening. I try it out. Pulling on the seams I am able to open up the shirt, much the same as a small child's shirt opens up with snaps on the shoulders. Just as easily they stick back together. I will be able to put his shirts on him. I quickly pull out a couple more and make a small stack of Velcro shirts to take with me to the rehab center. With this small success to buoy my spirits, I am much too excited to fall back asleep.

James has fallen into a routine of visiting the rehab center in the early evening and spending part, if not all, of the night there with his dad and Bryant. He slips in while I am in bed. I leave before he wakes up, and I do not have time with him.

When I check on him, I find he has uncrated the dog, and they are both curled up together on the bed. The comfort that comes from snuggling appears to be good for both of them. Pit bulls tend to imprint on one master, and Ali is really dependent on Bryant. He has not been separated from his master for more than twenty-four hours since he came to live with him.

Step two of my mental list: Now that we know Bryant has the capacity to swallow we need him to eat. The doctor told me to bring all of his favorite foods; it is important that we get him to eat something. It does not matter what. He will be far more tempted to eat familiar foods than hospital food. Bryant is a junk food junkie and with the tube going down his throat I don't want to bring anything like chips or snack type foods that could scratch his throat. I look around the house; the casseroles and food that are here are not going to tempt him. I put watermelon, bananas, oranges, and anything that I can find with a smooth texture in a cooler and take it to the hospital with me.

Step three, survive one more day at the rehab center.

Chapter 25
Something to Cling To

"Worrying does not empty tomorrow of it's troubles; it empties today of it's strength."
– Unknown

Walking out to the car, once again the Cicadas are everywhere on the ground, the remnants of another day of Cicadas. I have not been outside in the full daylight to grasp how many there are. Judging by the carnage on the ground, they must be plentiful. I remember how vulnerable they are at this stage, unable to spread their wings and fly depending completely on their instinct and a lot of luck to get them through. They crawl out of the ground and attach themselves to anything to survive while their wings dry out.

They spent seventeen years of their life underground waiting for this moment, only to emerge totally helpless. The comparison to my son hits me hard and I start to shiver. He has come out of the darkness; yet, he is helpless, totally at the mercy of the elements. His survival, his future is unknown. He cannot care for himself and we are relying on instinct to kick in and help him to eat. He has attached himself to us, to my hand, his lifeline. I crunch my way to my car, and then I realize that some of these Cicadas may not be dead yet. It may be that they haven't found anything to attach themselves to, and that I am crunching them to death. I gingerly try to make my way to the car, but in the early dawn there is no way to avoid them.

Putting the shirts and food in the backseat of the car, I roll down my windows. Once again, I am so happy to be sucking in the outside air. As I make my way down the highway and toward the rehab center my fight song comes on the radio again.

I sing my fight song all the way to the center; over and over belting it out as I drive.

The sun is starting to peek up over the horizon. I see a motorcycle rider without a helmet go whizzing by. The thought crosses my mind that a brain injury is a terrible thing to chance just to have the wind in your face. I realize that my outlook has changed in the past few days and a visit to a neurological rehab center has the power to change your views.

Steve, Bryant and James had quite a night. When I left that night, I told Steve that he was to watch Bryant closely. The feeding tube was not to come out. I told him how quick he was and to be prepared for a fight. Steve overheard me telling James that "your dad will never be able to keep that feeding tube in," and took it as a challenge.

When I arrived at the rehab center that morning Steve had left a journal entry for me to tell me about his night. Here it is:

Steve's Journal:

Between four-thirty and six in the morning Bryant was very agitated. It's real simple; he was begging me for a cigarette. You cannot convince me that he is not going through nicotine withdrawals. This cannot help his mood. Bryant has been smoking cigarettes for several years now. He thinks that we do not know. He at least respects us enough to not tell us about it or smoke in front of us. He has never mentioned cigarettes in front of me, until now.

He has been spitting up "hockers" all night long. The good news is he is bringing them up real well, the bad news...when I'm not looking he spits them over the bed and onto the floor. Quite disgusting, but yet it takes some brain coordination. I'm not sure, but I don't know if Catie could send luggies flying while laying flat on her back tied down to a bed. A nurse just came in and gave me a cup of coffee; she also changed the catheter bag. We were able to keep it on all night. He did not wet the bed on my watch.

Bryant has been really strong during phases of the night, especially when he was trying to go for the feeding tube in his nose. It was like isometric exercises; the good news is that he is very strong, with a strong grip in both arms and hands. He was pulling and squeezing my arms frequently fighting me for the feeding tube at times throughout the night.

The nurse gave him a sedative around eleven and he slept pretty well, for a while. He talked in his sleep all night. At one point he said, "Now what we do is..." He then woke up and seemed to be alert and was speaking clearly. I showed him a picture of him and his brothers and sister from the cruise we took this past Christmas, the first thing he said is, "There's me."

Unfortunately, he is still really upset with the feeding tube and that his wrists are tied down. The good news is that he was not agitated about going to the bathroom; what a relief. I guess the feeding tube has distracted him; it is now his number one priority. I heard your challenge to me about the feeding tube, WELL HE DID NOT GET IT OUT. I admit that he is really good at scooting down in the bed and getting his head/nose close to his hands.

The highlight of the night was when Bryant said he was thirsty. I had an ice cold bottle of water in the small cooler I brought from home. I asked him if he wanted a drink and he said, yes. I drank a bit of it first, just to show him how. He then drank and drank; he sucked it down. I could not believe how well and how much he drank, without stopping he must have swallowed four or five times. When he finished he let out a refreshing "AHHHHH that was the best water I've ever had." He went on to drink a few more sips and then was satisfied. It was a very special and satisfying moment for me to see the pleasure in his face.

You, Catie, called and Bryant has hit a new low. He is taking to bringing up luggies and spitting them out and onto the floor, the bed, his shirt, and five minutes ago onto the side of my face. He is in a rage because I will not pull out his feeding tube. We had an incredible struggle. I called and called for the nurses but they did not respond. I was holding onto both of his hands while he wiggled almost out of the bed... and he spit on me again. I am going to remain positive, Happy Sunday, praise God that my little man is spitting, thank you God for letting him spit his stuff onto me.

The nurse finally came in. I don't think she has the patience I have. She looked around at the room in disgust. She left to get a sedative.

I probably gave him the best aerobic workout he's had in a week. He is sweating out of all of his pores. He and I are worn out. He has just passed out, please Catie get here soon. The nurse and I restrained Bryant and put the waist belt back on him. Since he is sleeping I beg with her to not sedate him. Whew, I survived. Let's save the sedative for when we really need it. I've done my PT with Bryant for the day. By the way, he is stronger than shit in both hands. He was pinching me and bending back my thumb and fingers. Thank you God for giving him strength, he has it.

I hate to see him waste his strength fighting me. I would rather he learn to channel it positively. I'm sure he will eventually. I've asked the nurse to bathe him and clean the sheets. I think she is afraid of him, afraid of getting spit on. She still wants to medicate him because he has gotten the feeding tube out six inches; she has to re-tube him. She did it; we got it back in and taped down. I want you to know Catie; I did not lose the nose tube.

We just had another rough go. We had to give him Ativan. Let's chill him out. Yes, he did miss you, his momma. He has called out your name for the past hour since you called. He knew I was speaking to you. I'm tired. It was a tough night. I am going home to bed.

When I arrive at the rehab center and relieve Steve, he looks bushed and he is quick to leave. I try to remain positive and tell myself that this is progress. The sheets, walls, bedding and Bryant's gown are all streaked with gobs of spit. I survey the leftover evidence from their nighttime struggles. Bryant is bringing all of this up and out of his lungs and sinus cavities. It is good to get this out, it will improve his lung function, but it is disgusting. The harsh, nasty, crudeness of it all is foreign to the personality of our sweet, caring son. My son would never be this crass and gross, not in front of me anyway, and not to his father. He has taken great pride in sending spit flying all around the room. There is an aggressive nastiness to him that I have never seen before.

I count my blessings, he is alive, he is not paralyzed, he is breathing on his own, he can talk, he can move, he is strong, really strong, and really motivated to fight. This new turn of events is so depressing.

Steve and I do not get to talk much when we trade off. We cannot leave Bryant alone. He is keeping us so busy that we do not have time for conversation. With both of us missing so much of Bryant's recovery and of each other, we devise a plan to write everything down in a journal. I read Steve's entry while Bryant, who is newly sedated sleeps. Journaling is the only way Steve and I are now communicating. Although we had been keeping notes, names, comments etc., the new in depth journaling is a great way for us to keep in touch with each other. Steve starts keeping a really detailed journal of their nightly adventures. It turns out to work really well for Steve in the quiet of the night; I do not find it to be as easy for me in the busy day light hours.

It is a battle to get Bryant to cooperate. I am keeping a constant vigil during the day time to not let him take his tubes out and to keep him awake, engaged and calm; most of all calm. I do not want him sedated, and I do not want him sleeping in the daytime. I am fascinated with the "rebooting" of his brain. I want the rebooting to continue and not be slowed down. I want to be his support. I want to be the thing he can cling to for protection while he is so tender and vulnerable. I want him to survive and to spread his wings and fly some day. I have a lot of wants.

Even with a sleeping pill, Bryant and his dad are quite active most of the night. Usually, their nightly adventures end up with Bryant getting out of control and being sedated. This makes it almost impossible for me to get Bryant up and moving. All he wants to do is sleep during the day. He does not want to participate in his own rehabilitation and I am determined that he will. The real problem is that I don't often get the chance to read all of Steve's journal.

I am too busy in the daytime to finish it. It is not until much later that I piece together the sedation in the wee hours of the morning and his inability to get going in the daytime.

Today goes by pretty much the same as yesterday with the constant fight to get the IV or the feeding tube out. He is now drinking but has not eaten anything yet. He cries out constantly that he is hungry and is begging for food, but when we try to get him to eat his brain will not let him. I am hoping that his survival instinct will kick in soon. He is getting thinner and thinner by the day. We tried tempting him with all kinds of food but nothing has done it as of yet.

I spend most of the day bent over his bed preventing him from removing his tubes. We are both slowly going through the years of his life. He is growing up, once again, right before my eyes. He babbles on and I catch snippets of his conversations, he talks about field trips, teachers, vacations, his life in small pieces but all in sequential order. I am simply amazed at this process. He seems to know that I am Mom. Although he fights with me, he never crosses the line to spit on me or pinch me. I am grateful for that.

Steve and I are now settling into a new kind of normalcy, two ships passing in the night. When Steve arrives, I am exhausted. It is really difficult physically and mentally staying on point for so many hours. Keeping my eyes constantly focused directly on his eyes can make minutes feel like hours. I call a nurse to come in and stand over him for me to go to the bathroom. I have given up eating lunch, and am now munching on his cookie basket, grabbing a bite here and there to stave off hunger. I also utilize the cooler I brought with food to tempt Bryant, so far no luck.

When James arrives at the hospital that night, he tells me that my mother has called. She and my sister are staying at a local hotel, and she wants me to call her. I had told them we were not doing a graduation party, what is she doing here? It was good of them to come, but I cannot deal with much more right now. With my mother nothing is ever easy. This has been what I wanted: family; yet, somehow it is not.

Steve arrives at the hospital with Cheese Coneys, a local thing, small hotdogs, covered in chili sauce with a strange plastic-looking cheese on top all enfolded into a small hot dog bun.

"What are you doing with those," I ask.

"The doctor said to tempt Bryant with anything at all, he said it did not matter what he ate, well... he loves Cheese Coneys."

"Yeah, but don't you think it should be healthy?"

I don't tell him that I think it is really cruel to eat something that Bryant loves in front of him when he is so hungry and desperate for food. It seems wrong; yet, maybe it's right. What I am doing is not working. The whole world is upside down right now. I feel like Alice, and I have fallen through the looking glass, nothing is what it should be.

"No, I don't." He says matter of factly. "I think it is only important that we get him to eat."

He sticks a gooey bite of hot dog in his mouth.

"By the way, Elizabeth is going to spend the night with a friend tonight. She will go with them to the graduation ceremony tomorrow morning," he tells me.

"It will be tough enough for us to get out of here and get there," Steve says. "I arranged for a friend to come in and relieve you tomorrow morning. You come home and then we can drive to the ceremony together."

Steve and James munch on the Coneys making a lot of yummy noises as they smack their lips. Bryant is crying out that he is hungry, but when they get them up to his mouth he can't pull the trigger. They set one aside for him to try again later. I look over at them as they settle in for the night; they don't appear to feel the least bit bad about eating the Coneys in front of him.

Men, I think to myself.

Yet, somehow it seems so much cozier than my lonely quiet day. I stay with them awhile, and then head home; I am exhausted. Before I leave, I give them both a lecture once again, about the feeding tubes, IVs and the catheter. It gives me a false sense of control to be able to tell them how I want it done.

I walk out of the rehab center and into the warm spring night. The Cicadas, although not at full speed in the evening hours, are still buzzing around through the air. They are thick and everywhere. They have learned to fly, I think to myself. Their singing noise is deafening. They only have two weeks to live, and now they are airborne and looking for a mate. I cannot believe how many there are. The car is covered, and I quickly open the door trying my best to duck in without any of them getting into the car with me. Yuck, I shiver, bugs everywhere. I run my hands through my hair to see if any of them had landed in it. I do a quick check of my body and don't see any.

As I drive home, doing my best to decompress, I am really happy that James and his Dad are bonding through this ordeal. Right now, he seems to prefer his dad's attention, and I am a little jealous. I think that James has suffered the most because of his dad's traveling. The heavy travel had not happened during the early years with the other boys, but he had traveled all of James's life. I have been the one to toss baseballs to him and take him to most of his practices.

I am really bummed that Elizabeth will not be home again this evening. She had gone to a graduation party the night before and had spent the night at the same friend's house. I know that it is better for her to be around people who care about her and she has spent a lot of time with her friend's family over the years. She is like the sister Elizabeth never had. I feel that I am missing out on an important event in my daughter's life. I will never have this time again. I shrug it off, nothing I can do about it. I am feeling left out and alone.

Chapter 26
Hurts and Wrongs

"Therefore do not worry about tomorrow, for tomorrow will worry about itself. Each day has enough trouble of it's own."
– Matthew 6:34

Once again I return home to an empty house, except for the dog, waiting happily for me. I am used to our house being full of people, and kids; now it is Ali and me. I am hardly ever alone in my own house. Sometimes, life comes at you fast and you need to be able to adjust. I make my way into the kitchen and once again, like magic, there is food on the counter. A graduation cake is even sitting on the counter waiting for Elizabeth's celebration tomorrow. Who are these people, and how can they be so wonderful?

I look at the phone, then down at Ali and say:

"I guess I better get this over with. Here I go."

I do not have a motel name for my mother. I call a couple of local motels and locate her pretty quickly.

"Hello, Mom, this is Catie," I say.

"Well it's about time you call me," she replies.

"What are you talking about Mom," I ask. "I only just heard that you called."

I can hear the irritation and anger in her voice.

"We have been here for two days, and you haven't even called us. We are just sitting here. I don't appreciate being treated this way. We were talking about leaving."

"Mom, I did not know that you were here until an hour ago. Do you want me to come over and get you now?"

"No it's late, we are going to bed. What do you want us to do about the graduation tomorrow," she asks grudgingly

"Why don't you meet us here around ten in the morning? We will go to the ceremony together. I have someone staying with Bryant so Steve and I can go together."

I am waiting for her to ask how I am or how Bryant is; she doesn't say anything at all. A long pause lingers over the phone line.

"O.K.," I say. "You go to bed and I will see you in the morning, love you." I look around the kitchen at the food that is sitting on the counter, including the graduation cake. The outpouring of love all around me is in stark comparison to my own family.

My mother was the middle child of seven children. Her father died of cancer when she was twelve years old. Her mother made her quit school to watch her three younger siblings while my grandmother worked as a cook, supporting the family of eight. The older children and younger children were all allowed to finish school. Not having an education set my mother up for a lifetime of disappointments and poverty.

When she turned fourteen, while other girls were painting their toenails and dreaming about boys; my grandmother signed papers that said my mother was sixteen and off she went to work as Rosie the Riviter during World War II. She cleaned the steam engines at the terminal working long hours and handing her paycheck over to her mother. She loved that job, but when the men came home after the war she was forced to quit and went to work in the restaurant with her mother. After two failed marriages and never a support check from either of her husbands, she went to work in a potato chip factory to support her children. A lifetime full of people who did not support her has hardened her. She does not know how to offer physical love and emotional support. Knowing personally how important schooling is, she never misses a graduation. I was hoping she was here for me and not just the graduation.

I know her well enough and had expected something like this. I had unknowingly made her wait on me. I had not seen her since before the blow up over the funeral eight months prior. We had made plans for her to come back home with me after the funeral. We were going to attend a riverboat festival showcasing big paddleboats. Mom had been looking forward to this. I was so distraught by her casting me aside the way she did that I cancelled the trip. She and my sisters were appalled at my actions. I had spent my entire life anticipating and trying to fulfill the needs of my mother and for the most part my sisters. This was the first time that I had said "no" to her and my sisters. I simply did not have it in me to see her, afraid that I would do permanent damage it was best for her to stay away at that time.

This was a crucial step, the beginning of a turning point for me. I was so hurt that I reached out to my heavenly Father once again for help. I had not rejected Him the past few years, but I had turned away from Him. I decided that I had to forgive her for my own well being. I had been calling her and talking to her on the phone, but this would be the first time I had actually seen anyone in my family since the shunning. I had not spoken to my sisters in the past eight months. I simply needed space and time to heal, and I guess they did as well. I knew that it would never be spoken of again unless I brought it up. That is the way our family is. Hurts and wrongs are never brought into the light, and apologies are not made. No one has apologized to me, and I know they never will. I have put a stake in the ground about my worth. I cannot back down on this one. Bryant's accident is pushing me to face them before I am actually ready. If not now, when? Will I ever be ready to see any of them again? I need to trust that God has a plan and this is part of it.

Ali seems to be as lonely as I am. He is my shadow, never more than two steps away from me. He knows that I am part of the pack, that I am the alpha female of the pack. He accepts me as a second in command with no problem at all. He and I head out to the pool. I am amazed that there are no bugs in the filter at all, none floating in the water. That really baffles me; apparently they stay away from water. My shadow and I go upstairs to get my bathing suit. I find it hanging exactly where I had left it just seven short days ago. I put my suit on and jump into the water. My mind cannot help going back to the last time I was in this pool, and how that one phone call changed my life forever. The water feels great and it is relaxing as my hands slice through it. I swim around in the pool as evening turns to dark. I often swim in the dark; working all day it is often the only time I get to swim. I try to swim at least once a day. I love my pool. Ali does not get in the water, but races around the edge of the pool worried that something is wrong with me. Clearly, this is not relaxing to him at all. I finally get out, dry off, and we both go inside. I eat another great carb fest, and he has a bowl of dog food. I make a couple of phone calls to Paul, Elizabeth, James and Steve. Having touched base with everyone, I turn the TV on and try to relax and grab some sleep. Tomorrow is going to be a really interesting day. I hope I am ready for it all.

I wake around four in the morning, having slept fitfully throughout the night. I shower and head to the rehab center. I want Steve to have time to come home and catch a few hours of sleep before heading out to the graduation ceremony. When I get there he has, once again, had a mixed night with Bryant. He seems to go back and forth quickly between being sweet and childlike to being an aggressive fighting machine. He talked to his dad and James for hours about soccer, how to play physical, and how to be mean and tough. It was as if he was coaching James on how to play. He made them laugh out loud a couple of times over the funny things that he was saying. Apparently I had just missed James; he had headed home about the time I was leaving from home.

We trade off and I am now in charge. I make a milkshake in the kitchen with Boost and a thickener right before Steve leaves. I try to get Bryant to drink some of it, but he will not. This is really awful; I essentially am watching my child starve to death right in front of my eyes. His lean body did not have any fat on it to begin with and now, desperate for calories to heal his brain, his body is sacrificing his muscles. He is now beginning to look like a skeleton. I did not think it possible for a body to shrink this fast. If we can only get him to eat, we can take the feeding tube out and everyone's lives will be much easier.

Tomorrow morning he will be starting the next phase of his rehabilitation. One more day for him to rest up and then we need to get busy. I always put the kids in those white soft leather high topped walking shoes when they were first starting to walk. I look at these huge high-topped Nike shoes, and smile at the size. My relief arrives early and I am out of there around nine o'clock. I have not been away from his side in the light of day since the accident. I experience mixed emotions, I want to be there for Elizabeth's graduation, but leaving is really hard for me. This is the first time he has not been in the hands of a family member since the accident. I know that I must go. I need to let go and be there for Elizabeth. I miss our life.

Chapter 27
Celebrations

"Prepare for the worse; expect the best; and take what comes."
– Hannah Arendt

I drive home and to my surprise my sister and my mom are waiting for me. Paul, Leigh and James are there as well. I give everyone a hug and head upstairs to change. I have not thought about clothes for the graduation ceremony and remember that I planned to get an outfit this week. Oh well, I think as I pull on a sleeveless white top and a pair of black pants. It is really hot for the end of May. At that moment I remember Elizabeth needs a white dress for graduation, had she ever gotten one? She is walking today, and I have no idea if she even has a dress to wear. I feel like a loser mom.

We crowd into several cars and head over to the ceremony site. Steve's parents are meeting us there as well. We are somewhat late, most of the families arrived earlier with their students, and the seating is all taken. When we walk in I can feel the eyes on us, and hear the whispers. I know that we are the topic of conversation. One of Elizabeth's teachers spots us and helps us to find seating. She finds an area in the balcony for everyone, but we are two seats short. She escorts Steve and me downstairs to the main floor. She has tears in her eyes when she asks us how Bryant is doing. We realize we are both choking back sobs. The love and compassion that she is showing us is catching us off guard.

We sit down in the middle of the row. This is the first time we have been outside in public together since the accident. We lean into each other. We are not prepared for how raw our emotions are. From the first song of the commencement exercise we cry. Holding onto each other, I place my head on Steve's arm, we cry for an hour and an half throughout the entire ceremony. Tears are streaming down both of our faces. An older gentleman is sitting on the other side of Steve and he keeps talking to him. Steve says later that he helped him to stay focused on Elizabeth. Otherwise we would have been a real mess.

It is a beautiful ceremony, the part when they ask all of the veterans to stand war by war, we both watch as Steve's dad, Bernard stands for serving during World War II. Knowing that our beloved first son will be going off to join the Marines, we sob even more. Then, the speeches start all talking about carpe diem, the future, the past, nine students joining the military; it is all about everyone's lives changing and the new paths they will be walking. Our only daughter is leaving us, heading off to make her way. For us, the graduation commencement exercises and speeches sum it all up. Our new chapter has started. It will never be the same again. The past is in the past we need to look to the future; yet, we cannot help to think that Bryant's future is so uncertain. Whew, we were not ready for this.

After we dry our eyes, we head out front to meet up with our family and Elizabeth for a photo op. Steve's parents are there, and they are really quiet; it has now been three days since I last saw them in the driveway. They are staying at the local casino motor home park. They love to play black jack. They tell us that they will not be coming to the house; instead they are heading to Illinois to visit with other family members. We do not have a plan, and will not be having a party. Paul and Leigh will stop by for cake and then head to his apartment. We have not seen much of him. He has had classes every day this week and finals this coming week. We want him to graduate. Leigh has been a Godsend, keeping him on track and focused on the task at hand. When he was at the hospital, he always had his books with him.

The rest of us head home. I am planning to change my clothes and get back to the hospital. I feel that I have been gone too long. I sit in the back seat with my mother, giving us a chance to visit for a few minutes before I need to leave.

"I am hungry," she says, "what are we eating?"

"Well Mom, I do not have anything planned, I have been at the hospital every day since the accident."

"What do you mean you don't have any food, what am I suppose to eat?" I should be shocked, but I find it to be too funny for words, and I choke back the hysteria that is threatening to come forward.

"Well Mom," I say rather sarcastically, "other people have been really kind and understand that I cannot cook. They are bringing food to the house. They even brought a graduation cake for Elizabeth. I am sure we can find some leftovers for you to eat."

She thinks about this for a minute, "Well good, I guess I can find something to eat."

"I am going to eat something quickly and then head back to the hospital, would you like to come with me?"

"No, I don't think so," she says slowly. "I had a cousin once who got kicked in the head by a horse, and he was never quite the same, I think I want to remember Bryant the way he was. I don't think I want to see him."

"Well O.K.," I say.

I really do not have an answer to that one. I do not want her around him then. We make small talk as we head back to the house. She tells me again how awful it was of me to leave her sitting in a motel for two days. I really don't have the energy or the inclination to care what she thinks right now. What could have happened to her to make her this way? I feel really sorry for her.

When we get home I pull the food out of the refrigerator and set it up on the counter. Elizabeth comes in, and she is wearing a white dress. She is so beautiful. She pulls me aside and she is disappointed. She took an extra year of Latin to graduate with honors, only so she could have the medal to walk with during graduation, and she had forgotten it. Oh well, I didn't think of it either. We have cake, take pictures and relax. Steve decides that he wants to go to the hospital so that I can spend a little more time with my family...or said another way: he can not wait to get away from here. He wolfs down his food, wanting to get there to relieve Bryant's sitters as quickly as possible. I tell him that I won't be long.

My sister is wonderful; she hugs me and inquires about Bryant. She has faced tragedy and understands it. I had not been there for her. I apologize to her for that. I did not understand then what I understand now about the importance of being there. She has brought her grandson with her. She apologizes for not telling me they were coming, but she made plans to visit her son, and her grandson was excited about this trip, so she had decided to come anyway. They are leaving in the morning to visit with her son. I tell them to make themselves at home. Her grandson is having a fun time in the pool and with the video games. I say good-bye to my mother as they head back to the hotel for their nap. I tidy everything up, change my clothes and head back to the hospital. It has been a good day, all in all.

I am in for quite a shock when I get back to the hospital. The day gets even better. Steve stopped at McDonalds and got a vanilla milkshake, fries and a cheeseburger. He has continued on with the temptation, bringing in more of Bryant's favorite foods to eat in front of him; smacking his lips and making a scene while eating it. Bryant drank the milkshake and ate a few bites of the cheeseburger and fries. It is a miracle come true. His brain is finally sending the right signals, letting him eat. He has always been a fan of Mickey D's and the healthy food that I am trying to get him to eat simply is not tempting enough. I hate to admit it, but Steve is right and I am wrong. At this time, food is food, and he desperately needs calories. It doesn't matter from where the calories come; calories are king right now. This is such a different idea to me. I am always counting calories to keep them low. I know it is the right thing to do, but my mind is screaming good nutrition, not empty calories.

Steve is a man of action. He also had untied Bryant's hands and feet and had him sit up and then stand up for a couple of minutes.

Steve said that Bryant was really shaky and it was really hard. It exhausted him, because he then fell fast asleep.

Steve was never one for following rules; he does not think they apply to him. He makes his own way. I like to follow the rules, and it has been a constant battle in our family. This time, I am glad he broke the rules. We hang out at the hospital together for a while. Neither of us wants to leave. Bryant is pretty calm. I run out to buy more McDonalds just to watch him eat. It is awesome. I encourage Steve to go home to get some rest. He comes back around midnight to relieve me, with more Cheese Coneys in tow. Steve is so happy. He slept in our bed from six to eleven in the evening, five whole hours of sleep in his soft comfortable bed. He is amazed at how good he feels.

I have a surprise for him; they removed Bryant's feeding tube. Actually he had removed it once again, only partially, but the nurse had enough of it. I begged her to take it out since he is eating. She called the doctor, and he told her to remove it. If he continues to eat, no problem, if he doesn't eat, they will put it back. This is going to make things so much better for everyone, no more fighting with him over the feeding tube; I won't need to stand over him ready to grab his hands. Yes, things are really looking up. We are in business mode and ready to start rehab in the morning.

I head home, mentally checking off what needs to be done in the morning. I must get Bryant up, dressed and ready to go by eight in the morning! His shirts and shoes are ready, and the wheelchair was delivered to his room today. I need to send James out the door and to school by seven in the morning. James still has another week of school. Although the seniors graduated, everyone else has finals this week. He cannot miss. Steve has let Elizabeth spend the night away again. I object to this, but clearly I have lost all control. I am not home in the daytime, and he is running the show. His reasoning is that she will be leaving in ten weeks for college, and we will not be able to police her actions then. He tells me to let her go. She is a good girl; I need to learn to trust. I get home around 1:30 a.m. I am so tired by the time I get home that I head to bed for a few hours of troubled sleep, both excited and anxious about tomorrow.

Steve's Journal:

James did not come this evening as he has school in the morning. It is different here without him. Bryant is resting now, mumbling in his sleep, and he mentioned Grandpa Bryant's bass. He was my favorite Grandpa; I spent so many hours bass fishing with him, so many nights at his house sharing root beer floats. Bryant is named after my grandpa. He passed away shortly after Bryant was born. I don't think I have ever heard him mention Grandpa Bryant before. I have been praying to him, asking him to be an angel and to intervene on the side of Bryant. I am now convinced that he is here with him. Thank you, God, for this; thank you, Grandpa.

Bryant is extremely angry with me tonight. He is angry because I won't remove the "shackles" and the neck brace. I took his restraints off today and now he wants them off permanently. He is calling me names. I heard every name in the book tonight. Moments ago he was a sweet little boy fishing with my Grandpa, wow how quickly it all changes.

Well now Bryant has pulled his IV needle out that was a new one on me. I am watching three things: keeping his hands off his catheter; hands off the neck brace; wiggling out of his restraints. I was not considering the possibility that he would take the IV out. I thought he was only scratching his arm. He looked right at me and said, "What's this?" I called the nurses down, again. I can't help but feel that I let everyone down again, especially Bryant. He had to get re-stuck. The good news is that they stuck him in the right arm this time and then rolled him over to his left side. The nurse tied both arms down to the left side of the bed and he was able to curl up and fall asleep in a fetal position. He seems happy now. The nurse has warned me that he may be able to untie the restraints this way, so I need to watch him closely.

I am getting a reputation as being a bad night watchman. He pulled his feeding tube out last night and his IV tonight. I move my chair to the end of the bed to keep a closer eye on him. The nurse told me tonight what a saint Catie is. Bryant was cursing at her all day

*today; she does not get flustered and takes it all in stride. The nurses
are amazed at her ability to take abuse.*

*Bryant is sleeping soundly; he has slept for four and a half hours.
Then Houdini Bryant has spent the last half hour trying to escape. He
became incredibly angry with me for not pulling out the new IV and
the restraints. We went back to name calling, I heard it all tonight.
He even tried chewing off his restraints. I cannot calm him down.
Even though I am not fighting back with him physically, we seem
to be doing battle. When I call the nurses, he immediately becomes
nice and seems happy like I am getting in trouble. I asked the nurse
to sedate him again. It is now four-thirty and hopefully he will be
rested in the morning for his first day of assessment and meeting his
new team. I spend the rest of the night journaling and thinking, my
thoughts rambling as I journal and try to stay awake in the dark. At
one point I am laying on the floor using a penlight to write. Boy am I
tired. It is now seven-thirty and he has been sleeping for three hours.
The lab tech came in and took blood. Bryant did not even flinch. He
is really out. God I was praying for you to give him strength, boy have
You come through on that one, I want to adjust that prayer to give
Bryant patience and persistence.*

Chapter **28**
It's All Messed Up; It's Just Not Right

"A journey of a thousand miles must begin with a single step."
– Lao-tzu

It is good to wake up to a little bit of normalcy. I am anxious to get to the rehab center on time. I am sure that Steve will get Bryant up and dressed for therapy. I am leaving a little later than I have been lately, but James did not need to be at school as early as I thought. I do not want to rush him off, and I have not had much time with him. I cannot call Steve; he gave his phone to Elizabeth to use last night.

The sun is up and the Cicadas are up. They are pretty much in full flight now, buzzing through the air. Some are still coming out of the ground, some are flying around, and some are in the trees mating. They are in multiple stages right now. I am driving once again down the highway, and unbelievably my fight song has been on every morning as I drive to the rehab center, hmmm what are the chances of that? I belt it out, using it to psych myself up once again. I am prepared for today, I put my game face on. I hardly recognize my life anymore. It is hard to believe that I am in my life; it seems like someone else's. I hit rush hour traffic and that has slowed me down as well. I will need to leave earlier tomorrow regardless of James' schedule, but it was great to spend some time with him this morning.

I get to the rehab unit at seven forty-five, only fifteen minutes before Bryant's day is scheduled to begin. When I get to the room,

Bryant and Steve are both lying down. Bryant is not awake, dressed and ready to go. A breakfast tray is sitting in the room, untouched. Ha, I think to myself, is that really for Bryant? We will never get our son to eat hospital food.

Steve is lying on his back on the floor. I am really mad. He knows we have a schedule to keep. Steve tells me that he tried to get Bryant to eat and he won't, he also tried a Boost milkshake and he wouldn't eat that either.

I get Bryant up and use a wash cloth to both clean his face and wake him up. An aide has come in to help me. We untie Bryant's hands to slip a shirt over his head, velcroing up the side of his newly tailored T-shirt. She has brought in an adult diaper that we put on him. Then I pull his shorts up and put his socks and shoes on. I stand back and survey him. He looks pretty good, very young and skinny. There is a vacant look in his eyes. He wants to go back to sleep, he is not happy with me at all. He has been complaining through this whole ordeal. What's new, I am beginning to expect this.

A male nurse comes in. He has a lot of energy. He takes one look at Bryant and says:

"Hospital beds are for sick people. If you are sick we can send you back to the hospital. This is a rehab center; we must get you up and in your wheelchair."

Whew, what a difference between the weekend staff and the work week staff. I am grateful that we had the weekend for him to recover somewhat from the ambulance ride. This is a stretch even for today. He unties the restraints and brings Bryant's legs over the side of the bed. I hold him up so that he does not topple over. I do not know that he had been sedated in the early morning hours. I haven't had a chance to read Steve's journal. I only know that I have a job to do. Being the drill sergeant that I am accused of being, if there is a job to be done, I am the person to call on. Luckily for us, Bryant is out of it and does not punch us. The male nurse picks Bryant up by wrapping both of his arms around his torso. He has positioned the wheelchair perpendicular to the bed. He swings him off the bed and puts him in his chair. He then ties his arms and legs down to the chair, and wraps a waist belt around his midsection.

He looks at me and says:

"That's how you do it."

I don't know if I will ever be able to do that. I am impressed.

I brought bananas, watermelons, pudding and a few other things trying to tempt Bryant to eat. He eats a few spoons of a milkshake and a few bites of a banana for me. I find that funny because he has never liked bananas before. He seems to enjoy the taste of the banana, just one more new thing about the new Bryant.

The doctor was in to examine him. He is happy with his progress but reminds us that if we do not get food and quantities in him they will need to surgically put in a feeding tube. He tells us that he is not planning on using the feeding tube down his nose any longer. Bryant is too active. Bryant also swallows a pill for the doctor. Who would have thought that was possible? The doctor is amazed at how well Bryant is physically, considering the magnitude of his fall. He agrees that the alcohol was instrumental in his living, and his survival.

The therapist and her assistant then come in to evaluate him. We are asked to wait out in the hall while they visit with him. We stand out there for quite a while before she comes out into the hallway with us, while her assistant remains inside the room working with Bryant. She explains to us that his brain is confused. He cannot tell the difference between background versus foreground sounds. For example: one voice talking to him while a television or a sound out in the hallway are all going on at the same time confuses his brain. Our brains can differentiate, but his cannot, not at this time. She coaches us to only talk one person at a time; never to have more than two people in the room with him at a time, too many people are confusing. We are to keep the door closed, and not turn the TV or a radio on while someone is talking to him.

I ask her, "What can we do to help, how do we help him?"

That seemed to be a sensible question to me.

She looks at us, and then back to me.

"Tell me your story," she says.

"What do you mean by 'our story'?"

"You do not act like our normal family. Tell me the story of your family, any family history of concussions or learning disabilities?"

I am embarrassed to list the number and frequency that Steve, I, and our kids have suffered concussions. It is a pretty lengthy list. Then I gave her the information about the learning disabilities that we have been dealing with.

"Ah," she says. "That explains it all. We knew something was different about you; you are all about what needs to be done, about what you can do. It is not the normal action of a parent in this predicament."

I look at Steve, and he looks back at me. We don't know what to say about that. She takes us back into Bryant's room. She is critical of all of the photos and poster boards we have in the room. We thought that we were doing so much good by them. The truth is they made us feel really good.

She takes her hand and sweeps it all around the room. "This is a lot of distraction for someone who is confused. Just looking at that balloon could throw you off balance. I want you guys to minimalize this room. We want as few distractions as possible. Let's give his brain time to heal."

After she leaves Steve and I take some of the stuff down off the walls and fill a cart with flowers and things, including the eerily smiling balloon. Steve leaves for home and takes everything with him. This has all been before ten, what a crazy morning.

Bryant has been on his best behavior with the doctor and the therapist. We are amazed at how sweet and charming he is to everyone but us. A nurse explains to us that we should always remember that it's the brain injury talking and not the normal patient—both the charming, cajoling side and the nasty, name calling, angry side. Not to take it personal. Steve seems to be having a difficult time with this.

Multiple therapists are lined up and another one comes in to talk with Bryant. She questions him about his age, what high school he attended, the year, and today's date. He has no idea and cannot answer any of her questions. He has no idea where he is or how he got here. He is completely confused about everything. He is really tired and only wants to go to bed. He is unhappy and cussing me out and doing everything he can to escape from his wheelchair. The male nurse came back in and put something on the back of his chair to prevent him from tipping it over. He is far more active than they were expecting.

I keep trying to get him to take a bite here and there of food. Sometimes I am lucky, but most of the time he only cusses me out refusing to open his mouth for the food. An adorable physical therapist comes in and takes him to the physical therapy area down the hall. She and her assistant are able to get him to stand up for a few seconds and even take a couple of steps. The steps are not "completely on his own," the two women stand on each side of him and, with the aid of a harness, support his weight. His left foot is turned in badly and he seems to drag it. However, seeing him up and moving lifts my heart. They stretch his muscles out and work him. He is saying, "that hurts." None of the sessions last very long at all, just minutes. We still have a long way to go before lunch and a nap.

I am taking him for a walk in his wheelchair up and down the hallway, something to occupy him before lunch and naptime. My patience is wearing thin. At one point he is cussing me out so much I leave him in front of the desk and walk off, he reaches down and rolls his chair so that he can come after me and cuss me out. I don't care, all I know is that my baby is alive and he is rolling his wheelchair all by himself! I am elated. Let the cuss words fly. I continue walking to force him to follow me. If anger is his catalyst, I'll use it. We get close to his room and he can't make it. He is exhausted. I walk back behind his chair and take him into his room.

He is angry with me, "You want me to sit up and look normal because it makes you happy. I only want to go to bed."

He has tears in his eyes.

I call for the nurse; I cannot get him into his bed by myself.
I can see that he has had it; I agree he needs to sleep. I park his
wheelchair next to his bed. He is so tired that he extends his body as
much as he can, being strapped down in his chair. He lays his head
down so sweetly on the edge of the bed. His body needs some sleep
to recover and he is finished with all of his therapies for the day
anyway. I am sitting in a chair across from Bryant, I am watching
him, and he is eyeing me. The nurse is taking forever to get in here.
I am sure this is not their top priority.

Bryant starts crying, tears are pouring out of his eyes, and he
is sobbing. I cannot untie his hands for him to wipe the tears away.
I can't trust him. This is breaking my heart. Tears fill my eyes and
start to roll down my cheeks. I go over and sit on the bed, cradling
his head on my chest. He sobs as I wrap my arms around him.

He is sobbing, "Why, why me, why does everything always
need to be so hard for me?"

All I can do is comfort him, hold him, and love him. I agree
with him, everything has always been so hard for him. All of the
extra hours of tutoring, the special schooling, so much effort had
been put in to get him to where he was. After all that he has accomplished in his lifetime, he has now been taken back to square one.
No, he is even further back than square one.

Slowly I realize that the physical therapy was heart breaking
for him as well as me. He knows that he can't walk; that he is not
normal. All he has ever wanted to be was normal, not to be different than everyone else. What do I say to him? How do I help him?
I continue to hold his head on my chest wrapping my arms around
him, and the tears are running down my face now.

I finally find words. I know in my heart that I will not surrender. "Bryant, Dad and I will be here for you. You will walk again,
you will run again, you just need time," I tell him.

"Mom, everything is so confusing to me, it's all messed up, it's
just not right."

"Your brain is turning on again, it will take time."

I tip his eyes up to mine and look into his green eyes. The

vacant look is not there right now. We are having a moment. "We have come through so much you and I, we will come through this Bryant." I say it with complete confidence.

He knows that he can count on me, and I know that somehow I will make those words come true. I know it, I believe it, and I own it. I have the confidence of a mother who has beaten the odds once with him, once with James, and will do it again, somehow. This seems to calm him down. The male nurse comes in and puts him back into his bed. Thank God for the male nurse. Bryant sleeps for a couple of hours, but wakes up screaming that he is hungry, but he will not eat anything for me. It is so frustrating to sit here and watch my child starve, beg for food but not eat.

Elizabeth brings in a cheeseburger and fries. We are able to get him to eat a little bit. Elizabeth relieves me for a while so I can take a walk outside. I walk around the building a couple of times, needing some fresh air. The stupid Cicadas are awful. I had no idea that it would be this bad; the air is thick with them. I am so tired, so battered, and I have hours to go before I go home. Minutes feel like hours most of the time around here. The sight of my beautiful strong son in a diaper and a wheelchair, emaciated and weak, is hard. Watching him drag his useless leg around the room, and most of all, him recognizing that he is not who he used to be is the hardest. I am sure these visions will be permanently etched in my mind. I am the only witness to this morning's events, a day I tell myself that will one day be nothing but a sad memory. Walking around outside helps me to collect my thoughts and my composure. I head back in through the beautiful locked double doors for round two.

It has been a long day. I do everything I can to make sure that he is not sedated during the daylight hours. I am convinced if I leave he will be tied to his bed and sedated. I don't think that the nursing staff will or should put up with this behavior. I don't know that for sure, but I don't see any of the other patients up and acting this way. They are all in their beds, quietly lying there. A few are in wheelchairs but they are calm and, although a little goofy, not mean and abusive.

I spend all of my time when he is in his bed, bent over ready to grab his hands. He is now trying to pull out his IV. If it's not the ventilator, or the feeding tube, it's the IV, and when that is gone it will be his neck brace. I am convinced that he will never stop fighting us. My back is starting to hurt from leaning over him. I am now thinking that I may develop a bad back for the rest of my life. It is not easy, but I keep the tubes intact; and the sedation away. He kicked a nurse pretty hard today when she untied his leg for a couple of minutes. She won't make that mistake again, and I don't think she likes him very much. The abusive language is non-stop. I remind myself it is simply one of the stages through which he has to pass.

A friend stops by to stay with Bryant in the early evening while Steve and I go to a park for a walk. It is wonderful. The awful Cicadas are everywhere, but we are so happy to be together that we do not really notice them. It has now been ten days since Bryant fell. We share an entire two hours together. It's hard to not feel guilty, but we need this time together. We both seem to have a renewed appreciation for each other. I have said it before, and I will say it again; we are a great team in a crisis.

When we get back, a couple of Bryant's soccer teammates stop by to see him. He is sitting up in his wheelchair, but tied down securely. I don't think Bryant recognizes them, and they are taken aback by his appearance. He is now nothing but skin and bones, his ragged unbathed appearance is in stark contrast to the clean shaven young man they know. His head bobbles around on his neck brace, but mostly it is the vacant far off look that throws one. They are uncomfortable and seem to be at a loss for words.

To break the awkwardness we wheel Bryant down to the now empty physical therapy room. We untie his legs and one of his friends rolls a ball to him, he is not able to kick it back. Bryant tries a few more times; then, he says he is tired and wants to go back to his room. He has been reduced from being the Captain of the team and an All-American nominated player to not being able to kick a ball. I watch as the young men swallow hard and say their good-byes. It is hard on all of us, especially Bryant.

Steve's Journal:

My sweet boy is back. Thirty minutes ago he ate an entire banana. It was so funny; he looked at it and said, "What is this, this is so good?" I laughed, he has never liked bananas and he does not know what it is. He also ate half of a Cheese Coney and part of a Boost milkshake. The doctor stopped by tonight and he was really happy to see Bryant smiling. The Dr. asked him where he went to high school and this time he knew. When he asked him if he played sports, he said yes, "tennis, no baseball" (he has never played tennis and stopped playing baseball at the age of ten). We had been watching the Reds on TV, so it was on his mind. We telephoned Mom, James, Elizabeth and Jack (his childhood friend). He talked to them and told them goodnight. He seems to be at a young age in his mind. His good childhood friend Jack is on his mind a lot. He talks about the things that they are doing.

Bryant looked at me and said, "Thanks, Harrison Ford."

I said, "Just call me Indy." He smiled back at me. I don't think he knows who I am. I'm not sure, but I don't think he does. They came in at midnight and gave him his sleeping pill. We both slept through the night. It is our first peaceful night. I am hoping they will all be like this. I feel like I have been drugged. I cannot wake up. Catie woke us both up, she is here and taking charge. She has him up, dressed and is feeding him. He ate a little bit of watermelon and part of a Boost milkshake. I am heading home now.

Chapter

Fatigue 29

"When I approach a child, he
inspires in me two sentiments;
Tenderness for who he is, and
respect for what he may become."
– Louis Pasteur

Bryant is really groggy this morning. We had his round of speech, PT and OT. PT went just so-so; he was only able to make it through a half an hour. They plan to come back again this afternoon. Bryant finds walking really depressing. He is having a hard time getting the one side of his body to respond. All of his therapies are in the morning, with about an hour break before lunch. I am finding that hour is a long one.

I bring him back to his room to wait for his recreational therapy. He is so tired and angry because I will not let him go back to bed. He rests his head on the bed, leaning as far over as he can while tied down to his wheelchair. The male nurse walks in and gives him a lecture; he tells him that he has to stay up and in his chair, off the bed. He then takes Bryant to his recreational therapy session.

I am beginning to wonder if I am more of a hindrance than a help. I decide to stay away from his therapy sessions. He wants me to rescue him. Things are really looking good today. I am hoping that by the end of next week we may only be visiting him. Once he is eating on his own and all the tubes are gone, the rest is up to him.

I spend the extra hour between lunch and nap-time with him, getting him to wheel his own chair around. I continue walking in front of him up and down the hallway while he cusses me out. I take a few more steps, and he wants to make sure that I can hear how much he hates me, so he follows me. I know it is not me he hates, but it is his anger at the position in which he now finds himself. He is torn by his fatigue and need to sleep and his need to be up and out of that chair. He is mad at the world. He is as mad as hell, and he doesn't want to take it anymore. Who can blame him? Not me. I don't like it much either.

We continue this routine for as long as he can take it. He is unaware that he is pushing his chair and building up his arm strength. I know it is his frustration talking and not him. There is a fine line between letting him rest and recover and the open window of time to get his brain working again. Everything we read and heard says to get him moving independently as quickly as possible. I need to trust that they know what they are doing. Chronic fatigue is a real issue with brain injuries.

We put him back to bed after a few bites of lunch. He is in his bed now, once again we tie all four limbs to the four corners of the bed, and his waist belt is secured down as well. I never remove the straps from his arms and legs, but sometimes I loosen them from the bed, keeping the ends of them wrapped around my hand. To keep his attention I keep my eyes on his and let him have a little freedom with his arms. I am getting good at judging when he will become violent, and I quickly tie the restraints back to the arms of the bed. If I keep his eyes locked on mine, he does not notice what I am doing until it is too late. It is a game of cat and mouse.

He has such a vacant look in his eyes. We had the one moment yesterday when I could actually talk with him but that was short lived. I am not sure he knows who I am today. He does not use names for Steve or me. I hear snippets of conversations that he is having with himself when he is in his bed. He is spending a great deal of time with Jack, his friend that visited him in the ICU, right now in his mind. They were the best of buddies from kindergarten to fifth grade. He is somewhere midpoint in that relationship. We lived on a small farm during those years. He is running through the woods and fields of his youth. I find myself laughing at times as I recall certain events. He is unaware that I am here; he is just mumbling.

Then his strong will to be free and unrestrained surfaces. Things change rapidly, he wants the IV out, the restraints off, or the neck brace off. I get him off one thing, and he switches to the next one. He is often violent and the nurses want to sedate him. He is fighting for freedom, unaware that these things are for his own good. I do my best to keep my eyes locked on his during these times. If I stare directly into his eyes and talk softly to him, it seems to calm him down, somewhat. He cannot be trusted, his moods swing quickly, and he could be a danger to himself or someone else.

During one of these moments, with his eyes locked on mine, a woman enters. She tells me that she and her son, who is a friend of Bryant's, are here to see him. Bryant has his back to her, and I am facing her. He is laying on his side in the bed. I have been trying to prevent him from being sedated now for hours. I do my best to explain to her in a soft voice that now is not a good time, and she will need to come back during visiting hours. She is indignant that I am treating her rudely. I do not want Bryant to catch on that someone else is behind him. He seems to be unaware of that right now, and is focusing on my face, my eyes. I explain to her without breaking my gaze from Bryant's eyes and keeping my words monotone and slow that, "I am trying to keep him calm and she cannot bring anyone in right now, she will need to come back."

She lets out a loud "humph" and stamps out of the room. She does not return. I don't understand people; I have to do what I have to do. I don't want to be rude. Bryant stares back into my eyes, I recognize this look, it is the look of a wild barn cat that is cornered, pacing back and forth not taking its eyes off you. He is unsure of my intentions, gauging my every move.

A friend sits with Bryant again in the early evening so that Steve and I can be together. We go to the same park, but to my surprise Steve has brought the bikes with him. I am excited about the prospect of a bike ride; however, the Cicadas make it impossible. I am afraid one will go splat on my face; we decide to take a walk instead.

Simply walking side by side, occasionally holding hands, is really good. This is our only down time. I leave the hospital just in time to go home to bed, and Steve has been working all day. I know he is in contact with a lot of people; he is posting daily e-mails. He has reached out to so many people. In stark contrast I do not have anyone to contact. I made my children my world. I don't think of my customers as my close friends. Lots of people have offered to help in any way they can; yet, I don't know how to reach out to them to tell them that I am in need. I don't know how to take the first step. After an hour, we head back to the rehab center. We know that Bryant is volatile, and we would not want him acting out horribly with someone else there.

Steve's Journal:

I took Bryant down to the cafeteria tonight in his wheelchair. Two of his friends stopped by. Bryant is in a good mood but is acting a little goofy. He ate and ate down at the cafeteria. He loved the ham, beef and cheesy potatoes; he even ate a peanut butter cup. Boy things are looking up. He even swallowed all of his meds for me. He told his friends that he wanted a cigarette but said don't tell his parents they don't know that he smokes. They laugh at him and tell him that his dad is pushing his wheelchair. He looks up at me and says, "That's not my dad." He really doesn't know who I am, but it's all good. I am so excited it doesn't matter because that's not all. At nine in the evening the nurse and I let him out of the bed and we walked him to the bathroom. He went pee and poop and wiped himself. This is huge. I am so excited. I never thought I would be so happy about a shit. It's hard to believe that we had this much drama over elimination. That's the good news.

Now for the bad news, everyone is going to be really mad at me.... But I allowed him to remove his neck brace. I gave in. It is all or nothing. I either need to keep him restrained or take it off. He now knows that it is on with a Velcro strap. Bottom line it is a judgment call and I don't think he needs it. He should sleep much better tonight without the neck brace and no more restraints. He seems so much more peace-

ful. Tomorrow will be the real test; if he still stays positive then we will know it is the thing to do.

Bryant was sleeping peacefully at first, then he started calling out for James, over and over again. I wonder if he is back in the Gorge. Bryant woke up at one-thirty having wet the bed. He is really agitated. We have quite a struggle. A male orderly took him down to the shower. This is his first shower since before the accident. I stood out in the hall and listened to them, it was a hoot. He was moaning, "oh, yeah, that feels so good." We get him back to bed with a lot of trouble it takes four of us to get him in PJ's and back in bed. The nurse discovers that he does not have his neck brace on. They are really upset with me. They try to put it back on him, but he won't let them. After giving me a hard time they give up and put a call in to the doctor to see if they can keep it off.

He is so cold after the shower that I pile blankets on him. He tells me that he wishes that he could talk to his dad and starts to give me his phone number. He really doesn't know who I am. I get my phone out and dial my number, he misses the intro that has my name, he thinks about it for a while and says, "Hey Mike..." and leaves a message. OK so he thinks I am an Indiana Jones orderly, and he doesn't remember my name, that's fine by me. At least I think he likes me. It probably freaks him out when I try to kiss him and tell him I love him. Perhaps this is why he had all of that aggravation with me; he must have thought I was a pervert or something.

We were up at seven this morning on Catie's orders. I was standing with my back to Bryant and in a flash he was sitting up in the bed ready to walk to the bathroom. It scared me, we walked together and he sat down on the toilet. I still need to hold him up and help him to step his left foot. He shut the door on me. This is scary, wobbling and bobbing dragging his left leg and now he has shut me out of the bathroom. When he comes out he wants to walk down the hall, two male orderlies help him back to his bed. They are not happy. Bryant will not let me dress him but he does let the orderly help him. He is wary of me.

Chapter **30**
The Clash of Wills

"Success is not measured by the heights one attains but by the obstacles one overcomes in its attainment."
– Booker T. Washington

When I get to the rehab center I am in for quite a shock, Bryant sitting in the bed with the restraints and the neck brace off. Then I find out it is Steve's idea and not the doctors. I am upset. This is the same kind of crap that I have been dealing with throughout our entire marriage. It is a microcosm of our life together playing out right before my eyes. I need to be the heavy weight, I make sure the rules are followed, that everything is done the way it should be done, and then he comes in and he gets to be the fun guy, the nice guy, the guy who the rules don't apply to. I am pretty sure the doctor is not going to let a brain-injured person with a fractured neck roam around without a neck brace. And, oh yeah, there's a pretty good chance that he could fall over and hit his head again. One more concussion and the lights could go out permanently. That's what we have been told. Any small concussion from this point on could be devastating. Yeah, it makes sense that it is easier without the restraints and the neck brace, but life is not always about it being easier. I can't believe that he would do this now, after all we have gone through. How am I going to keep Bryant calm and in bed all day by myself? He is stronger than me.

Steve has never been above breaking the rules. In fact, he excels at breaking the rules. I will venture to take it even one step further: I don't think that rules even cross the threshold of his brain. They simply do not apply to him.

He doesn't think that he is ignoring them, they simply do not exist for him. Rules are made for people who can't think for themselves, he has the ability to make up his own mind; therefore, they are unimportant. He does not see that if everyone did his own thing, life would be chaotic. The rules are there to keep people safe, to keep society running smoothly. They are for the betterment of the masses. When you only think of yourself and your needs, the masses are not taken into consideration. It is an arrogant attitude as far as I am concerned, an attitude of which I have always been aware, but one that frustrates me to no end. I want to strangle Steve with Bryant's arm restraints; but the news about Bryant eating and going to the bathroom, is simply amazing. That he wants to walk by himself is unbelievable. The physical therapy ladies could not spark his interest at all, and most of the sessions did not go well. Steve's behavior goes against everything in which I have ever believed. I have always followed the rules, and it irks me to no end to watch my husband breeze through life disregarding the rules and always being so successful at everything he attempts.

I spent the evening last night returning e-mails and phone calls for my decorating business. The online store continues to do well, and I have orders to process and credit cards to run. I have drapery orders in all different stages of order from fabric arriving, custom draperies being made, and installations. I called and cancelled the consultation appointments. I simply cannot do anymore than I am doing. The thought of discussing someone's interior decorating wishes seems superficial to me. I am unable to get my mind wrapped around it.

The doctors are telling me that recovery will be really slow, and not to expect much. After two years we will see what we have, there is no way to really know. I started discussions with a friend to build wheelchair ramps so we will be able to get Bryant's wheelchair in and out of the house. I don't see how I can have a handicapped child at home and still run a business.

When Bryant's teammates stopped by the rehab center the

other night, right before they left they asked if there was anything they could do to help. I was finally able to say "yes." I asked them to empty out Bryant's apartment and move his furniture to our house. They agreed. They are so excited to be able to help. I am not sure what I am going to do with it all, but it is clear to me that he is not moving back to his apartment. Steve, Paul, James and the young men from Bryant's soccer team are going to move his stuff this weekend and just dump everything in the large porch room still filled with the celebratory tables and chairs. Life's changes are coming at me fast.

I have absolutely no drive to talk to my customers. I do not seem to be able to talk to anyone, certainly not about the interiors of their homes. I have a customer giving me a hard time about a tiny scratch on a drapery rod. I had it repaired, but she is insisting on getting a huge discount. I am disgusted with humanity right now. I thought we were "friends," at least good acquaintances. Yeah, that's what I get for spending all of my time at work and not at home these past few years: an ungrateful, non-caring customer. I suddenly understand what is important and a scratch on a drapery rod, well it is not.

I have always been so sure, thought I had all of the answers; now, all I know is what I don't know, and that's a lot. My world and everything I believe is flip-flopping on me. The lack of sleep, the worry, the stress, the countless hours of keeping my eyes trained on my son's without conversation, the quiet solitude of the room and the constant care are all breaking me down. Many of my beliefs and walls are breaking down, too. I am beginning to see a whole new world out there. Maybe, just maybe, it defies the odds. Maybe it does mean breaking a few rules. All I know is that I am angry about the unfairness of it all.

The nurse's tell me that they called the doctor at three this morning, about the neck brace, but they have not heard back from him yet. They will not let Bryant get out of bed without the doctor's approval. They will not even put him in his wheelchair until they get approval. They switched his schedule around to allow for the occupational therapist to work with him first from his bed. They spend some time with him trying to get him to comb his hair. He is not cooperating. I slowly back out of the room to give them some space to work with him. I can hear him calling for me as I stand outside of his room. I can hear him arguing with them and refusing to brush his hair, or maybe he can't follow the steps. He continues to call out "Mom, Mom, Mom." The good news is that he knows who I am today. He isn't brushing his hair, but he knows who I am.

I am really nervous since he does not have his arm restraints. He is not allowed out of the bed without his neck brace, so I keep him as calm as possible. He finally drifts off to sleep. They stop by to get him for group therapy, but he cannot go. The doctor has not called back yet.

I think, *thanks, Steve. He is now missing his therapies because of your inability to keep his neck brace in place.*

I am still in my half bent over position at the ready to subdue him if necessary. He is really starting to get agitated. He is moving around in his bed and that is when I notice that his waist belt is missing as well. I feel the hair on the back of my neck start to rise. I can't believe that this is happening. No waist belt, no neck brace and no arm restraints. I know that help will not arrive in time if I need it, and I will be in for the fight of my life if he is so inclined.

He then smiles at me, raises his hand up to his chin and scratches his face. "My whiskers hurt," he says.

He has not had a shave since the accident. I bet they are bothering him.

"I will let your dad help you shave tonight," I tell him.

The nurse walks in with the bad news, "The doctor called and he will need to keep his neck brace on for a minimum of at least six weeks. We have to put his neck brace back on."

I look down at my son and swallow hard. I know that this is going to be ugly. Now that he has the ventilator out, the feeding tube out, the IV out, he wants the neck brace off. He has been persistent about all the others, and he thinks that if he fights us hard enough he will win. It has worked for him time and time again. Six weeks sounds like an eternity right now to me. Six weeks breaks down to forty-two days, or 1008 hours, or 60,480 minutes that I will need to keep this nasty neck brace on him. Now that he knows it comes off with a pull of a Velcro strip, I am screwed.

The nurse picks up the neck brace to put it back on him, he knocks her hands out of the way. She explains to him why he needs it on, thinking that she can reason with him. She asked him if his neck hurt, he replies "yes."

"Well that is why you need your neck brace on."

He is not buying it. You cannot reason with a brain-injured person. He is starting to get really angry and sits straight up in the bed, preparing for battle. He has a crazy look in his eyes, that of a trapped animal fighting for its life. You must admire the fight in him. He is not willing to take any more of this crap. She calls for reinforcements, and it takes three of us to hold him down. While they hold him I put the arm restraints back on him, securing them around his wrists. I then wrap them around the side railings of the bed. I am amazed at how fast and efficient I am becoming at this. I then get the waist belt and wrap it around his waist as well, once again holding him down in place. The nurse then takes the neck brace, placing the back of it on first behind his neck; she then places the front of it on his neck and secures the Velcro straps.

All the while my son is screaming at me.

"I fucking hate you," he yells. "Oh look, you've made friends with the nurses, isn't that nice. You just don't care at all about me." Really who can blame him? I have become the enemy. He is fighting for human rights, and I have become one of the oppressors.

I am pretty much hating on my husband right now. None of this would have happened if Steve had left the neck brace in place. My heart is pounding.

After the nurses leave and it is the two of us, the barrage keeps coming.

"You can waste your life sitting in that chair," he says. "You cannot make me do anything, I am not going to do anything that anyone wants me to do."

He then sobs out, "I just want to die, let me die."

Wow, what a tantrum, I think. *You have met your match, Bryant Hartsfield. Your safety is my primary concern. You can scream, kick, yell or throw as many tantrums as you want.*

I steel myself to his words. I tell myself *they do not matter, but deep down they hurt, I love him so much. I don't want him to know my weak spot. I don't want him to stop eating or drinking.* I don't dare speak those words out loud. This is a battle of wills, and I am as stubborn as he.

The tirade continues for about an hour until he finally falls asleep exhausted.

What a shit you are, I think as I watch him sleep, and yet as an after thought I can't help but be a little proud of him for his tenacity. He has tried to bend my will to his with every trick he has from anger to pleading. I want to give in to him, but I cannot.

This has all taken place before noon. I will let him sleep until lunch and then I intend to get his butt back in his chair. They refused to let him even get into his wheelchair today without the neck brace. Let the games begin. His fight or flight adrenaline may be in full swing, but so is mine. I grab a cookie out of the basket and eat my cookie lunch while watching him sleep.

After lunch, of which he ate very little, only a couple of bites, I had the orderly help me get him into his chair. He is still furious with me. With the waist belt on, I loosely tie his hands down, leaving him enough range of motion to reach the wheels but not his neck. He rolls his chair up and down the hallway calling me every name possible. He rolls himself back into his room. A dry eraser board is in his room. The speech therapist has written on the eraser board, "Your name is Bryant Hartsfield, you had an accident and fell at the Gorge, and you are at the rehab center."

Bryant has not paid any attention to this board up until this time. We do not know if he can read or not. He wheels himself over to the eraser board and picks up the marker. He writes on the board in a huge sweeping hand, FUCK YOU MOM. I stare at it in disbelief; all I can think of is that my baby can write. These are his first words. I should be shocked, but all I can do is smile. I find it hard not to think back to his baby book, if this is his rebirth, perhaps I should be keeping a "baby book" of all of his firsts. My child can write and if he can write he can read.

I am so happy, an exhausted happy, but happy. My mind goes back to the story of Helen Keller. I am reminded of the scene in the movie that includes the week-long fight between Helen and her teacher Annie Sullivan, when she first spelled out words into her teacher's hand. This is one of those moments. My heart soars.

I rush over to him and kneel down next to him. "Bryant" I say, "you can write."

He looks up at the board, with a strange look on his face. "You can write Bryant," I say again. I am filled with amazement.

He looks up at the board and then over at me. "Of course I can write," he says, "do you think I'm stupid?"

He continues looking at the board and slowly it is sinking into his head as well. He can write and he can read. He reads the board for the first time.

"I fell at the Gorge," he repeats the phrase.

I realize that he now has no memory of the fall. It is all so strange to me. He had perfect recall only a week ago, now there is no hint of it at all. I am not sure if it is because of the trauma and his mind has blocked it, or if he is simply not there yet in his mind. The rebooting of his brain is stuck somewhere around the age of twelve or fourteen. In his mind he has not visited the Gorge yet. Nowhere in any of the literature that I read, have I heard of this process. I am not a doctor, I am not a nurse, I am simply a mother who knows her child. I know every moment of his life. I have been there for almost all of it. I have watched this process and I know that, in his case, this is happening.

We are making real progress here, I hold his hand in mine, and we share a moment. Then in a flash, the moment is over and he is back to being angry with me—really at life but I am a pretty good target right now. I am living for the good moments. I know that he has made incredible progress, and if I simply looked at his chart, clinically speaking I would be amazed at how fast his abilities are coming back. Somehow living it moment by moment it does not seem fast at all. It somehow feels agonizingly slow, even though I know it isn't, it is all so hard. I keep telling myself that it is his ability to fight that has brought him back, but his ability to fight is wearing me down.

The nurses are frightened by his outbursts and steer clear of him as often as possible. Several of them sport large bruises from our fight to put his neck brace back on this morning. They comment to my husband that they do not know how I can take this much abuse and let it roll right off me. They are amazed.

I want to laugh at them. I have had an entire lifetime of my own mother and some family members throwing nasty comments my way. I learned from a very young age to let it roll off me, like raindrops on a highly waxed car. I try not to absorb them. I always understood that it was never about me. It was about them. It was about their hurt and their need to lash out at the world. What I don't understand at this point is that I take it and take it; letting it roll off, or so I think. Then bam! I explode like a powder keg, not unlike Bryant is right now. The person I explode with may or may not deserve the explosion that they get, but it happens. At this point in my life I believe that this is "normal behavior."

The days are hard. The doctors have a schedule that must be followed from eight to five, no visitors allowed, and therapists are coming and going throughout the day. The evenings are far more lax. Friends come and go throughout the evening. Bryant is highly social, always has been. He is on his best behavior most of the time when he has visitors, and at his worst when he is alone with us or when asked to perform an activity.

In the evening there is no schedule to keep, the nursing staff is laid back and do not pop in unless called upon for help. This allows Steve a totally different approach with Bryant and his rehabilitation. I know that we are both working to our strengths; it would be a total nightmare if Steve were here with Bryant in the daytime,

because he would never make it to his therapies. Rules and proto-
cols would be broken right and left. He would get out of control
and need to be sedated. As hard as it is for me to accept, Steve is far
more equipped to bring Bryant along with his own brand of "therapies" in the evening. The staff seems to turn a blind eye to both of
their behaviors at night. I am feeling really left out and jealous of
the activities that are going on in the dark of the night.

So far I have been successful at keeping him from being sedated
in the daytime. It is not easy, but I am generally able to keep him
somewhat calm. I am looking forward to the weekend. We will
enjoy two whole days without therapies and maybe I can share a
more relaxed time with my son. Maybe we can laugh and talk and
have visitors. That's what I am holding out for anyway. Right now
it is Thursday afternoon; Saturday is a whole lot of minutes away.

The day has been a total waste for therapy. They make no
progress at all with him. He refuses to cooperate. He is angry about
being tied down again, angry at the neck brace, angry at life, angry
with me.

This afternoon, an unexpected visitor stops by, while Bryant is
in bed. He has been very agitated and I am training my eyes on his
and doing my best to keep him calm. He is in a slump and is down
again. Gee, so am I.

When she leaves he comments, "Who was that lady? Was she
here to talk to Bryant the idiot?"

We have had a tough day. Steve does not receive a warm wel-
come when he comes in that evening. The nurses all work long
shifts and many of them are still here when Steve arrives. Allowing
Bryant to take his neck brace off has made it a tough day for all of
us, and they carry the bruises to prove it. Steve is given a stern lecture by the head nurse. Bryant's foul mood continues throughout
the night. Visitors are cancelled for the evening, and we try to keep
things calm and quiet.

I finally head home that evening. The Cicadas are out thick,
singing in the dusk, looking for a mate. I am whipped. Bryant is so
depressed and so am I. He is really beginning to understand how

much he has lost, and at times it is really hard for us to cope. I need to stay positive, but right now I want to be depressed. I allow myself to be down in the dumps. By the time I drive down the tree-lined street toward our house, I am trying to get in a better mood. I start to list all the accomplishments and the things I should be grateful for:

My child survived the fall.

My child was rescued.

My child is alive.

The paralysis is gone.

He has been reborn.

He can breathe.

He can drink.

He can eat.

He can use the bathroom, if allowed.

He can write.

He can read.

He knows who I am; he does not know his father yet.

With that thought, I let my mind go to the point that I am trying so desperately to avoid. I don't know who my son is anymore. Is the son I knew gone forever? I want to mourn for the loss of my child. I am beginning to think that the person that he was may have died in that canyon.

Everyone wants to tell me how wonderful it is and what a miracle his recovery is, and I know that they are right. If I had the time, I would like to mourn for the passing of what was and will probably never be again. It is all moving so fast. No one else ever mentions this. I want to embrace and love this new person, my new son, with the love of a mother. I also want to honor the passing of the son that came before this new one. I need to sit with this for a while.

I relax as I come down my long driveway in my car. I immediately go inside and take Ali outside with me to sit in the dusk while the Cicadas buzz around us. I sit down in a chair and stare up at the sky in amazement. There are so many Cicadas. The trees and the air are alive with them. I want a quiet moment to mourn, but Ali has discovered that he likes to eat the buzzing bugs. He has eaten quite a few and I now begin to worry if he can become sick from ingesting too many. So Ali and I, the two pit bulls, head back inside. My moment of mourning has passed. Life continues.

Chapter 31
The Crooked Tree

"Nature does not require that we be perfect, it requires only that we grow, and we can do this as well from a mistake as from success."
— Rollo May

The weather has really warmed up. It feels like spring has turned into summer. I take the dog out to go to the bathroom the next morning; as I do, I check on James. He is still asleep curled up on his bed. Ali and I are starting to bond; he follows me everywhere I go. It is as if we share a wire connecting the two of us. He even follows me to the bathroom and back and forth as I walk around the kitchen. Ali is never more than two feet away from me, but he is not allowed to sleep with me. He is still sleeping in James's room with him in his bed.

Bryant was still agitated last night, and Steve asked James not to come. It was the first night James and Elizabeth have been home with me. We finally broke down the tables and chairs last night. All remains of the celebration that never was are now history. The room is now empty waiting for the contents of Bryant's apartment to be deposited there.

If falling asleep is difficult for me, staying asleep is even more difficult. I wake up after an hour. James and Elizabeth have a few friends over and while I am upstairs sleeping someone has snuck into my room and left a fan. They have turned it on and turned off the TV. I wake up to the whirring noise. Confused, I assume that the soft humming noise is there to conceal the noise of the people downstairs. I angrily go down to confront the person who came in my room and put that fan in there.

James explains that he put the fan in my room. I accuse him of trying to be devious, trying to be sneaky and fool me. I am so angry, and when I look into his face I realize that I am being completely irrational. He explains to me that many people find fans soothing and helps them sleep. He thought it might help me. I apologize profusely but the damage is done. Why am I such a bitch sometimes? Even if someone tries to help me, I lash out at them. I do not trust anyone, always looking for ulterior motives.

I stagger back upstairs, curl up in my bed to listen to the soft sound of the fan. Somehow the soft whirring sound does help to comfort me; I also like the air movement. The knowledge that it is placed here out of love also comforts me. I fall back to sleep and sleep the deepest I have in weeks. I am completely unable to sleep without a fan now, one of the many changes in my life.

I walk around outside in the soft light of the early summer morning with Ali while he does his business. The Cicadas and most of the neighborhood are still asleep in the dawn of the day. Although I slept well last night, I stretch and rub my sore back. The lower curve is quite sore. The constant bending over in my half-ready-to-tackle position is really taking its toll. I never had an aching back. Humph, I am thinking, the key word here may be "never had," so many things are changing in my life, a bad back may be a permanent change as well.

While I walk around, I survey my newly-planted trees. One of the newest trees is a white dogwood that Paul and James had planted in the back yard for me. They dug the hole, and I surveyed to make sure it was straight. It had looked very straight from the back yard; however, when viewed from the kitchen window, it is slightly off kilter. They had already back filled it and had high fived each other for a job well done when we realized it was not level. The three of us had stood at the kitchen sink and discussed the prospect of taking the tree out and replanting it. I laughed out loud as they looked at me.

"Leave it as it is," I said, "It will be my crooked tree, planted by my crooked sons."

And that is how it stayed. I love my tree. I am sure I will always remember that moment. I survey my crooked tree, and I can see that the Cicadas hit it hard. It looks like someone has taken a pocketknife and slit the undersides of each and every branch. I don't know if this newly-planted tender tree will be able to survive this onslaught. Mother Nature has a plan and a purpose for every animal, plant and bug. I know that they say the purpose of the Cicadas is to aerate the ground and to prune the weakened branches on the trees, but to attack a perfectly young and healthy tree like this seems to have no real purpose to me. My mind goes to all of the other young, tender trees that we just planted, I do not have the time or the ability right now to go out and find netting to wrap around the trees. It will need to be survival of the fittest. That is the best I can do given the circumstances.

I go into the kitchen; it is still amazing to me. I have not been to the grocery store in weeks; yet, somehow the fridge is still full of food. The church ladies, coordinated by Brad's wife, have now taken over the food deliveries. It is mind-boggling. These women who never even met me are making such an impact in my life. Casseroles, bread, fresh fruit, salad... it is all right there in my kitchen every night. I pack my little cooler for the day, with fresh fruit and veggies, planning once again to get back on my diet. I scour the kitchen for food that Bryant might eat. Although he is eating, generally it is very little and never the hospital food that arrives on his tray. He continues to lose weight at an alarming rate. There has still been talk about inserting a feeding tube directly into his stomach if he does not pick up the food intake

I put Ali back in the bedroom with James. I stand over James and kiss him on the cheek. He rolls over, his blond curly hair against the pillow. He opens his sleepy eyes and tells me that he loves me. This is his last day of school. He will be a junior as of tomorrow. My baby is growing up. He too will be out the door before too much longer. He kisses me good-bye.

"James, I am so sorry that I yelled at you last night," I say. "The fan really worked, I slept good last night."

"Don't worry about it Mom," he says. "I will come by this afternoon, before you come home, to see you guys. I missed being with Bryant last night. The grass is getting tall. I will cut it before I come to the rehab center."

He has been working hard around the yard, going to school and spending evenings with his dad and Bryant. He does not seem to want to slow down. I don't know what is going on with him emotionally. I wander around James' room, folding, picking up, trying to be useful to him, but I cannot turn off my mind.

Paul will be graduating next weekend. He walks next Saturday. We will need to find someone to sit with Bryant so that the family can attend. I make a mental note to ask someone. I feel bad that he will not have a celebration. There is not enough of me to go around. I feel like I am failing on all fronts. I have not seen him since the last time at the rehab center. He has stopped by to visit with Bryant and his father later in the evening. Everyone is too busy and too sad to really celebrate.

I do not want to be the hard ass all of the time. I know I need to be, but I do not want to be. I want to be the fun guy. I want to be the one everyone likes; I think I want Steve's life.

I keep telling myself that Bryant is upset, unsure, unhappy, and afraid, and it is always the one you trust the most, the one you know will love you no matter what, at which you lash out. I am the safest one he has to whom to be nasty. I feel my throat tightening as I want to cry out. It is so hard, so very, very hard. I know we have made great strides. No, *he* has made great strides. He is breaking records with his recovery, or so it seems to me, which should make it all better. In a way it does, but it is still agonizingly painful to watch. The greatest comfort is that he knows who I am. I feel so alone. I walk out of the room and close James' door; his alarm will be going off before long.

I go across the hall to check on Elizabeth. Her long dark hair spills out over her pillow. I choke back a sob as I realize that she will not be in her room much longer. I am missing the last weeks of her life here at home. She met a boy at his graduation party last week. They have been seeing each other every day. I have not even met him. I am going to need to trust her judgment. She is still sleeping; she has always been the best sleeper of the family. Even as a small child, she took long naps and went to bed at night like a champ. I am sorry that I did not spend more time with her last night. I am feeling the sadness of her leaving the nest. I was exhausted last night, after yesterday's fight. Not only is she my only daughter, but she has worked side-by-side with me at the store for the past three years. She is quick and smart; she has completely set up our on-line store. She also has a great eye and can put fabrics, color and patterns together, which is a gift that you either have or don't. She is keeping things going for me at work while I am with Bryant. I kiss her on the cheek as well. She does not wake up. She makes a small noise and snuggles deeper into her pillow.

I back out of her room and head down the steps and out to the car, picking up my cooler as I go. I am not alone. I have so much love in my life. I am not focusing on it, I am only focusing on the alone part. I don't want my children to leave me. I want them to stay. I don't want them to leave; and yet they must.

I feel like Scarlett O'Hara, I will worry about that tomorrow. I prepare myself for another day of tough love. I send a prayer up to my Father, asking for patience. I remember when they were all babies. Each day started with a prayer for patience. Funny, everything is different; yet, the same. I am still praying for patience. My favorite saying goes like this: Patience is not something that you are born with; it is something that you learn. Clearly I needed a lot of practice because I had more than my share of lessons in that department. I still do not have it right.

I look back at our yellow farmhouse with the green roof. Steve did not want to buy this house, and financially it has been a bust. He was here when the inspector advised him not to buy this house. I was still living in St. Louis with the kids. The inspector took Steve aside and said "young man there are thousands of houses out there on the market, don't buy this house." He bought it for me anyway, because I loved it, and because I said I would not move to the new city without this house. When we moved here it needed so much work, it had been on my bucket list to restore an old house, and I love painting and repair work. I love being a part of the history of this old house; it has been a labor of love.

I have started on the yard, and I dream big plans for the gardens. I want to create fabulous, old-fashioned gardens in the yard to go with the house. The house is above the pond on a slight incline and is surrounded by giant old trees. The trees are falling down at an alarming rate, but we are replacing them as they come down.

The longer the ground has been undisturbed the larger the Cicada population. In a newer subdivision the Cicada larvae would have been scooped out of the ground by the developer's bulldozers. Our yard and the surrounding area is a beacon for the Cicadas, a hot bed of undisturbed ground. It looks as if someone has come along and dug holes in every square inch of our yard. The Cicadas also like mature trees from which to drop their eggs. I am really starting to hate these bugs. They are making a hard time even harder. Ugh.

As I get into my car to head to the rehab center, my fight song comes back on the radio. I laugh to myself as I roll down my window and sing. What are the chances of this? I love that I can get prepared for my day this way. It gets me into the right frame of mind. Put me in coach, I'm ready to play. Once again I sing at the top of my lungs, "I won't put my hands up and surrender. There will be no white flag above my door. I'm in love," (the unconditional love of a mother), "and always will be." Yeah, that's right.

When I get there all pumped up and ready to go, Steve looks beat. He has had a tough week, staying up most of the night with Bryant and working in the daytime. Apparently James showed up at Bryant's room last night. He must have felt like he needed a friend after I yelled at him over the fan. They had a good night. James was telling stories and talked Bryant to sleep.

Steve and Bryant both slept until I arrived at six forty-five. They had gone for another walk last evening, but it was not as much fun as the other day. While Steve had him out in the hallway, he took him to the men's room and let him use the toilet. The problem is, he won't let anyone go in the bathroom with him; he fights you. He wants his privacy and shuts the door. Hospital rules do not let him go in alone because he is not walking independently or with a walker, but it seems wrong to all of us to ask him go to the bathroom on himself and not let him use the bathroom. We are all getting frustrated with the rules.

There has to be a solution to this problem. His safety has to be our first concern, or does it? We also need to encourage his independence and his desire to be a dignified person. The bathroom issue at least takes his mind off his neck brace for a while. It brings some minutes of a reprieve. The neck brace is on this morning, but I am not sure if Steve left it on all night or not.

Bryant's old soccer team has been wonderful. They are visiting off and on at night. They called Steve last night and told him that they have a truck and a trailer and they will be at Bryant's apartment to empty it out this weekend. Wonderful! They are unbelievable. I am so impressed with them. They are able to band together and to help when adults, at least the ones in my family, are frozen. *Kudos to today's young men,* I think.

Bryant ate about ten bites of watermelon for me this morning. Later on, when Steve brought in Cheese Coneys and fries for lunch, he chowed down. He discovered catsup for the first time, and he enjoyed dipping each fry in the catsup. Steve and I sat with him and watched him eat. It brought such joy to our hearts. It has been such a long road, and to watch him dip those fries and eat them... well, it was like Christmas and our birthdays all wrapped up into one. So far we have had a great morning.

Chapter 32
The Escape Artist

"Never give up, because it aint over 'till it's over."
– Yogi Berra

Bryant is out in the hallway in his wheelchair. I smile at my son. He is not smiling back at me. He is dressed for the day in his high top shoes, pull-on elastic shorts that are puffing out with an adult diaper, and Velcro shirt. He looks so child-like in his PT outfit. His hair is dirty again and Steve has not been able to shave his beard. He is looking really rough. The inability to keep him tidied up is really starting to bug me. His appearance is nothing at all like my well groomed handsome son. He continues to lose weight despite his Cheese Coney and McDonald's diet, not enough calories going in I guess. His incredibly strong legs are now sticks with knobby knees. He is skin stretched over bone. His left foot is pigeon toed and sits at an awkward angle on the foot rest of his wheelchair.

"Hey Bryant, how about we go for a walk?"

I give him a push to get us started down the long hallway. This is our usual route by his room.

When we get to his room which is a little less than half way down the hall, he says, "Why don't you wait here Mom, I want to go down the hall by myself."

I am wary but elated. This is such a turnaround.

"Sure Bryant, I will wait right here."

"Why don't you wait in my room for me?" he says.

We are having a "normal moment." I look around and see

nothing for him to get into. He is strapped down in his wheelchair and I can peek around the door, so I agree.

I walk into the room to sit down. He looks at me, he appears to be lucid and focused at the moment. He backs his chair up and turns it around to continue his walk. I walk over to the door after a couple of minutes and peek around the edge, as the alarm goes off.

I see Bryant at the stairwell doorway trying to get the door open. The alarm is piercingly loud. I race down the hallway and get to his wheelchair before anyone else. I get into a tug of war with him. He will not release the door and I am trying to pull him backwards, not wanting him to fall down the stairs. I am sure it was only minutes but it felt like an eternity before my friend the male nurse shows up and wrenches him loose. I am so embarrassed. I can't believe I let him do this. He could have fallen down the stairs head over wheels. I am so stupid. The nurse wheels him back to his room.

Bryant is so mad at me. He sees me as part of the problem. He would have been free if it were not for me. He starts cussing me out again. Using the only thing he has, his mouth, to let me know how miserable he is. He is really starting to reason things out, I think. He knew that was an exit and he had planned his escape.

After a while the verbal barrage is getting really ugly. I decide to take him outside to the courtyard. We go out there to sit. The sunshine, fresh air and the occasional Cicadas buzzing around seem to get his attention and keep him preoccupied for a while. I am buying minutes. He asked about the bugs, and really seems interested. Everything at times seems to be new and wonderful, like the fries and catsup.

"Mom can you help me to get over to the grass?"

This does not seem like a strange request. This is the first time he has been outside in the daylight hours since the accident. I don't blame him; I would want to be closer to nature too.

"Sure, why not?"

I help him get his chair off the patio and onto the grass, and he seems to be happy. He has a huge grin on his face. We are having a good moment. I take a deep relaxing breath. We are both happy to be outside. He gives his chair a big push and is at the gate; freedom lies just beyond it. Grabbing his chair, I fight to pull it back towards the patio. He is angry at my interference. He slides out from under his waist belt. I reach down over the handles of the chair and grab his underarms. We struggle for quite some time and I realize that I do not have the strength to pull him back up. He has lost too much weight and can slide under the bindings. Suddenly his neck brace gets caught on the waist strap. He is now dangling from his chair being held up by his broken neck while the ugly red-eyed bugs buzz all around us. Still he fights me and will not let me pull him up. I must let go of him, run for the door, and scream for help. It seems as if I am in slow motion, faces slowly turning to look in my direction, everything becoming strangely quiet. He is slowly strangling himself on the strap. A man turns and rushes forward to help me, and suddenly we are back in real time. I look up and Steve is there as well. They are able to hoist him into his chair. Apparently he had not been restrained properly. I will not make that mistake again. He is known as Houdini Jr. after today.

Apparently his fight or flight instinct is still engaged. He is doing both. What will power to live, to fight, his never give up attitude is amazing. I am humbled at the sheer strength of his desire to be normal. He is not willing to accept anything less than a complete recovery. He is not going to accept limited bathroom use, the limits of a wheelchair, the limits of a neck brace, and the limits of restrictions of movement. I appreciate his will and drive. It has been a trademark of his life, to accomplish things that he was told he could not accomplish. I admire him for it. His father and I have quite a will and drive as well, only we have a job to do, to keep him safe until he can fully recover.

I understand him, and I want all of these things for him as well but first he has to master one step at a time. He needs to rest, recover, and rehabilitate. These things take time. He wants it all now before he is ready. We are having a serious clash of wills. I am on the side of the rules and the doctors, he and his dad are on the side of rebellion.

He is really furious with me for the rest of the day. He acts like a child who has missed a nap and is having a tantrum. We get him back into his bed and tie him down. His nurse wants to sedate him, but I talk her out of it. I finally calm him down, and he falls into a deep, deep sleep. Steve comes in to relieve me, and I am ready to go. We are all amazed at his ability to plan and execute his escapes. He has really come a long way in a short time. Now, if we can only get him to like us.

I head home, allowing only a few stray tears to escape down my cheeks. My stomach is hurting. When I head into the bathroom I am amazed. I had gone through menopause early. I'd had a blood test six months before that had proven that I was completely post-menopausal. I had not had a period in a long time, but there in the bathroom was a surprise for me. My body is reacting to the trauma and the stress. Mother Nature's way of feeling for me over the loss of a child? Was she giving me the chance to create a new life? I am amazed. If I grow another head tomorrow, I will not be shocked. Nothing is as it was. I head into Elizabeth's room to look for supplies.

Steve's Journal:

Catie just left; she looks so defeated. I am worried about her. The nurses are all telling me that Bryant is really hard on her. They praise her and can not believe the patience that she is showing. They all think she is an angel. I do not think she knows how amazing she is; we are all in awe of her ability to hang in there.

Elizabeth and several of Bryant's friends stopped by tonight and brought a pizza. We all went out to the patio and ate the pizza. It was really a good time. He is so good with his therapists and with other people. It is like he can turn the charm on and be nice to others. The doctors had told us that whatever skills he possessed before the accident would probably be his strong suit and his ability to charm teachers and such was always his strength. They told us that he will never be able to learn anything new. That what he had before the accident is all the he will ever have. I cannot get my mind around that one. Will he be a twenty-one year old for the rest of his life?

James came in tonight as usual, and this time he brought a portable DVD player and a comedy show. We watched it and laughed; it was really funny. When Bryant is in his bed resting, I let him take his neck brace off. As long as he is not moving around I don't see any reason not to let him take it off. I also take him into the bathroom and let him shut the door. I think the rules are stupid and there is no one around to stop me. He still does not know who I am.

I am really excited; they brought a fold out chair for me, and I get to lie down tonight. I have been sleeping on and off sitting up in a chair, or lying on the floor when my back hurts. I slept some but every time he moved I woke up. He woke up at two-fifteen this morning. He is trying to use the phone to call his (girl) friend. They were best friends, never girlfriend, boyfriend but good friends starting when he was in seventh grade. I am guessing that is where he is developmentally right now. We are guessing at that by who was important in his life at the time. It was so funny. He talked about her brother and parents; they are pilots, so he started talking about airplanes. He even thought we were in an airplane and I was piloting the aircraft. He can be so lucid at times, and so out there only seconds later. We then went back to sleep.

When he woke up he ate a large bunch of grapes, which he thought were great and then two more pieces of pizza. It is so much fun for me to watch him eat. I get a great sense of joy watching him rediscover food. The nurse came in to change him and put clean clothes on him. The nurse is upset with me and put the neck brace back on him. We are up and ready for another day. Saturday the first day of the big move with Bryant's apartment. The work never lets up. I stretch, I am sore and tired, and another long day is in front of me.

Bryant is agitated once again. He is so mad about the neck brace that I get out my cell phone and let him make a few phone calls. He tries to call his friend but she does not answer. That makes him even madder. It is almost time for Catie to get here so I call her. When Catie answers: I hand the phone to Bryant.

Chapter 33
Circling the Wagons

"If you obey all the rules, you miss all the fun."
– Katharine Hepburn

Two weeks since the accident. How could so much happen in two weeks? I check the calendar, recounting the days, how is that possible. We are starting week three. I am down today, but really I should be rejoicing. If I think back to where we were two weeks ago, this is nothing short of a miracle. We have so much for which to be grateful. Bryant is doing great. He is even able to form a plan of escape and follow through on it, our first real sign of mental-thought process. It is strange, we get glimpses of progress and then, poof it is gone and, we are back to an angry disoriented person. Bryant is amazing. Helping him come through this is the hardest thing I have ever been asked to do.

I am surprised and especially grateful that Steve is here. I always felt before that he was a disconnected workaholic, but he is now putting that focus on our family. I am seeing that wonderfully focused side of him that he reserves for work, a part of him that has been missing in our family life. I have a new respect for him. Although he was always around for games, practices, and dinner when he was in town, somehow he never seemed connected to us the way he is now. He always backed off the family stuff and let that be my domain, not his.

I have not told him how I feel. Part of me is still mad and is not ready to forgive him for the distance he built between us over the previous years. My emotions are stuck in the middle, probably because we have not had any real time together.

I am enjoying reading his journal. It gives me a peek into his thoughts and emotions. I know that the double shift is hard on him; but he is enjoying the support he gets at work from his contemporaries. I am really jealous.

My days are filled with getting Bryant to therapies and having him calm and ready to learn. I don't know at this point if I am really making a difference or not. I only know that the other patients are not up and moving around like Bryant is. They are all quiet and reserved. Is the difference that I won't let him be sedated, or is it his undying will to be normal and to be free of all restrictions? I don't know anymore. Today is Saturday. Maybe I can have friends and family visit, maybe he will be nice and I can have pizza and fun. I am so ready for some fun.

The name calling and the abuse take me back to my childhood and the times my mother would come home after a night on the town. She was a woman who had known great disappointments in her lifetime. I was the light sleeper and often woke up to open the door. She would then ramble on with slurred speech about how horrible I was, how I thought I was so special and so smart. She did not like my attitude. I know now that these were her demons not mine. These were her own insecurities not mine. Those words hurt back then, and they hurt now. It is an old wound that has not completely healed and I am finding it harder and harder to let the insults roll off me. I know she loved me, but I don't know if she liked me, or maybe she did not like herself.

When Bryant yells at me, he does not know it pushes on this old wound. I need to separate the two (Mom and Bryant), but it is hard at times. I would not let my mother ever know she hurt me, and I will not let Bryant know he is hurting me now. I know he is in pain, he is lashing out at the world; and it is easiest to take it out on me. He knows my love is constant, and I will not turn away from him. What my mind knows, my heart does not seem to understand. It is like the universe is giving me a second chance to deal with this crap, and I do not like it very much at all. Maybe, my own mother was lashing out at the world as well, and she knew my love was constant. Something to think about....I did not like it from my mother, and I do not like it coming from my son. I don't think I could make it through the nights too, and I am really grateful Steve is relieving me. He is my knight in shining armor.

I have not been expecting much from the other kids, yet. I know when Steve leaves to work in Florida, in only a week, I will need to rely heavily on them. It is going to be a really hard two weeks without him. I feel ill just thinking about it. I don't know how I am going to cope. I breathe in and out slowly and send a prayer up to my heavenly Father. I tell myself He has a plan. I need to trust in Him. If worse comes to worse, He will be at the rehab center with me, and I will need to give it up to Him.

It has really been a hard week. I think to myself: Where did that clear-headed young man in the ICU go? I should have insisted we not move him. If I had only known what would happen. I am blaming the nonstop bumping and pounding of the rough ride for the setback to his fragile brain. Why didn't I do something? I somehow feel responsible, I'm sure I'm not, but what if I am? The guilt, stress and fatigue are starting to wear me down. I am so wrapped up in my own pity, I cannot see the love that is here: people praying, people moving furniture, and people sending meals. My children and their friends are here. My nieces and nephews have come through.

My mother did come. She was not able to give me what I needed, but she had made the long drive here. It was all she was able to give. She isn't able to give me compassion, I don't know why, but she cannot. I spent a lifetime sending out love, time, and compassion to family members, and they are never able to reciprocate. I do not know why, I only know it is not forthcoming.

My in-laws have given me the space I need. I am grateful for that. I am sure Steve is communicating with them. They plan to come back in a few weeks.

I am at the beginning of the rest of my life. I am being given a rare chance to see how wrong I have been living my life. I can pick my circle of influence. Perhaps I keep picking the wrong people. I decide to make changes in my life. I am never going to be this alone again. I am going to have a minister, friends, and people that I can be there for, and who will be there for me. I do not know how I am going to make these changes, but I am determined they are going to happen. I am going to share emotional intimacy, the kind Steve and I had before. I want my thoughts known, my sentences finished. My fears, my happy thoughts, I want to share all of these things with a man. I am hoping it will be with Steve; but regardless I am going to have it in my life. Like I said, I don't know how, but I am never going to be this alone in my life again.

I make a solemn vow to myself that morning. It will be a while before I make a break for the light; before I can find my way, my voice, but the seed is planted that day. When things were bad when I was a child, a voice in the back of my mind always told me *never forget how this feels. Move forward and make it better. This same voice encourages me now to never forget how this feels. Move forward once again, to break the cycle, and become the difference.*

I am taking a few minutes to myself, sipping a warm cup of tea before I head out the door. The phone rings. I answer it; it is Steve.

"Someone wants to talk to you," he says.

I hear a slow, child-like voice come over the phone line, "Mom, this is Bryant."

I can't believe my ears. My eyes fill up with tears, my son is calling me.

"Mom, when are you coming to see me," he asks.

I tell him, "I am on my way right now, I will be there soon." I am finding it hard to keep the tears out of my voice.

"Good," he says. "I want to come home."

Steve is now on the phone. I tell him I will be right there, and thank him for the phone call.

That phone call gives me wings to fly on. I sing my heart out once again on the way there, with my windows down all the way, the wind blowing back my hair.

When I get there Steve is in a hurry to take off. They are starting to empty out Bryant's three-room apartment this morning. They are going to box up everything they can, but Steve is planning to take advantage of the soccer team's help by letting them move the heavy furniture down the stairs. They are planning to set all of the stuff inside the long narrow porch room of our home. I say good-bye to him.

I am excited it is Saturday—no therapies, no up and at it. We can have a lazy day, maybe a fun day. Elizabeth is coming up this morning to visit. Maybe I can take time for a walk or something. I am looking forward to the break.

The morning is tough. He wants his neck brace off, and I am not going to take it off. I don't know that Steve is taking it off for him at night. The sweet young man who called me this morning is now gone. We make it through the morning. Elizabeth comes in to sit with him. It was really funny when she walked in he said, "O.K., now I'm really confused. That's Elizabeth, but an older Elizabeth."

I realize he does not always recognize us because we do not look like we did when he was a child. I have gained and lost a lot of weight over the years, altering my looks. I think this is why he likes to look into my eyes. He recognizes them. I have no idea why he doesn't recognize his father.

I go for a walk around the grounds. I am so excited. I take my phone with me, just in case. I am grossed out by the Cicadas; they are everywhere, so much thicker in the daytime than I could imagine. By the time I leave in the evening they are usually calming down. Their sound in the daytime is almost deafening.

I check out the rehab center more thoroughly. I am amazed; they have an indoor pool for therapy, a nursing home attached to the facility, and a huge courtyard located in the center of the building with access for the entire center. It is quite lovely with lots of flowers, a basketball court, pergolas, tables and chairs. I realize at the rate Bryant is improving, hopefully I can take him out here for a walk. Of course I will check to make sure his restraints are tight before I ever do that again.

About this time I get a phone call. Bryant is agitated, could I come back, like now? I head straight back. Elizabeth is in a panic and does not know what to do with him. I quickly ascertain the problem and realize he needs to use the bathroom again. This is ridiculous.

He has to have a bowel movement and is now mentally too advanced to go in his bed. He will not sit on a bedpan and the staff refuses to let him go into the bathroom. We argue for an hour and a half, Bryant insisting he be allowed to go in there by himself. I inform him it is not possible. I am so frustrated with the rules. They finally bring in a portable toilet. We try to get him to sit on it, but he refuses. He wants to do his business in the bathroom with the door shut. I try to redirect him, no such luck; it is a rough afternoon.

Fortunately, Steve and Paul show up. While we distract the nursing staff out in the hallway, Paul takes him to the bathroom. We are all starting to cop an attitude. It just doesn't need to be this difficult. We are not feeling like we are on the same team anymore with the staff. We make a shift, the family against the nursing staff, well against the stupid rules anyway. Let me correct that, I am converted, I am now in line with Steve's and Bryant's thinking. The rules are now getting in the way of progress.

Steve and I take a walk together while Paul and Elizabeth stay with Bryant. It is good to spend some time with Steve. He is a little upset, or confused. He spoke with his mother today on the phone. He said it was not easy. She does not listen when you talk to her. She does not deal well with stress or reality. When he tried to tell her how tough it is, her only response was "I understand it's tough, and we're praying."

"I don't know what I wanted, but the positive, everything-is-going-to-be-fine attitude and her not wanting to hear the dirty details is really starting to annoy me. I appreciate positivism, but I simply want her to listen. We don't know if everything is going to be all right," Steve told me.

Actually, all we know is that nothing will ever be the same.

I know he really doesn't want a response from me, he is thinking out loud to himself. I find it interesting, because I have been thinking the same thing for a lot of years not only about his mother but about him as well. I am quite pleased he is experiencing this for the first time himself. I could not say how I felt for a while any clearer. I am suddenly feeling closer to him than I have in years.

Our small family is starting to circle the wagons around Bryant. I spend the rest of the evening sitting and talking with our family in Bryant's room. It is good. Paul is really excited about his upcoming graduation. This will be one of the few times I have left with him. I head home well after dark. I am reluctant to leave, but morning will be here before I know it.

I arrive home to let the dog out, clean out the pool, and return work e-mails. To my surprise, there is an apartment full of furniture in an unorganized pile right in the middle of the porch room. It looks like it was dumped right out of a truck into the front room of the house. Boxes are spilled out. Cushions are everywhere, in no exact order. A mattress and box springs are shoved on top of the couch and love seat. I don't know what I expected, but it was not this. My house now looks exactly like my mind, totally disheveled and disorganized, everything upside down and knocked over, spilling out in places where it should not be; a big step back for a huge leap forward, I tell myself.

Steve's Journal:

I had a breakthrough with Bryant last night. I took a long walk outside with him. I pushed him in his wheelchair. Although it is warm outside he likes to wear a blanket bundled up around him. He has had an especially lucid moment. We were walking along with me pushing him in his wheelchair taking in the night when he said, "How's your business?"

We talked about all the people at my business, the business he has always planned to join after graduation. He remembered interning, he even asked about his job.

We walked out past the hospital and turned around to walk

back. He really liked getting out of the unit. He sees the big red brick building from a distance and reads the words "Rehab Center." We start talking about the kind of patients they see. He is so with it right now. I take it one step further.

"Bryant do you know what kind of accident you had?" I asked.

"Nooo," he answers, kind of slowly like he is thinking about it.

"Do you want to know?" I ask him. I don't know if I am going where I should be going or not.

"Yes, I want to know," he answers.

I proceed to tell him the entire story of falling at the Gorge. He listens to me and then says "Oh my God...that's high."

I point to the five-story building and say it was three times higher than this building.

I think he realizes for the very first time he should not be alive. He also starts feeling really stupid. He starts putting himself down based on how he thinks others will view him. He keeps saying, "I'm stupid, I'm ignorant."

We talked about God and our belief that God has a special plan for him. After a while, he thinks it through and he agrees.

We continue to walk for a while and then he says "I am a little shaky and woozy even thinking about falling that far. I need to use the bathroom."

I am a little concerned that I upset him. He has had a physical reaction to this information. I don't want a fight with the hospital staff, and I don't like their way of thinking anyway. I take him upstairs to the bathroom near the cafeteria. He is not walking on his own. I help him up, supporting his right side with my body weight. I let him go in and use the toilet while I stand outside in the hall.

I am so excited about the breakthrough that (when we get back to the room) I immediately call Catie. I hand the phone to Bryant and he seems to have forgotten the entire "accident" discussion. When Catie asked him if he knew where he was he said, "a hotel." I am really befuddled as to how his memories can go back and forth and in minutes, it is really discouraging.

I brought Bryant's cell phone up to him and he called a few people last night. Funny, how he knows how to use a phone with no problem at all. He gets so upset, and then out of nowhere he is happy. James came in with ham sandwiches Catie made, and we pigged out. It comes and goes, from moment to moment.

He did not sleep well and tried making phone calls most of the night. I take him outside for another walk, thinking it will cheer him up. It seems to tire him out. He is now really agitated, just in time for Mom.

Chapter **34**
Moving Forward

*"Though no one can go back and make
a brand new start, anyone can start
now and make a brand new ending."*
– Carl Bard

Bryant is exhausted from not sleeping the night before, he does not need therapy today. I am able to let him nap off and on. He has visitors throughout the day and, as a result, I have mini-breaks.

We have entered a new phase; violent mood swings, along with his memory coming and going from moment to moment. If I look at the positive side, his memory is now lasting for a few moments. He will ask us a question and then not even a minute later will ask us the same question. We need to be patient with him. I remind myself patience is not something you are born with; it is something you learn.

It is amazing how many times he can ask the same question over and over and over again within an hour. The good side of this is that we can redirect him easily. I find I am using the distraction/redirection technique as often as possible to get him off a subject. His favorite subjects are: when can I go home, and where is my car? Right now the short-term memory is working for us, but he is changing rapidly, morphing right in front of our eyes on a daily basis.

I am trying to distract his anger and redirect it moment by moment. I am using every technique I learned over the past two decades. I am pulling out all of the stops, using every coping skill I learned to teach my children.

I am now grateful for the years of researching and discovering new ways to educate my own children, ways to teach what worked for them, to get through to their specific strengths and abilities that were not the "norm." I never thought I would consider those countless hours a blessing. Now I see them for what they were. Had we not gone through that experience we would not be up to the task now before us. I am using "we" because Bryant and I are in this together. I feel I am uniquely qualified, self-taught; I clocked many hours in the field of motherhood and educating. Bryant has clocked many hours in learning new concepts, techniques and coping skills. I hold onto this thought, it keeps me from feeling overwhelmed.

He is understandably angry, angry from the effects of the brain injury, angry that he has to start all over again, angry at himself, angry at the world. Who can blame him? This has been an uphill battle for him from the beginning. In many ways he is still in the bottom of the Gorge fighting to get back up to the top of his mountain.

Perhaps it is his anger that fuels him to overcome. I only know it feels really personal when he directs the anger at me. Understanding this and not taking it personally is easier said than done. Human nature has its limits, and mine are being tested as well as his.

I am happy that Steve took Bryant outside for a walk in his wheelchair to see the stars. As I have said before, he is his mother's child, and he needs to feel the wind in his face as much as I do. Being kept inside all of this time in the air conditioning feels like imprisonment to him as well as to me.

I have constant supervision over my every move here in the daytime; and even if I did not, I feel overwhelmed by the size and strength of my son, I would be uncomfortable taking him that far away, outside, away from help should I lose control of him. Steve, being larger than me, must not feel this way, or if he does, he does not show it. I do not share the amount of fear that the nurses do, but I must admit that I do have some fear. I fear that he could get away from me and hurt himself, and I fear that I will not be able to contain him.

I look over at my son, and he is a mess. His hair is filthy, greasy and stuck to his head. His gums are angry and red; he needs better hygiene. I realize now he is going to live. I am not sure when the real fear of his imminent death left. It slowly stopped being a concern. We now need to focus on his person. If his teeth are not brushed, he is going to develop serious dental problems. I am his mother; yet, I am not going anywhere near his mouth. He could bite my fingers off. His acne has come back with a flourish. The oil seems to be pouring out of his pores. It appears that as he is mentally entering his teenage years, his body is also responding as if he is going back into puberty. Along with his oily skin, the natural rebellious nature of a teenager is also making itself known.

We struggled with the teenage years the first time around, now we get to go through it again. Yuck, and it looks like I'm going to get to go through menopause one more time as well. This really has to be a sick joke. Menopause and adolescence should never go together once in a lifetime, certainly never twice. I make a mental note to speak with his doctor about his personal cleanliness first thing on Monday.

Chapter
Houdini Returns 35

"Character consists of what you do on the third and fourth tries."
– James Michener

This day is not starting off well. As I walk into the room this morning, Bryant takes one look at me, and starts yelling, calling me "Miss Piggy." Wow, this is going to be a real pleasant day.

I know this is his embarrassment, his own image problem, but I am tired, run down, and I simply want a little respect and love. "Miss Piggy" hits right to the heart of my insecurities about my weight. I arrive at six-thirty, and Steve is just as crabby. The pair of them in the morning are not usually much fun, but this is really the pits today.

Steve hid Bryant's cell phone last night. Bryant then used the hospital phone next to his bed to call people all night, or to try and call them. He has not yet figured out you need to dial nine first. The problem with him calling people is his short-term memory. When he gets it into his head to call someone, he is not aware he just called them. That can be annoying all night long. His childhood friend Jack has been awesome. No matter how many times an hour Bryant calls him, Jack always acts as if it is the first time he has spoken to him in months. I love that about him. It's so heartwarming to have people help out like that.

I don't know what has happened, but Bryant is delusional this morning. He seems to be getting worse instead of better. He has no idea where he is or who I am. He is in his bed, hiding under the covers, pulling them up around his face. He is screaming about a boat in Canada. He went fishing in Canada with his uncle when he was thirteen or fourteen. He believes he is in the boat, and it is sinking. I try to reason with him, but there is nothing I can do. Therapy will be useless today. Sometimes I wonder why we are even here.

The roller coaster continues. He sleeps for thirty minutes, wakes up in a good mood and asks for food. He eats all of his food, everything on his plate, and then lets the orderly take him to the shower. He looks so much better. The shower must feel really good to him. I stand outside of the shower door, and he is making all kinds of happy sounds.

We are now off to physical therapy. It should be a great experience, but he cusses me out the entire time we are in therapy. I usually do not do therapies with him, but they invite me in today. He stands up all by himself, and he does ball bounces. He can catch great, but he refuses to do an overhead toss. We walk back to his room with the PT person and me helping him. His left foot really toes in a great deal and his left side is weak, but he is walking. Steve has taught Bryant to walk at night. He advanced rapidly by walking up and down the hallways throughout the nights. I am short and cannot get a shoulder under his arm, forcing him to lean way over with me. The therapists do not want me walking him at this angle.

Now we are back in Bryant's room; I am hoping he will go back to sleep and wake up in a better mood. With the help of the therapist, I get him into bed. We have not been successful in turning his days and nights around. He reads his name on the dry marker board. He is angry his name is there and wants to know who put it there.

He is almost asleep when they come in to give him his daily seizure and blood clot inhibiting shot in the stomach. He has been fortunate so far, but they warn us that seizures could start at any time. The shot in the stomach really angers him. He babbles on about snakes biting him, which reminds me of the many rattlesnakes in the Gorge. I wonder if he saw snakes throughout his time alone down there? The paranoia comes and goes.

I just get him quieted down, and then the speech therapist comes in. Bryant is smiling and pleasant so I leave the room for them to work. They take off his restraints and sit him up to eat. He is so pleasant with them; I am jealous.

I walk back into the room as they finish up. He smiles at me and takes off his neck brace and throws it across the room. Ooops... that does it, now we need to restrain him once again. He is calling me every name imaginable. He is so violent we call for help. After we get him restrained, the staff member picks up the neck brace and roughly puts it back on. The staff is having as hard of a time as I am dealing with the foul language and rough treatment we are all receiving. Patience is wearing thin for all of us. I do not know what I would do without them. They deal with patients like this day in and day out, over and over again. They must have great patience.

A therapist comes in to speak with me. We go out in the hallway to talk. He tells me he is speaking for the team. He suggests I not come in from now on until noon.

"It is common for patients to act out with family members. The safer they feel with them, the more they act out with them," he tells me.

I look at him dumbfounded. I do not know what to say. I know Bryant's behavior is a form of abuse and to let it continue is wrong, but isn't this just a stage? I am afraid he will be sedated if I leave him alone with them. On the other hand, no one but a parent would allow this abusive behavior to continue. Perhaps it should not be allowed and I do not know how much more I can take. However, I am not comfortable leaving him alone with them. I no longer know what is right or wrong.

We strike a deal. I agree to wait out in the hallway the rest of the day in a chair. He will not know I am here. I will not enter his room, and I will let the staff take care of him. I will be out there should they need me. We will see how it goes. If they are right and he behaves better; then I will agree to sit outside his room in the mornings—possibly not coming in at all. I take a seat on my hard plastic chair. I look at my watch. I cannot grieve yet; it is only one in the afternoon!

I sit here for an hour. No one has gone into his room to check on him since the speech therapist left. I have not heard him calling out, it has been quiet. I sit there boiling in my own stew. Perhaps I am wrong; maybe I am upsetting him too much. Maybe I should go home and stay away. I am feeling unappreciated for all that I have done. I have been sent out to the hallway like an errant child.

I hear a faint clinking noise coming from Bryant's room. I cannot place it, but there is definitely a noise. I fight the urge to enter. I listen more intently. There it is again, I am sure I hear movement in there. I cannot be positive because they shut his door when they left. The aide who came to my rescue an hour ago walks by.

"I think I hear something in there," I say, while motioning with my head to Bryant's room.

This aide has helped me out a number of times. He reminds me time and time again that my son will not remember any of it, although I will never forget any of it. I disagree with this philosophy; he may not remember, but I believe the seed of being treated as a human being is terribly important. The "feelings" left behind from that non-memory could last a lifetime. But then, I am only a mother, not a professional, maybe I'm wrong.

He listens at the door, telling me nothing is going on in there, and then walks away.

I sit listening for a while longer and am convinced something is going on in there. I am completely irritated they do not go in to check on him. I am getting angrier by the minute. The nurse comes along and I tell her of my concerns and she tries to open the door to check on him. The door will not open. She tries again, the door still will not open. She calls out for help. The doors do not lock and something is preventing her from opening the door.

Two men show up, they push against the door but they cannot get it open. I hear the orderly catch his breath when they realize Bryant is on the other side of the door holding it closed. His tiny body is holding the door closed against the power of two full strength men. They force the door open a couple of inches, and I can see the thin emaciated body of my son holding them off.

The nurse disappears for a moment and then shows up with a straightjacket. This is how they are going to look after him? I am angry. The mood of the orderly, who was so gentle with Bryant in the shower earlier today, has darkened along with the frustrating events of the day. The two men, after a lot of effort, finally push the door open. They manhandle Bryant between the two of them. He is fighting for his life. I am now in the mix telling them they are not putting my son in a straightjacket because they did not do their job. It is a heated battle with my son and me on one side and the two orderlies and the nurse on the other. One orderly has Bryant's arms pinned behind his back with Bryant's back to his chest the other orderly is preparing to put the straight jacket on him when, out of nowhere, a cute young PT girl comes along with a wheelchair.

"Hi," she says with a brilliant smile. "I am here to take Bryant to PT. His regular therapist is not here today."

The two orderlies look at her in disbelief.

"Not now," they yell at her.

She looks at her watch completely unaware of the battle that is taking place.

"Well," she says with her cute little perky mouth, "it is two-thirty and he has PT at two-thirty, so if you want to come with me Bryant, I'm ready to go."

He looks at the men, smiles a dazzling smile back at her and he says, "Yes, I'm ready to go."

She puts him into the wheelchair and off they go with Bryant flashing a shit-eating grin back at the orderlies. He knows what happened. Maybe he won't remember it, but the orderly is right, I will never forget. I believe this feeling of success will propel him onward.

The two men exchange a look of shock on their faces. They and their straight jacket leave, having been outsmarted by a twenty-one year old TBI patient. I walk into Bryant's room to survey the scene of the crime. There in his rumpled bed is the evidence. His lunch tray had been left on the table in his room. He was able to get his restrained leg over to the tray and get it close enough to the bed to kick the tray onto his bed. A lunch knife was on the tray. He then got the knife up to his hand where he sawed through his restraint on his right hand. From that point on he was able to untie his restraints and get out of the bed. Hmmm, they are right, Houdini has nothing on him. That explains the clinking noise I heard, it was the tray landing on the bed. I have a mixture of pride and anger, both pride in my son's ability to process and work through his plan, and anger that he had been left alone to orchestrate it. He could have really been hurt! They don't want him walking into a bathroom by himself, but they let this happen! Yeah, and I'm the problem; right.

While I am waiting for Bryant to come back from his PT, his doctor stops in to see me. He informs me the team has decided they will get better performance out of Bryant if I am not around. They would like me to stay away for three days. I am in shock. After all of the hard work I have done, they want to throw me out. This is the last straw to a very large haystack.

I voice my concern, that he is not watched close enough. I relay the story of the escape and that Bryant was not monitored by the staff. I also tell him that until today he has not been bathed regularly and they need to take better care of him before I will leave him alone in their care. He looks down at Bryant's chart and tells me he has been bathed every day. I tell him he has not; it is a lie. He calls for the head nurse. We then have a meeting right there in the hallway. He is now on a quest to find out exactly what has, or better yet, what has not been happening.

By the time Steve arrives that evening the doctor has interviewed the nurses and the team. A new plan has been formed and they ask me for my cooperation. The doctor assures me he has spoken with the staff and Bryant will be receiving better care. The team really believes Bryant is far too reliant on me and they feel he will progress better if I am not around. I have a vision of the neck brace flying across the room and I know, in part, this is true. Regardless, I am out of my league. Am I really going to argue with these professionals that I know more than they do? Ultimately, I want what is best for my son.

I gather my things and leave the rehab center, agreeing not to come back for three whole days. This is breaking my heart but I have seen him through a lot. If my leaving is best for him, then that is what I will do. I walk out to my car. I don't know what to do with myself. One thing I do know is that after three days I will be back here. They can bet their boots on it. I drive home feeling pretty deflated, adding the rehab team to the long list of people who don't appreciate me. I want to check my backside to see if there is a sign with "Kick Me" on it.

The bon-fire shaped mass of Bryant's belongings greets me when I walk in the door. I realize immediately that this is a way I can help out. For the next three days I am going to organize his belongings and assimilate it into our home. I know an inspection of our home has to take place before they will release him from the rehab center. I certainly would never release someone into a mess like this. I survey the downstairs; the remains of the never-to-be party are at one end of the room, an entire apartment is stacked in the center of the room and a business going on in yet another room. This job will keep me occupied, a task worthy of my intensity.

Although my mind has been occupied, I have not used any physical energy since the accident. I am actually quite excited by the whole process. I will need to clean up clutter and make our house "handicap safe." I spend the evening eyeing everything from a different vantage point. I look for anything that could make an unsteady person trip. A seat for the shower and a hand held shower sprayer will need to be installed. I start to feel better about myself. I develop an action plan.

I look around at the business I put so much into. I know myself so well. I know if this business is still running when my son comes home, I will be tempted to go back to it. I could be seduced to turn away from my promise to take him any way I can get him and immerse myself into my work if possible.

Our children had been the center of my world while I was a

stay-at-home mother for the first thirteen years of motherhood. I think I was a great mother of young children but had a really hard time adjusting to teenagers. Steve and the kids told me I was too intense and needed to back off. Certainly my style of mothering wasn't working with teenagers.

When I started the part-time decorating business from our home, ten years ago, it was a way to express myself. I needed to feel worthy, and it helped. However, I still felt lost so I thought that going bigger and opening a retail store would be the answer. I was sure it would fill that hole, or emptiness inside of me. It was something creative to focus my time and energy, other than the kids. It did take a great deal of focus, in fact too much of my focus.

I must assume Bryant will always be living with us. He is now handicapped and will always need me to be around. This will be a new chapter in the book of our lives, and I want to make space for it. I want to make myself available, and I do not want this business to get in the way.

As I sit in my office, looking around at the hundreds of wallpaper and fabric books, all of the samples, the countless hours of work I put into growing this business, I simply do not have the drive anymore. I do not want it. Somehow it feels like a sickness to me; a place to hide away. I want and need to take temptation away from myself, like an alcoholic throwing out the booze, or a dieter purging the sweets. Sitting in that room, gazing at all of my hard work, I know in a heartbeat what is important and what is not. I know what I need to do.

Steve and I talk on the phone and although it is going to be hard on him, we agree that he will leave at six in the morning and not go back until after lunch, giving the rehab team the time they need alone with Bryant. Steve is planning to sit outside of Bryant's room and work on his laptop the rest of the afternoon, to be there if he is needed. After this morning's incident, we have little confidence they can turn things around.

Talking with the doctor today, we agreed that if Steve can walk Bryant around enough; they won't need to give him the injection in his stomach. That will help out a great deal. We are trying to wean him off of a few things. This is all part of the plan to get him home as quickly as possible.

Now that the doctor has signed off on Steve walking Bryant, it is making it much better. Steve walks him up and down the hallway during the evening. We seem to have turned a corner with the staff. Bryant still does not know who dad is, but he has a good time with him.

Steve seems to miss the sneaking around and comes up with a new game. The two take Steve's flashlight and walk up and down the halls pretending to be James Bond and looking for a way to escape. They are being "sneaky," so the nurses won't see their "moves." Probably not the best thing to do, but they laugh and have a good time. He won't remember it anyway, and laughing is always good. Paul comes by later that night and brings Cheese Coneys and ice cream for a late night snack. Bryant sleeps most of the night. Steve will be leaving in the morning and not coming back until one in the afternoon. This will be Bryant's first morning since the accident without his parents—a huge step towards independence.

Chapter 36
Three-Day Leave

*"Ask for help; if you think you
are in over you're head, you are."*
– Unknown

I wake up the next morning with a plan. I drive to the local decorating store, a former competitor of mine. I am there when it opens. I explain my situation to the manager. It is a huge step for me to go to the decorating store and ask for help. He has known me for years and has watched me as I built my business. We share a mutual respect for each other. I ask him if he would like any of my samples for free. I could sell them but that would take time, and I simply do not have time. I do not have a garage in which to store them, so that is that. Plus, I do not trust myself. I think a clean sweep is best. He has a pickup truck and after several loads we throw everything into the back. He is wonderful and tells me what he does not want he will put in his dumpster and for me not to worry about it. By evening, all that is left are the shelving units. I plan to move them upstairs to a small bedroom and turn it into a storage closet.

It was really hard to watch ten years of my life go out the door. What had started as a seed in my mind had grown into the beanstalk, and the ogre was climbing down the vine. It was time to cut it down. Everything has a season and a purpose, and now something else is more important. I know it is the right thing to do, but it does not make it the easy thing to do.

I stand in the middle of my now empty living room, all signs of my former business life swept away, and I survey the change. This huge room is going to make an excellent living space for Bryant. I will give him the downstairs bedroom and bath, and will then put all of his belongings into this living room. It sounds like a great plan. I am hoping he will be comfortable back at home.

I also accept the offer of help from a friend. The next day she and her son help James and me, along with another young man from James' high school team move all of the furniture around and reorganize the living space. James is discovering a few things as well. Unlike Bryant's teammates, when James asked for help with the move from his "good friends" from his high school soccer team, they blew him off. The one person he always disliked, or was jealous of, showed up and spent the day helping him. In times of need you find out about someone's true character. James view of life is changing.

With the boy's strong backs, we quickly put things in order. I occupy myself for the next few days and am amazed at how quickly the time flies by. When you are not living second to second time flies. After three days, my house is now clean, organized, and handicap ready.

I have taken huge steps in the past three days; Step one: I gave up control over Bryant. Step two: I asked for help. Step three: I accepted help. Step four: I gave up on a business I had tied myself to, and accepted the loss. Step five: I trusted Steve with our son and did not judge him. These are all huge steps for me. My healing has begun.

Meanwhile back at the rehab center Steve is learning much. When you keep Bryant up all night, the days are really difficult. The second night, Bryant did not sleep at all. He still does not know who dad is; he called him Tony that night. He now wants to escape. This is his newest thing; forget the neck brace, he wants out of there.

Steve and the nurse tied Bryant down and sedated him last night. However, since Steve is not on shift until one in the afternoon, it is the team's problem and not ours. Steve is thinking less of us may be better. Bryant ate breakfast and lunch today and he had another breakthrough by realizing he fell. He has not remembered it on his own since the night in the ICU before the ambulance ride. They say once he can string together the events in a conscious stream—fall, rescue, hospital—it will help him to move forward. He does not remember falling, but he remembers camping in the cave.

Steve talks to Bryant about God and how He saved his life. Steve tells him he should say a prayer and then Bryant responds with "you should pray every day." About that time a huge bolt of lightning hits the ground somewhere close. They exchange looks and take it as a sign from above. Then again, when Bryant wakes up from a catnap, he asked Steve very seriously if he would do him a favor. Steve said "sure." Bryant asks in a serious tone that he wipe down both his Humvee and his helicopter. He wants to make sure they are real clean. Steve thinks maybe he has taken the James Bond thing a bit too far. One moment we think he is divinely connected, and the next moment he rambles.

Bryant does not do so well this morning without us in the room. The PT person does not make sure someone is in the room with Bryant and leaves him alone tied down to his bed. He has to go to the bathroom, and when he did not get help he peed all over the walls and floor. Who can blame him? I would do the same if I had the body parts to pull it off. Good for him! The nurse was really upset and wants to know where I have been. She talks with Steve about it, and she is furious when she finds out the team asked me to stay away. She tells Steve the team has no idea how much good I have done. It feels really great that someone appreciates my efforts. She speaks with the doctor, and they assign a male sitter to Bryant. They say they only do this in special cases. He now has a sitter assigned to him twenty-four/seven. I feel vindicated.

With the sitter in charge last night at nine-thirty, Steve left the rehab center and came home. He drove home in a light rain with the top down. Steve and I swim outside in the fine drizzle, it is wonderful. This is the first night Steve and I have slept in our bed together since the accident. Steve tosses and turns all night.

His sleep patterns are all messed up as well. I wake up with a mild panic attack, sucking air with a power surge and adrenaline pulsing through my veins. Not unlike a fight or flight response, my cortisone levels, along with Bryant's, must be running on full throttle. I wonder if we will ever adjust. Regardless, tonight is a good night. We do not discuss recent events. We do not discuss the dismantling of my business. It is simply a non-event to Steve. We do not discuss his upcoming two-week trip to Florida. We simply enjoy the peace and quiet.

Chapter 37
A Shave and a Haircut

*"There aint no rules around here!
We're tying to accomplish something."*
– Thomas Edison

Per our agreement, I arrive at the rehab center at noon the next day. I am so excited to spend time with Bryant again. I really missed him. When I walk into the room, he is sitting in his bed looking really lost and afraid. The sight of him melts my heart.

He looks at me and says, "Mom, I was so afraid. I am glad you are here."

This is so much better than "Miss Piggy." Maybe they knew what they were doing after all. He looks great. Steve took him to the barbershop here at the center. He got a shave and a haircut. Clearly, they picked up on his hygiene since the doctor became involved. I spend the afternoon with Bryant. I can tell he has aged a little more in his development. I am guessing he is around sixteen or so. His memory is getting better. He is starting to string some memories together but his short-term memory is still really bad. The amount of time between asking a question a second time is longer, but it is now getting harder to get him off subject and to redirect the question to something else.

He thinks he is out of town for a soccer tournament, downtown Chicago, or St. Louis. This makes sense to me, probably not the therapist, but we spent a large part of his childhood out of town for soccer tourneys. He is now old enough mentally to remember driving and wants his car back.

He is now obsessed with where his car is. He is getting angry because he wants to leave. I am amazed at his reasoning abilities. Although he is hard to deal with at times, his anger, is perfectly rational. He does not think there is anything wrong with him! He has not put the pieces together yet, but he believes we are keeping him unjustly and he wants to go home. I don't blame him. This must be terribly confusing to him, no wonder he is mad at us. He wants to leave, to get on with his life.

He has come so far. It is truly a miracle. He is able to eat and is now walking around on his own back and forth to the bathroom. Yes, they are now letting him go to the bathroom by himself. I think the team has learned a lot and loosened up on the rules. He is wobbly, but it is simply amazing to me that he has come this far. How can we expect anything more than this? Steve and I plan to go back to church as soon as Bryant is released. We want to go and celebrate this miracle. Certainly God must have a great plan for him or He would not have saved him. I am not much of a church person, but after all of this, I really do think I need to start attending. Steve is already there, I am the one dragging my feet. I pray all of the time, but church hasn't been for me.

We spend the afternoon basically going back and forth and changing the subject. He wants to go home and I can't take him home yet. It was much easier moving furniture around than this constant battle.

I take him outside to the beautiful big courtyard containing the basketball court and gazebo. He wants to walk, but he has to stay in his wheelchair when moving around hallways. We have a really nice time in the courtyard. Bryant is completely distracted by the Cicadas. They are out in force once again. They seem to love the heat of the day. There are also lots of dead little Cicada bodies lying around as well. Clearly we are getting to the end of the season. When the sitter arrives I leave.

Paul's graduation ceremony is this evening. Now that we have a sitter, we can take Paul and Leigh out for a steak dinner at a really nice restaurant. It will be only the four of us. It's kind of nice really, but not what we had planned.

The evening turns out to be lovely. It seems quite strange to be doing normal things. Elizabeth and James meet up with us, and we go to the ceremony. I am amazed at how many people graduate from this university each year. The walks are broken down into different schools at different times. Steve, Elizabeth, James, Leigh and I watch as the first child in our family receives his college diploma. I am bursting with pride at his accomplishment. Given the last few weeks and the stress, the way he stayed focused on what he had to do is nothing short of a miracle. We do not share the traditional cake and family waiting at home. Instead, he goes back to his apartment where he and his friends are planning a huge party. We say our good-byes and head back home. This evening did not turn out at all like I planned, but it is nice. It is, after all, what he wanted.

The weekend goes by in a blur. We do not have the team around and there are no therapies. I expect this to make things better; however, Bryant is not accepting being held against his wishes at the rehab center any longer. He is anxious most of the weekend, and at one point tears all of his family photos off the wall to pack up and go home. I finally give in and let him be sedated.

He is now paranoid about the male sitter sleeping in his room. He does not want him sleeping in there with him. Paranoid about his personal items such as his clothes and things, he keeps hiding them and then does not know where they are. He accuses the staff of stealing from him. Perhaps the paranoia is only another stage. He appears to be acting more and more irrational at times. We are all frustrated. I am being as patient as I can be, but he is really acting strange. Elizabeth, James, Steve and I are all using our distraction and redirection skills to deal with Bryant. We all understand it is not his fault, and we handle him with kid gloves, taking a great deal of verbal abuse from him. Paul spends the night with him Sunday night to give his dad a break.

I am really getting nervous because Steve is leaving Monday afternoon for Florida. He usually would be gone for two weeks, but he is planning on coming home on Friday for the weekend. It is going to be a long two weeks. I am not sure how I am going to handle this by myself. I feel myself tensing up at the mere thought. I will need to depend on the kids to help take up the slack, especially if Bryant refuses to sleep in the room with his "body guard."

The team told us on Friday that they are probably going to release Bryant in two weeks when Steve comes home from Florida. They are going to do their home inspection this week, and take Bryant out to lunch for his trial public experience. The plan is then to move him into the residential apartment in the complex to work on his independent living skills. They asked me if I had any other concerns. Boy, do I have concerns, but not too many they can help me with. I am concerned Bryant may not yet have the physical ability to swim. They worked it out with the PT department to test his swimming skills. We have a really big week coming up.

Before heading out to the rehab center this morning, I survey my downstairs; nothing is as it was. I walk around the house admiring my handiwork. I had screws put into all of the downstairs windows. They are really great, and you can only remove the screws with a special key—that I keep in my pocket. We have old casement windows and way too many to install a security system, plus hospital expenses are going to be out of this world. We do not have the money to cover the expense of a security system as well. My plan is to keep on the air conditioning. This alone will bother me, but with the air conditioning, I can screw the downstairs windows shut. I put keyed-only dead bolts on all five of the outside doors so he cannot escape that way. He does not yet have the ability to climb steps so I feel pretty good about having the downstairs secured. I know my son and he will find a way out if I leave one. I need to be one step ahead of him at all times.

His "apartment" is now set up downstairs and the bathroom is equipped for his use. I put twin beds in the downstairs bedroom. I am hoping he will let me sleep in the room with him. If not, then the video monitor I installed will help me to keep an eye on him. I read and followed all the general instructions they sent home with me, including the part about removing all knives, scissors and sharp objects. Yikes, that one will put the fear of God into you. I am feeling good about the security measures I put in place and hope we will pass inspection.

Chapter **38**
Snap Out Of It

"One of the advantages of being young is that you don't let common sense get in the way of doing things everyone else knows are impossible."
– Anonymous

I drive to the hospital, singing my fight song. I feel as if they put it on the air especially for me each and every morning only to pump me up. I park my car, walk through the beautifully appointed lobby and head down to Neurological Rehab.

I press the buzzer and wait while the night nurse lets me enter. We are now on personal terms with all of the nursing staff. I stop in the kitchen area to mix up a Boost milkshake for Bryant. We are still working on putting weight on him, and I should be working on taking it off me. I go into the room and there is Paul, as crabby as his father has been each morning. Sleeping here at night must put everyone in a really bad mood. Bryant got up to use the bathroom and I went to help him.

Paul looks at me and says, "Hey Mom, he can do that himself. Why don't we go out in the hallway and talk?"

We go out in the hallway and he looks at me, "Mom, Bryant has been acting really crazy, I mean really crazy. I finally lost it with him last night. I grabbed him and told him he has to snap out of it. He has to stop saying all of this crazy shit. I told him people are going to start thinking he is crazy. He really listened to me, Mom. I think you are babying him way too much. Don't let him get by with this crap. He is really much better. That's all I have to say, and I am going home now to go to bed. Love you, see you later."

I watch as he walks down the hallway and out the door. I stand there dumbfounded. What right does he have, after all I have gone through, to come in here, spend only one night and say that to me? I shake my head in disbelief. If this is the help that I am going to get for the next two weeks I tell myself, I am in trouble. I need support, not judgments.

I walk into the room and there is Bryant sitting up on the side of the bed.

"Hi Mom," he says to me. "How are you?"

And right then and there is the beginning of the big change. After all of the love, the coddling, the patience, my burly matter of fact oldest son comes in, gives him a lecture and he is more like his old self than he has been. Paul does what he is meant to do, at just the right moment, unbelievable.

We have an extremely pleasant morning. We talk about his fall while he eats breakfast. The partially open window into his mind about the accident is now open. He understands he has fallen, is at a rehab center and that certain things must happen before he can go home. He has not been this sharp since before the horrible ambulance ride. I am talking to my son, be still my heart. I am talking to my son in a rational manner.

The doctor comes by and is impressed with the progress. This is what he has been wanting. He also tells us he really wants to try Ritalin on Bryant. He feels it will help him to focus. If we will give it a try for a week, we can then judge for ourselves. We agree hesitantly. I have opposed medicating him before, but the thought of him coming home in two weeks and the doctor's insistence that this is all he does, and he has seen remarkable progress when administered at this point, pushes me to consent.

He receives his first dose that morning and we are amazed. Within hours it is as if we have our son back. He is able to share a normal, rational conversation and goes to all of his therapies with a new purpose.

As we talk throughout the morning, the one thing Bryant keeps coming back to is how sorry he is that he put his younger brother through something so traumatic. He feels really bad about this. He is asking question after question trying to put the pieces of the last few weeks in order. He does not remember anything about his recovery at all. He comes back after lunch and takes a nap. Just like the movie *Fifty First Dates,* the moment he falls asleep he forgets everything and we need to explain it all over again. He faces it each time with the same intensity, shock and awe. It is so cruel to watch. His short-term memory still has a way to go before it is recovered.

Like everything else, maybe it will improve, maybe it won't. With brain injuries you never know what you're going to get. The dry marker board in his room becomes even more important. Each time he wakes up now he reads, "Your name is Bryant, you fell at the Gorge and hit your head, and you are at a rehab center. You are O.K." This message immediately helps him to process where he is and what is going on.

Steve stops by to visit with Bryant before he leaves town. We are both relieved about the progress Bryant has made. The angry paranoid Bryant is now much calmer. We are both amazed at how our prayers are being answered right before our eyes. Each time we are faced with an insurmountable task, somehow it is always taken care of.

I am a stubborn woman and I should be trusting God, and completely giving control over to Him; but I learned from the time I was small that I could not depend on anyone but myself. It is ingrained in me. This is a very big struggle for me. I am doing better at this point than I have ever done before. Here I am an unknown, only an average person, a mother, not a minister, not a great thinker. I don't lead large groups of people, and yet, He is revealing His love for me and for my children over and over again. I am starting to get it. God loves me as much as I love my children. It's that simple, there is nothing I will not do for my children and there is nothing He will not do for me. There are things I need to do for myself, and for others. I do, after all, have free will.

I watch as Steve leaves the rehab center for the airport. I am feeling more confident than I thought possible. We both know when he comes home in two weeks Bryant will be returning home with us. It is a big step for all of us, and like Bryant said in the ICU while still in his coma:

"Won't we have a jubilation when I come home."

I shake my head as the memories and thoughts buzz around in my mind. He proclaimed his own prophecy and yes, it will be a jubilation: he will be talking, eating, using the bathroom and walking. Yes, my partially paralyzed son will be walking, when he comes home.

Bryant, James and I go out to the courtyard and they play basketball. Bryant has to stay in his wheelchair, but he accepts it. He still beats James, and James does not throw the game. We eat dinner out in the courtyard, which is where I prefer to spend as much time as possible with him. I am able to go home to sleep. Bryant is now accepting of the male orderly and understands why he is there.

The next morning is a big day. The team is taking Bryant out to lunch at his favorite hamburger joint. It is closer to our part of town and it will be a thirty-minute drive to get there. The team explains to me that he will have trouble for a while discerning the different sounds and motions. Sometimes this is upsetting and they may need to make several trips before Bryant is comfortable in public. He has had limited stimulation here in a controlled environment. It will be a good test to see if the Ritalin is doing what it is supposed to do. Bryant is really nervous as he dresses for his big day out. He is so concerned he will blow it and they will not let him come home. I am nervous as well.

I wave good-bye to him as they walk him out the door for the first time. It is like the first day of school, when you are no longer in control of what will happen to your child that day. You trust the teachers and the school district to do the right things. I say a prayer for it to go well. I decide to go down to the computer lab and research brain injuries. I am too nervous to leave and want to be here when he comes back.

When they come back into the room he is a little anxious. I ask him how it went?

"It was O.K., I really didn't like it. It took us forever to get there and once I got there I only wanted to leave. I don't know if I did good or not," he answers.

He is really anxious and shaky. I finally get him to lie down to take a nap. When he wakes up it is a new day, and I must re-tell him about the accident and everything all over again. I don't mention the trip to the hamburger joint, really no need to relive it right now.

Shortly after his nap the adorable PT girl is back, she has her bathing suit on and is going to take him swimming this afternoon in their huge pool. He is so shy and insecure, nothing at all like my confident, aggressive son. He is the same, but he is different. He certainly knows how to smile sweetly at the girls though. He would follow her anywhere.

The three of us walk down to the pool and by the time we get there he is already tired. I help him get into a small handicapped dressing room to put on his trunks. He shoos me out, he wants to do it himself. I wait outside the doorway.

The pool is amazing, completely equipped for handicapped swimming. It has a floor that can be raised and lowered. They completely raise the floor for Bryant as he enters the water. The trick is to slowly lower the floor to see if he can swim or not. He still has his neck brace on and they are making him swim with it. I don't see how he can possibly swim with his neck held erect. He has trouble and they quickly end the session; no need to make him feel inadequate. He has been a strong swimmer since he was a child and I am honestly surprised.

While Bryant is dressing she tells me it could be the neck brace but he is absolutely not to swim without it. I will need to replace the pads inside the neck brace after he swims. She recommends he swim with a noodle. She thinks it will come back but for now he is not a strong enough swimmer yet.

Chapter 39
Making the Grade

*"What counts is not necessarily
the size of the dog in the fight-
it's the size of the fight in the dog."*
– Dwight D. Eisenhower

When I arrive at Bryant's room this morning he is awake and has already read the board. We talk about his accident and once again, I watch as he relives the shock and guilt. I then explain how and when he will be going home. He goes to therapy and the team informs him they are inspecting our home today. When he gets back to the room he is really anxious and has a frightened look in his eyes.

"What's the matter, Bryant," I ask.

"I want you to go home, now. I don't want you to wait around. I want you to go home and make sure everything is good. I don't want there to be any problems. I mean it, Mom. I want you to leave now and make sure everything is perfect. I want to be sure I will get to go home next week. It is really important this goes well. I want you to make sure everything is cleared out and I won't trip. I want it to be safe," he adds.

"Are you going with them," I ask.

"Yes," he answers. "I told them it is really a long way away, but I am going with them. So leave now Mom. Make sure it's all good, this is really important."

I had no idea they would be bringing Bryant along with them. I grab my purse, give him a kiss and head out the door. They are going to be there sometime this afternoon. I feel butterflies in my stomach as well. This is so important to Bryant. I don't want to fail him.

He is hanging onto the thought and dream of coming home. I drive down the drive and try to look at the surroundings with fresh eyes, the eyes of someone looking for danger. I am so grateful I had those days to organize and tidy up the downstairs, otherwise I would be a nervous wreck.

"Oh my gosh, Bryant is coming home for a home visit," I tell Elizabeth and James. We are so excited.

I see the sedan pull up the drive and watch as everyone gets out of the car. I quickly run out to meet them. I want them to come in the back way. Our house is on a hill and the front and side entrances have steps, but the two back entrances do not. Bryant is looking as stiff as can be. He looks like he is about to freak out. I thought he would be happy to be home.

I lead them around and show them the safety additions I made. I show Bryant his new living quarters and am expecting some kind of reaction. The neck brace keeps his neck stiff, but he only looks straight ahead, only turning his eyes on occasion. It is like robot Bryant. Although he is walking under his own power, he still is shuffling his left foot and drags it on occasion. He is not picking it up all the time. We go into the family room for him to sit down, and I cannot take it anymore. I am so happy to have him home. I tell him to sit down on the window seat.

"I have a surprise for you," I tell him. "Someone who is really going to be excited to see you."

I run upstairs, and let Ali out of his huge crate. He has been crying upstairs; he knows Bryant is here. He bounds down the stairs straight into the family room. He jumps up on Bryant and licks his face. His exuberance cannot be controlled. This is simply too much for Bryant. This powerful dog could easily topple Bryant with his high energy.

He looks at me and says, "We gotta leave. We gotta leave now."

I grab Ali by the collar. Ali is crying and trying to get away from me.

"I only wanted him to know you're alive," I explain to Bryant and the team. "This is Bryant's dog and he has missed him so much."

I realize now I made a terrible mistake and should have left him upstairs. I have grown attached to this dog, and I couldn't keep him away from his master. He has been missing Bryant as much as Bryant has been missing him. I ask James to take him upstairs and James manhandles him and takes him back upstairs to his crate.

Bryant stands up, "O.K." he says, "it's time to go. I will see you back at the rehab center."

Bryant cannot wait to get back into the car. This has me terribly confused. I thought we would have trouble getting him to go back, I never expected him to bolt back there. He is already walking out to the back door, leading the others. They are all turning and thanking me for the visit. They are very different outside of the hospital setting. They seem more like real people to me than they did before. Now that I think about it; we probably seem more real to them as well.

I stand out in the blacktopped driveway batting the Cicadas away from my face. I watch as they all load up in the car. Bryant is sitting in the back facing forward. He does not even look over at me as they drive out the long drive. I do not understand what has happened. I am thinking that I have let Bryant down. I wish I had not let the dog out. I chastise myself all the way back on the long drive to the rehab center. I am thinking to myself this has not gone well at all.

When I walk into Bryant's room, he is sitting there in his bed by himself. He is looking very "shell shocked." He has had a glossed over glazed look in his eyes since he has "woken up." It is hard to explain. Everything about him is my son, but there is a different look when I look into his eyes. I find this upsetting at times, but I tell myself it is to be expected given the circumstances. I expect him to be really upset with me.

I start to apologize to Bryant and right in the middle of my apology he cuts me off.

"Mom, we just need to do what those dumb therapists tell us

to do in order to pass and graduate. I was afraid if they knew I had a pit bull, maybe they wouldn't let me come home. I wanted to get out of there and get back before they realized it. I need to do these things to graduate."

I am taken off guard. This was why he was so stiff, he was afraid of not passing, not making the grade. He was staying focused on doing exactly what he thought they wanted. No more, no less. I am thinking he is going to do very well next week when he does his independent living skills. I am hoping he does anyway. He has not really showered by himself as of yet, but they are letting him do more and more. He is working toward a goal and that is so much better than fighting with us. Even now it is them versus us. I guess we will never really be a team. I was the only one on their team, and I switched over to Team Family a while back.

I stay until late into the evening. Since Steve is not here, I am staying as late as possible. We spend the evening once again out in the courtyard. It is really quite lovely out there. We do not hear how all of the visits have gone. We don't know if Bryant has passed or not. We do know Bryant's doctor seems to be really pleased with his recovery. He thinks he will continue to recover, but how much he does not know. Things are looking good. He warns us when Bryant is released the two things that will prevent recovery: alcohol and drugs. The brain will not progress with either of these in his system. He cannot stress this enough.

Although Bryant has not lost his license, they do not want him to drive until he has passed a driving test, which will be administered by one of his therapists. The timing will depend on his rate of recovery. Most brain injury patients die in car crashes. Bryant's reaction time is much slower than it used to be and will probably never be as good as it once was. I agree, but keeping this stubborn young man out of his car is going to be tough. I will need to pull a wire or something. My sons never listen to reason. They, like their father, do not think the rules apply to them.

The other shocking news is no soccer from now on. Soccer is the sport with the leading brain injuries or concussions. One more concussion, no matter how small could be catastrophic. This seems plausible to me, but as Bryant's recovery is progressing at a really good rate, this may be a problem down the road for him. Soccer is his identity and one of the things of which he was really good.

"I really think his prognosis is good," says the neurologist.

Not being able to tell me anything about my own child is really starting to bother me. Up to this time no one has told me his blood alcohol content because of HIPAA rules. I can change his diaper, feed him and care for him, but not know about his blood alcohol level, come on. Although he has the mind of a sixteen year old at this time, he has all of the legal rights of any twenty-one year old out there, including the hospital bills. We can pay them or let his credit go bad. The choice is ours. We are in a real pickle.

We do not want Bryant starting off his life with this debt hanging over his head. It is already going to be tough enough. I am told because he is a student and does not have a job, he cannot get Social Security or Disability benefits. It is a catch twenty-two. He has recovered to a higher level because of family support but, because of his level of recovery, he will not qualify for any financial services. The bottom line: it is our problem and no one else's.

No one is taking up collections for us. Steve's dad has generously offered to loan us money for the hospital bills, with interest. It is the best offer we have, and we will probably take him up on it. It's that or risk a financial meltdown.

I drive home later with all of these thoughts going through my mind. The ripple effects are penetrating every aspect of our lives. I know the accident happened to him and not to us, but we are all feeling the ramifications. Having been in almost solitary confinement with my son for the past several weeks has changed my thinking patterns. The lack of sleep, the stress and the void of stimulation to my brain makes me feel as if I have ADD. I have not really had much contact with the outside world and frankly, I find it over stimulating now. My brain feels as if it has been reprogrammed.

James came to the hospital tonight as always. Bryant had a friend stop by, and it gave James and me a chance to talk. I think the reality is starting to sink into him as well. With his father gone, he is realizing it is only going to be him and me at home with Bryant. Before he had been the youngest brother of four siblings. With Paul and Elizabeth leaving in a few weeks, and Bryant mentally at a younger age, James will now become the older brother. The roles have been reversed. This is new territory for him as well. He is feeling overwhelmed by it all.

"James, you can do whatever you want to do," I tell him. "Our old life is over. I look at life as a book, with a lot of chapters. That chapter is closed; yes, it ended abruptly. It was a great chapter, but it is now at an end. I am going to enjoy my time with the new Bryant. I may be spending time going to the zoo, watching movies; I don't really know what it will be; but, I intend to embrace this new chapter."

He looks at me. I can tell he likes this analogy.

"Yeah," he says. "I can see that. I never thought of life that way before but it makes a lot of sense. I'll be there with you guys, Mom."

This is a good moment in time, and really what more can I ask?

James stays a little later with Bryant and Paul. I head home. I will be back early in the morning, and I am exhausted. It is Wednesday night and Steve is coming home on Friday night. I am feeling pretty good, like I am going to make it. Steve and I talk more on the phone than we have in years. We are communicating three or four times a day. He really hates being away. Although it is hard not having him here, I love the fact that he is missing us. I have been missing him for years. I finally feel we are more important to him than the people he is coaching.

Section Four
New Beginnings

NEVER QUIT, NEVER GIVE UP
LINCOLN'S ROAD TO THE WHITE HOUSE

Failed in business in 1831
Defeated for Legislature in 1832
Second failure in business 1833
Suffers nervous breakdown 1836
Defeated for Speaker 1838
Defeated for Elector in 1840
Defeated for Congress 1843
Defeated for Congress 1848
Defeated for Senate 1855
Defeated for Vice President 1856
Defeated for Senate 1858
Elected President in 1860

Chapter 40
Facing Your Fears

*"Courage is being scared to death;
and saddling up anyway."*
– John Wayne

I am in for quite a shock this morning. I walk in the door that morning at six-thirty and the nurse informs me Bryant is going home today. I look at her like she is crazy. She tells me she was told to get him ready for discharge this morning. I sit around in Bryant's room waiting for the team to enter. The nurses already informed Bryant, and he is so excited. How am I going to do this alone? Steve is not home until tomorrow and will be gone all next week.

What if he turns aggressive at home, and I cannot control him? I do not have a bed with straps. I cannot give him a shot to calm him down. My heart is racing, and I feel like I am developing a full-blown anxiety attack. How could they put me in this position! They know Steve is out of town, and Bryant is scheduled to come home at the end of next week. How can I disappoint Bryant and tell him he cannot come home? He will hate me. The team finally arrives at eight. I am beside myself. I pull the speech therapist aside.

"I hear you are releasing Bryant today. Is that true?"

"Well, yes he is really recovering at a very fast pace, we feel he is not responding to us anymore because he is so fixated on going home. We decided he can continue with his therapies on an outpatient basis. It is really the best thing for him."

I look at her like she has three heads popping out of her neck.

"My husband is out of town. You know he will not be home

until the end of next week, how am I going to deal with him by myself? Why the big hurry, what happened to our plan?"

This seems like a reasonable question to me. I want to add, *because you can't get him to respond to your therapies anymore you want to move him on out,* but I keep that part to myself.

"If you do not feel you can deal with him, then I can discuss it further with the team, but as of right now we feel it is best he be discharged this morning," she says with a smirk.

This is a really big decision. I want to wipe the smirk right off of her face. I really feel like this is a gotcha for the stink I caused with the doctor over the lack of consistency with Bryant's care. I am terrified, but I am not about to let her know. I take a deep breath, suck it up and look her right in the eye.

"I will take him home this morning then, when can we leave?"

"As soon as the paper work is completed. That should be within the hour," she answers.

I paste a smile on my face and go back to Bryant's room. He is ecstatic; I am ready to throw up. I call Steve and tell him the "good news." He wants to jump on the plane and come home immediately but the best he can do is noon on Friday. He will, however, need to go back on Monday. But once again I am dealing with seconds and minutes. Monday is a whole lot of seconds and minutes away. I call home to tell them the news as well. Everyone is in shock. We did not see this one coming. Only twenty-five days after he fell 150 feet and suffered a broken neck, a massive stroke, a serious TBI and paralysis on his left side, he is walking out of the rehab center and coming home. We should be having a jubilation, I should be jumping for joy, but honestly, I am so afraid, I am frozen. I am being tested and asked to do something that is the most monumental thing I have ever done in my life. This is scarier than coming home with the fourth baby. I have done everything I can think of to prepare for it, but I do not have anyone to lean on. I feel terribly alone.

Bryant and I pack up all of his belongings. I leave most of the flowers in the unit, on the reception desk and such. I load the plants up in the car with the rest of his things. This is beginning to feel real. I am doing everything I can to keep busy and keep myself calm. We are sitting in the room waiting for the release papers.

I look at him in disbelief. What else am I going to be asked to do, end world hunger, bring about world peace? These things all seem as possible to me right now as taking him home alone without Steve.

I look at my son, he is a grown man trapped with the mind of an adolescent—and with super human strength. I know in my heart this is the right thing, but my palms are sweating and my heart is racing. Good thing we haven't checked my blood pressure over the past month. I try to slow down my heart rate, breathe in one, two, three, four, then out one, two, three, four.

The release papers are signed. I am given instructions on how to schedule the five outpatient therapy visits per day. I will be driving a great deal. They give me a handful of prescriptions that need to be filled immediately and detailed instructions on when to administer them. They recommend I go to the pharmacy immediately. How do I do that? I certainly cannot leave him in the car alone; yet, the thought of taking him in with me terrifies me. I am in such shock right now that if Santa Claus and the Easter Bunny both jump in the car with us I would not even flinch.

The car is loaded and I walk out of the doors with my son. It is lunch time, I ask him if he would like to stop at McDonald's, his favorite. He climbs into the front seat of the car, and I think nothing about it. We are in the drive-through line when I first notice his anxiety.

Suddenly he tells me "go, just go, it's too much, let's just leave."

When we are whizzing down the highway, his eyes are open way too wide and he is holding on with both of his hands.

"It's really strange, Mom, but the cars are all going so fast, and it looks like they're coming right at us. I don't understand it, it is really scary."

I realize he is having trouble with his depth perception with moving objects. I suggest he close his eyes and try to relax. I explain that his brain is waking up, and it has to learn about depth perception all over again. I now have a better understanding of his reaction over eating out and his home visit. I'm not sure either he or I are ready for this, but here we are anyway. I offer to pull over and let him get into the backseat, but he tells me to "just go."

When we get home, we are greeted by balloons hanging all up and down the driveway. My mind drifts back to the eerily smiling balloon in his room. Oh boy, I think, this is going to be tough. I get Bryant situated inside the house with James. I make sure all of the doors and windows are locked tight. The pharmacy is only down the street, it is not busy and they fill the prescriptions quickly. I am a nervous wreck.

I race back home, unlock the door and when I get inside, everything is just fine. Bryant and James are sitting in the kitchen talking and laughing. "So far, so good," but I remind myself things can turn on a dime.

Chapter
Against All Odds 41

"It is not enough to do your best; you must succeed in doing what is necessary."
– Winston Churchill

I am afraid, I am afraid of what my own son might do with his outbursts. I know it isn't really my son I am scared of but the traumatic brain injury. This is simply another phase, and he will eventually outgrow it, or at least I hope. Of course, no one can really tell me anything, what we have is what we have, blah, blah, blah. I am afraid I will not be able to handle him without restraints, without Ativan, without nurses, orderlies and my husband. I am afraid I may do something that will jeopardize his recovery. I am frightened I will miss something important, and nervously walk on eggshells around him.

The first day he is really quiet. The drive has worn him out. He looks around the bedroom not really recognizing it. He has never slept in this room on the first floor, which had been the master bedroom when Bryant was growing up. We took the bedroom under the staircase, so I could hear if anyone snuck down the stairs at night. His bedroom had been upstairs, but he is unable to climb steps now.

The day passes pretty uneventful. At this point, every time he falls asleep—no matter the length of time—he still has absolutely no memory of anything that happened before that. I put a marker board up in Bryant's room so he will not panic when he first wakes up; it becomes a lifesaver. He wakes up, reads it and is ready for the next step. This has really been helpful at the rehab center.

We lie low today... no visitors. I want to keep it quiet to limit confusion and therefore the potential of an outburst. James and Elizabeth are here with us. He is calmer at home, and we make it through the first day without any serious problems. It appears most of his aggression was simply because he wanted to do something and was not allowed. He gives me some grief over the neck brace, but not much.

Things are going well. I keep the doors and windows locked with the key in my pocket. No one goes in or out without my knowledge. I am still a complete and total control freak.

Elizabeth goes out this evening with her new boyfriend, but James stays by my side. Bryant does not want me to sleep downstairs with him, but he agrees to let James sleep in the bed next to him. He still gets agitated easily, and we want to keep him calm. We do not have a plan if he explodes; therefore, I have no idea what we will do. I am grateful for the sleeping pills. They knock him out completely. This is the only way I will ever get any sleep; yet, the first night I hardly sleep anyway. I keep the video monitor next to my bed and stare at it all night long, drifting off occasionally for a couple of minutes at a time. Seizures are still a concern. I am on constant watch for them.

The new surroundings keep him confused, and he doesn't recognize me at first in the morning. I panic when I walk into his room, because he has a wild look in his eyes and is confused and angry. I develop a pit in my stomach the size of Texas. I back off and give James room to work his calming magic; he recognizes him. I make breakfast and he is happy to be sitting up eating with his dog by his side. I am happy to see him here, back in my kitchen eating so well.

We have a quiet morning and once again when he gets up from his nap, we play out scene two of who we are and why he is here. The confusion and anger become the norm when he wakes. I wonder when this will stop. His friends stop by in the afternoon, and they all hang out by the pool. I am nervous someone will say or do something to which he will react negatively, but these friends are wonderful to him throughout his recovery stage, and he needs their support.

The words he proclaimed in the ICU float by in my head: *Won't we all rejoice when I can swim in the pool.* Bryant wants to swim and I am glad I covered this with his therapist and with Bryant. I explain to him he will have trouble swimming only for a short while and he needs to protect his neck. I do not want to tell him he cannot swim, it would not go over well at all. The minute I tell him he can't do something he is determined to prove me wrong. I suggest he float around the pool with a noodle. That way no one will need to know. I sit out by the pool with him and his friends. I am on edge ready to jump to save him, but he handles it like a champ.

Steve arrives home that night, and we keep Bryant occupied. The first few days with him home are pretty uneventful. He has taken up fishing, something he has never really wanted to do much before the accident. I think it is his memories of fishing in Canada and the dreams he has had about fishing with his great grandfather, his namesake. He passed away when Bryant was two, but Bryant has talked a great deal about fishing with him while in and out of cognition. Steve is convinced it was Great Grandfather Bryant by Bryant's side when he fell and also the man who was with Bryant in the room in the ICU. I think he would somehow have made himself known to Steve, and not me, if this were the case. However, he would use the words jubilation and rejoice. He was an old fashioned Christian and an avid fisherman. I do believe those who pass before us, can be around us: angels if you will.

With that being said, I am not so sure after the scary scene in the ICU. Would a gentle soul like him turn into a wolf with the scary red eyes? I haven't shared the events or my thoughts with Steve. I am keeping my fear and guilt to myself, and I do not know with whom to talk about it.

More visitors come and go over the weekend and things are going pretty well. He is now fighting me steadily about the neck brace. He jumps in the pool for only a couple of minutes at a time only to get the padding wet on the brace. I have one set of replacement pads, and he cannot wear it if it is wet. It is a constant game, me drying the old pads before he gets the new ones wet. I keep diverting his attention onto something new all the time to give the pads time to dry.

A reporter has called and wants to come by and interview James, and perhaps Bryant, next week. I mention it casually to Bryant. He is not for it, at all.

"Mom, I know how you get," Bryant says. "When you get going on something, you can get really negative. I love the Gorge, and I will not have you say anything negative about it. It's my own fault I fell. I want you to promise me you will not get negative about it."

I promise him, but I can hardly get the words out of my mouth. I know he loves the Gorge, but the number of accidents there each year is astonishing. They could at least have cell phone coverage for the emergencies. I feel I share a responsibility to tell other mothers to not let their children go there unsupervised. I know that Bryant's mood can change quickly, and I will need to hope for the best when the reporter arrives.

Sunday is Father's Day, and I cannot think of a greater gift than having our son home. We plan to give thanks and go to church. We called Paul, but he has not called us back. After a family discussion about which church to attend, we settle on a non-denominational mega church. James really wants to go there, so our sons lead us back to church.

We are all lined up in the large, dark, theatre-style room with large screens and even louder music. I am thinking to myself I will never be able to embrace this. I am also nervous thinking all of the lights and loud music will cause Bryant to have a seizure. We were told to keep him away from flashing lights and such. Then, this young Pastor comes onto the stage in his blue jeans and Harley-Davidson tee shirt. I try to keep an open mind, then it hits me: this is really the same as a traditional church. The music, then the informational talk, the sermon, the offering, and then music again.

It is done in a hipper, younger-person format. If this will hold the attention of my kids, I'm all for it.

I am a little irritated because it is Father's Day, and Paul is not with us. Apparently, he called Steve while we were in church. Steve calls him back on our way out to the car. He did not want to tell us, but Leigh is in the hospital. They have been there since Saturday afternoon. He took her swimming in the river, and she broke her lower back. He does not want to leave her side and asks us to bring some clothes for him to the hospital as he is still in his swimming trunks. They will do surgery today and put a plate in her back. As of right now, she cannot make her legs work.

The hits keep coming. This is awful, I feel so bad for both of them. We now drive over to get Paul clothes from the same apartment house from which we moved Bryant. We are waiting for an argument out of Bryant, but fortunately that does not happen. It takes a couple of days for Leigh to have her surgery. She is in a trauma hospital and her surgery gets bumped time after time. Paul never leaves her side, not even to eat or get clothes. He feels responsible for this accident. Watching him in the hospital I realize the events of the past month have bonded them as tightly as super glue.

I want to let Leigh come home to our house to recover, but I cannot. Bryant is still quite vulnerable and any chaos or change can set him off. I do not trust him enough to recognize her. I cannot get my head around him waking up confused and not knowing where he is and then seeing a stranger in the house. He is getting better and better, but outbursts are still the norm. Leigh's mom and dad come to town, and she recovers in a hotel close to the hospital. I feel bad about the situation, but I cannot risk it. I do not want to rock the boat.

Monday morning Steve leaves for Florida, and a reporter comes by to visit with James and Bryant. Bryant becomes really irrational. He keeps saying over and over again that he loves the Gorge, and he does not want anything bad said about it. James is excited to talk to a reporter and is irritated at Bryant's response. He wants his moment to shine. He deserves his moment to shine.

Looking at Bryant sitting on his couch (but in our house), I think how strange this must all seem to him. The young man who cannot remember anything after falling asleep, who is dazed and confused about everything, now sees his furniture and his things, in our house. This must be as confusing as the wild smiley face balloon in the rehab center. He was right when he said back in the rehab center, "it is all messed up, it's just not right."

Bryant is getting more and more worked up. He is up on his feet, pacing back and forth across the room, opening and closing his hands. He is starting to have memories of his camping gear and wants to know where it is. I sense his mood is spiraling out of control and things could get ugly quickly. My main priority is to keep Bryant calm.

I look over at the reporter, who is in a deep conversation with James, and say: "I need you to leave, I am sorry, but I need you to leave."

The reporter pauses and looks at me in complete confusion. Having been so involved with their conversation they have not paid any attention at all to Bryant. I nod my head in his direction.

Without raising my voice I repeat myself, "I need you to leave, now."

He looks at me in disbelief. I do not have time or space in my life right now to deal with manners. Standing, I usher him to the door. This is our first real incident since Bryant has been home and I want to regain control before it gets out of hand. With a huff and hurried exit, I finally get him out the door. I never hear from him again.

Spending the rest of the afternoon redirecting Bryant's attention to other things, I finally take him to the movie store. He has always loved movies, especially action-adventure. I am being careful what movies we select. He is no longer taking anti-seizure medication and there is a chance blinking lights could trigger one. His brain is impressionable. I do not want him watching violence or things of that nature. If he is being "reborn," I want him to ease into the adult stuff and spend some time experiencing the kinder, gentler things in life. If I could get him to watch, _The Walton's_, or _Little House on the Prairie_, I would, but fat chance of that. We spend quite a bit of time picking out movies on which we can agree. His thoughts are now on movies, and he quickly forgets about the reporter and his anger. When we check out the young man behind the counter asks if I want to upgrade to a "one-price-for-all" plan. All the movies you can rent for a year plan. I tell him to sign me up for it. We could be in for a long year. The car rides to and fro are getting easier for Bryant and me. They still leave him feeling a little off balance; however, he is starting to get his depth perception back.

Another reporter is due at our house early the next morning. I do not want a repeat of yesterday. I quietly let myself out the front door and hang out on the porch watching for him. I meet him out in the driveway and explain to him, that now is not a good time. I am really nervous and keep looking around for Bryant or James to come outside to check on me. The last thing I want is a scene in front of the reporter. I am careful what I say to him because I know anything I say is on-the-record. He is kind and sympathetic and left right away. James is disappointed, but given the circumstances it was the right thing to do.

The reporter writes up a story, regardless of interviewing us, and the next day it is on the front page of the newspaper and on one local news channel. I do not want Bryant to know about it. The reporter handled the story with class. It is quite touching. He apparently interviewed the park ranger and he said he had never seen such brotherly love. The ranger said something about being convinced the only way Bryant survived was the love and attention James had given to his brother. I am so moved by these comments. Some of the facts are not completely right, but then again we had not been interviewed. The boy scouts are given a lot of attention, and it makes for a sensational story. I feel sorry James and Ace do not get to tell their side of the story; they are not given the credit they so rightfully deserve.

Chapter 42
Weathering the Onslaught

"Even if I knew that tomorrow the world would go to pieces; I would still plant my apple tree."
– Martin Luther

I am not prepared for the reaction the morning the story breaks. Walking through the therapy door all heads turn our way and the therapists are all abuzz. This is Bryant's fifteen seconds of glory and I do not want him to know about it. They all read the story and want to comment on it. I quickly change the subject time and again. I pull them aside as quickly as possible and explain to them Bryant will be upset if he knows the story broke and not to mention it. I am not exactly sure why it is such a big deal to him; I don't know if it is his love of the Gorge or his embarrassment over the accident. They act as if they have a celebrity in their midst. Keeping this quiet is going to be tougher than I think.

We keep several more appointments that day and somehow make it through without Bryant hearing about the article. I feel so deceitful and hate keeping the information from him. To be perfectly honest, I probably wanted to protect myself, from him being angry and disappointed in me.

I watch the evening news report upstairs in my bedroom with the door closed and the volume turned down low so Bryant will not hear it. It is the first chance I have to see the news. They end the story saying something about the mother calling for more cell phone capabilities in that area. A lot of naturalists are not going to be happy with me, I think to myself. That part alone would send

Bryant into a frenzy; he is a purist when it comes to nature.

The first full week is really tough on all of us. Getting my arms around therapies, medications and a new "norm" is taking a great deal of concentration. Reminding everyone to keep the windows and doors locked and carrying the key in my pocket is an adjustment for all of us. I am grateful I no longer have customers calling me; it is the one bright spot in my new hectic schedule.

Bryant's car is a big worry for me. I continue to tell him it is not working and redirect him. Much to my surprise, it is not such a big issue for him. I think he is afraid to drive at this point, objects coming at him are still unnerving to him. We are both trying to understand the boundaries of our new lives.

He is quiet and pensive, looking like a deer in headlights. I am on edge, blunt, direct, consumed by keeping such a rigorous schedule and still constantly on the alert for things that could cause a blow up. My family starts to call me Nurse Ratchet from the movie _One Flew Over the Cuckoo's Nest_. I agree, I am wound pretty tight.

Bryant's recovery is happening at warp speed. It doesn't seem like it when you are living minute-to-minute, but after the first week he only needs to be reminded of something once, and it comes back. We are introducing things slowly, but when you think about the million little things you do in a day, from brushing your teeth, to writing it is amazing. Although his handwriting at this time is weak, he is able to type and use a Palm Pilot as a calendar. He quickly starts calling it his brain. The therapists want him responsible for recording his schedule and daily activities.

Losing his memory when he sleeps is strange since he does not forget the new things he has learned that day, or the day before that. Bryant only forgets about the accident and why things are different. I believe the confusion is because mentally when he wakes, he is at a younger age and everything was different back then. When he first opens his eyes, I would look younger, he would not be as physically advanced and he would be in a different bedroom, everything is different and it is confusing and scary to him.

And then, one day he walks out of his bedroom as if it is no big deal. After all, it is normal to wake up and remember where you are, or who the people around you are. He stands there....and then it dawns on him: He always forgets about the accident and how it confuses him when he naps, and he is surprised he remembers. I am ecstatic, we high five it. It gives us hope that one day he will wake up in the morning after a long sleep and remember. I look around the house, but there is no one else with whom to share the news. I call Steve in Florida and leave a message on his voice mail. I miss him; I miss the "us" we used to be.

Bryant continues expecting to be treated with respect. One day, while talking with his therapist out in the lobby after his appointment, I mention something about his handwriting being weak. Bryant is standing next to me, and he is livid. On our way out to the car he looks at me with disgust.

"How could you talk about me like that," he demands? "Right there in the middle of the room where everyone can hear you."

I look down at the key to avoid his gaze and push the button to unlock the car doors. I know he is right! I was wrong.

"I am sorry, I should not have done that. I will never do that again."

Sometimes sorry is simply not enough. He is insecure and I crossed a line, publicly humiliating him. I had known when I did it that it was wrong. I did not want to ask him to wait in the hall so I had seized the moment and had embarrassed him. What I don't know is that Bryant believes he is normal and his handwriting is fine. He is embarrassed and frustrated with me because I see it differently. He doesn't understand that his communication skills are not yet sophisticated enough to express how he wants things to go down, and neither do I. The only control he has over the situation is to act out.

He refuses to get in the car with me. I beg him to get in. He takes off walking toward the sidewalk. I get out of the car and run after him, chasing him down trying again and again to get him in the car. He refuses to speak to me. The thought crosses my mind that he knows how important it is to me that he not walk home down the five lane road without me. He wants to make me squirm, and it is working. He turns his back to me and takes off walking. I have no choice. I cannot go home without him. I follow behind him in my car, with the flashers blinking, begging him to get in the car. He refuses to even look at me or to speak to me. The sight of him still as thin as a prepubescent boy, favoring his left leg, wearing a blue neck brace and looking straight ahead while walking down the busy street is crushing me. I finally call James and ask for help. Bryant is almost home by the time James arrives, but he is willing to get into James' car.

I am greatly shaken by the turn of events today. I am reminded of the straightjacket scene, when he barricaded himself in the room at the rehab center. It is not quite so funny to be on the receiving end of his stubbornness. I learn a valuable lesson that day. I am embarrassed by my actions both in the waiting room and in the car. I realize I cannot do everything by myself and that I must call for help when I need it.

That afternoon while Bryant is inside with James, I go out to survey my garden. Spring has turned into full-blown summer. It is hot and sticky outside and my garden looks bad. It looks as if a war has been waged here. The Cicadas are gone, except for an occasional dead body a bird hasn't eaten yet. Surprisingly, the reminders of their invasion into our world come up in both expected and unexpected ways. Our yard looks as if a giant aerator has plowed through it, leaving numerous holes every inch or so. Wrapping my arms around myself to offer myself some comfort, I realize I am confident these gaps will fill in over time. I know now this is the time for recovery.

The trauma of the summer is evident. The trees, both the hardened mature ones and supple young ones have suffered. From where I stand every tree appears to have some damage, none are spared. It appears they will bear those scars for the rest of their lives. At first glance it looks as if the young tender trees have been the hardest hit. I really don't know how they will survive, but they do, in time. Mother Nature is admirable. Looking at these young branches split open with their insides exposed, it seems impossible that they will survive. The younger trees, although scarred, continue to grow and flourish, hardly losing a branch.

I discover over time it is the more mature trees that actually suffer the most. The older the hardwood is, the less likely the branches will recover. As the years go by, the scarred, weakened branches fall from the trees, self-pruning themselves with every windstorm, while the young, supple trees take the damage in stride.

Chapter 43

New Growth

"Sometimes if you want to see a change for the better, you have to take things into your own hands."
– Clint Eastwood

Bryant's strength continues to grow throughout the month, as does my waistline. Now that I am home, I need comfort and find it once again in food; same old story for me, different year. I am not sleeping much at night as my sleeping patterns are severely altered. I worry about Bryant and wake several times a night to check on him.

Unbeknownst to me, he is now able to climb steps. I do not realize he can, but he walks right up the steps one day and into my bedroom where I keep the monitor and I follow him.

He quickly looks around my room, which was his room growing up, and without hesitation walks over to the video screen, "What's this?"

Luckily I turned the monitor off this morning. I think I can bluff my way out of this one.

"It allows me to hear you, should you develop a seizure in the middle of the night," I answer.

He looks at the monitor and pushes the button on the top, and the screen comes to life.

"I don't want you watching me," he states.

With that he steps back down the stairs and walks into his room. He looks around the room and quickly spots the camera, which he had never noticed before, unplugs it and hands it to me.

I completely underestimated his skills, not only of climbing stairs, but his skills of perception. That is the end of monitoring his nightly movements... and the end of my sleeping.

Time marches on, the world spins, and before we know it, we are all sitting around the table celebrating Paul's twenty-third birthday. It is the middle of July and I set up the same round tables I had for the "graduation party that never was." I move them outside to the front porch overlooking the pond. Now that the Cicadas are gone, we can go back outside again.

I look around the table. It is really impressive, our patched up little family: Bryant in his neck brace, Leigh in her back brace. Paul, Elizabeth, and James are here as well. Steve is home and I am grateful. This is a huge celebration for us. Paul and Leigh are leaving tomorrow. He is going to take Leigh home to her parents on the east coast, and he is going to stay there with her for rest of the summer. While he is there, he will be looking into Officer Candidate School. He is really leaving, and probably never coming back home to live near us. Leigh's back surgery has moved this along. She needs to go home, and he needs to be with her. I have barely seen him as he has spent every moment of the past month with her and her mother. He has been as protective and caring of Leigh as I have been of Bryant. I miss him already.

Rose and Bernard are here as well, and a funny thing has happened, it is a non-event. I am so preoccupied that it does not bother me. I have a new power about me. It does not matter what I imagine they think about me, what really matters is what I think about myself. They really do not know who I am. It is that simple. They are good people, but we do not really know each other, having misunderstood each other completely for years. Open, honest communication between us has been non-existent.

I took back the power in my own home, without even knowing it happened. All this time I wanted to blame Steve's parents and really all I had to do was take my own place, to not feel (or be) inferior. I had given away my power, and when I did, it allowed someone else to fill in. I have made a huge shift in my own personal growth.

Bryant is having a tough time coming to grips with the new living conditions, the rules, and the new "him." It can be depressing at times. Rose and Bernard are shocked when they see him. They have stayed away since the driveway incident and graduation. They do not know anything that has transpired since the ICU. I guess they thought he would simply get up and be the old Bryant. We need a diversion for Bryant and they offer to take him on a camping/fishing trip to get him away for a while. I am so grateful. I know every week brings about new growth and strength for him, and one week older at warp speed is huge. I am hoping a week will change a great deal of things for him right now.

Allowing Bryant to go with them is also a real testament to my resolve to make things right between us. Trusting them with my precious child at this stage says much. Although we have not always seen eye to eye, I know them to be, loving and caring grandparents. I am sure they will watch over him and care for him.

We finish up the yellow cake with homemade chocolate icing, a family favorite. One of Paul's gifts is a small red toolbox. Bernard gave it to Steve the first year we were married, he even put Steve's name on it. My husband polished it up to give to Paul. He filled it with tools, to pass it onto the next generation. I cannot help thinking this is really a funny symbol, as all three generations are anything but handy.

I stand out in the driveway watching as Paul and Leigh drive away. I have a lump in my throat and want to cry. I know in my heart he is leaving home for good. He will not be back to live, only as a visitor. I know my job as a mother is to give my children wings and the courage to use them, but I do not want him to go. I do not want him to leave the nest. I fight the urge to run after him, and stand there and wave instead.

As I walk back inside; I am greeted by both Ali and Sadie. I now have two dogs for the summer. Did I mention Sadie, Paul's dog is a lovable, slobbery boxer? I am going to need to make adjustments, once again. I want to support him; it seems the least I can do. I find one dog alone is fairly calm, two dogs, well they can be pretty rambunctious. They are tearing through the house chasing each other; as slobber slides out of the side of Sadie's mouth.

With both Bryant and Leigh cared for, I now have my first guilt-free week. It is a really good week. I open up all of the windows and doors and leave the keys in a drawer. It is great, once again, to have non-canned air fill the house. Funny thing, when I open the windows, I find several dead Cicadas trapped between the window and the screen. It is a sharp reminder of the carnage of the summer.

It is a good week with James, Elizabeth and the dogs. I spend the week helping Elizabeth get her things organized for her new adventure in San Diego. She has a long list of items she will need for her dorm, some we will purchase out there, some we pack away in boxes to go with us in her car. She will be leaving us before long. Soccer practice starts the day after my birthday. I know better, now that I am an older mother, nothing will ever be the same. She is here, but emotionally she is already gone.

Rose and Bernard bring Bryant home. The week flew by really fast. They were wonderful with him, and he really enjoyed a week of quiet fishing. He had a great time with his grandparents. They both are surprised and comment on how tender Bryant is. We see him as stronger compared to the wobbly legged son we brought home. I would not have let him go with them if I did not think he was strong enough. It is all about point of reference.

Bryant looks rested and a little older after his trip. He is still thin, gangly and walking with a limp. His neck is still encircled by the brace which forces him to stand very erect. He has such a "young" appearance, you are thrown off by the thick facial hair. He shaves each morning but his beard is thick and tells the truth about his age. Maybe someday the rest of him will catch up, I think to myself.

He talks so softly now, our confident, outgoing son, is only a memory. He still has a far off, vacant look in his eyes. He has experienced things the rest of us cannot imagine and sometimes I don't recognize the person behind those eyes. I don't see Bryant, but a different person looking back at us. This is the hardest part of all for James and me. But all in all, it could be worse, much worse.

Now that he is back from his fishing week, Bryant will be starting his driving class at the rehab center. I am afraid and he is elated. He has followed the rules and has not tried to drive until he passes the class. I am almost secretly hoping he does not pass. I lie to him and tell him his license is revoked until they can test his reflexes. I feel really bad about this lie. I justify it in my mind that he is a danger on the road to himself and to others right now. I shiver at the thought of him driving in a couple of weeks.

At this stage of his recovery even a day can make a difference in him. I feel like he is growing on fast-forward. The best way I can describe it would be to watch a seedling grow with a time-lapse camera. Growth is happening daily, sometimes hourly but not easily seen by the naked eye. He only needs to be reminded about how something works by either watching someone else or by being told. His reading and writing abilities improve daily. He seems to do really well with technical gadgets, like phones and planners; yet, he still shies away from the computer and video games.

We spend a great deal of time sitting around the kitchen table talking about things, looking at photo albums reliving his life in photos and stories. He is coached on simple daily tasks by the occupational therapist. It is not very long before they cannot teach him much more. Things are coming back quickly to him. It's hard to believe, only weeks before he did not know who I was or how to use a toothbrush. Now he is casting a fishing rod. We continue with all of the therapies for the summer, but by the end of the summer they are not necessary.

I decide not to join the parent support group of traumatic brain injury victims. My child has recovered at a very quick pace. How can I possibly complain to them? How can I ask someone else for support? I think I am suffering "survivor guilt." Bryant should be in a wheelchair right now unable to hold up his own head. This is such a miracle; yet, I have no idea how to cope, how to keep up with these day-to-day changes. For what is he ready, for what isn't he ready for? Am I pushing him too hard or not hard enough? I wish he came with a manual. I am conflicted with my own emotions.

He has a really great sense of humor, which gets better by the day. He still wears the dreaded neck brace. He swam at first with a noodle wrapped around his waist and then one day he pushed it aside and swam freely. With proper nutrition, the vitamins I give him, and the increased physical activities of walking, swimming, and daily living, his muscles quickly strengthen. The increased muscle function helps lessen the severity of his limp. He is walking straighter and stronger day by day.

He takes great pleasure in accomplishing the things I think he cannot do. It is only another form of the wheelchair game, cussing me out while he pushed his own chair. He wants to push my buttons and make me "say" why I don't think something is a good idea. It is so frustrating. He knows I won't say he can't accomplish this or that, I'll only say that I don't think it is a good idea. He is so determined to prove me wrong at every turn.

I cannot say enough wonderful things about his friends at this stage. Someone has stopped by almost every day. With his friends visiting so much, fishing and swimming with him, I eventually need to let him out. They take him out on field trips, out for a drive, visiting other friends, or out to pick up movies and such. I could not keep him a prisoner in his own home indefinitely. I kept him in lock down for quite a while. He has done really well. My mind had made up some really worse case scenarios. We have not had any of the events about which I was so worried. I had feared so much, and either through good planning or sheer luck it has not happened.

Slowly the trips with his friends get longer and longer, the newest trend is to go to concerts at the outdoor venue down the road from us. We are sometimes able to hear the music filtering through the air, which calls to him. I am a nervous wreck the first time he goes. I lecture his friends to death about all the things that could happen. He comes home just fine and happier for the experience.

Bryant wants to show his friends he has not changed, and he

desperately wants to be accepted by them. His friends are your typical young twenty-somethings, and I warn them not to drink around Bryant. I hope they are listening. Like I have said before if you want to know what your children are doing, look at what their friends are doing.

Once his memory returns after naps, I start cutting the sleeping pills in half and then fourths, and then the day comes to not give them to him anymore. This frightens me; I am upstairs, he is downstairs, I no longer have a monitor on him. I do not have the comfort of knowing if he will sleep. He does not sleep well at first, but finally starts sleeping through the night. One day he wakes up and remembers what happened the day before, all about the accident and why he is here!

Bryant looks at me after waking and says, "You can move the dry marker board out of my room now. I don't need it anymore."

His recovery happens without any real incidents, each day a new one with more discoveries. He keeps many of the discoveries to himself. He believes it will all come back to him, and it mostly does. He does not mention these "discoveries" to me and takes it all in stride as a non-event. Men. What are you going to do? They hardly ever make things into a big deal, the way I do.

Finally, he is bored and starts looking for something to do. He is curious as to why he isn't going back to work. He does not believe he is different in anyway. He is certain that he is the same as he was before. He asks to cut the grass, and I am not quite ready for that yet. We use a huge commercial walk behind mower, and it takes some strength. I compromise with him, and he starts doing things in the yard, light gardening and washing cars. I have a wheelbarrow that is not working; he takes it apart and fixes it. I marvel at his reasoning skills. I never imagined he would be able to do something like that again. He is still unpredictable at times, but not that bad. He is learning to calm himself down when he reacts angrily because of the impact to his frontal lobe. He is more and more normal every day. His ability to learn, process and remember new things amazes me.

I am probably suffering more trauma at this stage than he is. He seems to be blissfully unaware (most of the time) that he is different. I am always on edge and looking for the "what ifs." If we have any area of contention, it is over his neck brace. He still has to keep it on, even to sleep. He takes every opportunity he can find to take it off. It is a constant, day long, old battle. I am sure he does not wear it when he sleeps, even though he tells me he is. He now locks his door at night so I cannot check.

Chapter
Driving 44

"A good scare is worth more to a man than good advice."
– Ed Howe

A little over two and a half long months after the accident, the dreaded morning comes for Bryant's first driving lesson. He is ecstatic; I am ill. They do not offer driving lessons at our local occupational therapy facility. We must go back to the rehab center for this. As I approach the building with Bryant in the front seat with me, it seems surreal. Everything has moved so quickly. When we were in the thick of it, I thought time was standing still. Now, here I am facing my worst fear, testing for Bryant to be allowed to drive again. All I can hear in my mind are the words *"most traumatic brain injury patients die in a car crash, their reaction time is so much slower."*

Staring up at the building, I cannot help but think that the last time we were here we were still arguing about him using the bathroom by himself, and now someone thinks he can drive. I cannot accept this new twist; yet, I knew this day was coming. I feel a knot in my stomach. We need to go in through another entrance for the Occupational Therapy Unit. Following the directions, I turn the corner. The car suddenly goes bump and then up and down. My knuckles tighten on the steering wheel, and I feel my stomach wretch. These are the same bumps we went over in the ambulance not so long ago. I am having a serious flashback, and I feel my chest tightening. I look over at Bryant, who is totally unaware of the bumps. I slow the car down and inch over them as slowly as possible, fearing that these bumps could cause serious setbacks.

Bryant continues talking as I park the car, no reaction at all. He is excited, and he is scared. I wipe my sweaty palms on my shorts before walking inside. I look over at him, remembering to myself how devastating those same speed bumps were only a few months back. I don't mention it to him, instead I take it all in stride like any mother would do.

I am expecting and hoping this will go on for weeks, but like everything else they completely release him to drive within a couple of days. My immediate reaction is to argue with them. This cannot be possible, but here we are. He also discovers he never had his license revoked. He could legally drive at any point in time, amazing. However, they do convince him it was a good thing to test his reactions before starting to drive again. I am pretty sure he knows I lied to him, but gratefully he does not mention it to me. I try to be completely honest with my children. This experience has changed everything about me. I hardly know who I am anymore.

The parent of any child that has just gotten their license can understand the trepidation one feels when your child drives away for the first time. I have done it four times and, let me tell you, that is a piece of cake compared to watching Bryant drive out the driveway in his cherry red Jetta. Freedom comes with a car. Some kids are ready for it and some are not. I am really certain Bryant is not, but I am not in control of this situation. He is the most bull-headed person I ever met in my life. There is no stopping him, he is legally an adult.

He drives his car for a few days, and suddenly he is sixteen again. He loves it and is now over his fear of driving. He wants to drive to St. Louis to see his friend Jack. No way am I going to let him drive that car to St. Louis by himself. I am not a stupid woman. If I tell him no, then the fight will start. I will wake up one morning, and he will simply be gone. I use the distraction technique. Each time he brings it up, I change the subject and redirect him. I never give him an answer. He is still forgetful and is easily distracted right now.

Steve is in Florida working again. I make it through the entire week without giving Bryant an answer by redirecting him. I explain the situation to Steve on the phone. The minute he gets home, Bryant asks him if he can drive to St. Louis. Steve says, "sure." I want to kill him. I cannot believe my ears. How could he cave like this after a few seconds? How could he completely disrespect my wishes and grant permission after I danced around the issue without a showdown for an entire week? I am enraged with him; Bryant is of course in love with him. Once again, I am the bad guy and Steve is his friend.

I pull Steve aside and tell him, "that since he gave Bryant permission, he will need to go with him."

He tells me. "I am babying Bryant; he is perfectly fine to drive by himself. That he has done it a hundred times in the past."

The words "babying" comes back to me, it was not that long ago when Paul had used those words. He had become a new person after that night. Maybe I am wrong. Regardless, I cannot stop the two of them.

Bryant packs his bags and is out the door within the hour. Off he goes on a six-hour drive to St. Louis by himself. This is more stress than I can take. I head over to the apartment house with Steve in tow. We work on cleaning up the vacant apartment Bryant had occupied. Paul has decided to stay out east and is coming home before the new semester starts to empty out his apartment. It seems like a good idea to get started on the cleaning of his apartment as well. I missed the small window of opportunity to find new student renters for the year. Most of them made their rental decisions before they left last spring. The entire three-story house is now empty, with no renters on the horizon; lost revenue when we so desperately need it.

I watch the clock, as the minutes tick by while scrubbing the kitchen cabinets with much more aggression than they deserve. Steve and I argue the entire time. I am sick with worry, while Steve is telling me I am too protective. Our marriage and the weather have turned into a storm, with thunder and lightning cracking all around us while the rain pelts the windows. I scrub even harder, trying to ignore the tightening in my chest.

Four hours later we get a phone call from Bryant. He has wrecked his car in the pouring rain and is having trouble driving it. He mentions that the air bags deployed. The car is still moving, and he is limping along toward St. Louis, along the shoulder. He is having trouble and has to go slowly because the car pulls sharply to one side. He thinks he may need some help, and he suggests calling his friend Jack.

We tell him to pull over at the next exit and wait for us. I do not want to leave him alone for four hours. My first instinct is to jump in the car and go. Steve then tells me he cannot go because he has to head back to Florida on Monday. His flight has already been booked. I realize calling Jack is the best thing to do. He is only two hours away from Bryant. I quickly reach Jack on the phone, and he starts out immediately to go and retrieve Bryant and take him on to St. Louis. I give him permission to make an assessment of the car. I cannot get much information out of Bryant. Jack promises to call me the moment he gets there.

I do not understand why, but the gravity of the situation does not seem to be registering with Steve. He is in denial. I want to jump in the car and fetch my child home. I know the best plan was to call Jack, but waiting those two hours is very hard. All I can do is glare at my husband. It is everything I can do to not pack my bags and walk away from him at this moment. This is one of the lowest moments of our marriage.

Steve is really quiet, and somehow I think he finally gets it. The reality of what he has allowed slowly sinks in during the long two-hour stretch. Not knowing the outcome of our child's fate is beginning to unnerve him, and he is completely responsible for this situation. He should back me up, I am the point person here, and I should be allowed to make the decisions.

I look over at Steve. I am really upset with him and me for allowing this to happen.

"If Bryant is seriously hurt, if he has hit his head and suffered another concussion, we are through," I say.

Steve doesn't say anything as we wait. I spend the time furiously scrubbing. I take out all my stress and anxiety on any piece of dirt I can find, wanting to wash away all of the dirt from our lives.

The two hours tick by slowly. When we finally get the phone call, Jack tells us the situation is not good. It looks to him like the car is possibly totaled. He does not know how Bryant drove it at all as the axle is bent and the tire is leaning in and rubbing the fender. We call a tow truck, and Jack takes Bryant to St. Louis.

Steve makes plans for me to go and pick Bryant up on Monday. Steve and I argue about this. It is his mess. He should be the one to go and retrieve both Bryant and the car. I want us to go get Bryant now. I call Bryant, and he adamantly refuses to come home early. Jack reassures me he has him and will take good care of him until Monday. It is one of those situations where the damage has already been done. Steve needs this consulting job, and we need this extra money. It is not a good weekend at our house.

On Monday I head over to St. Louis. Jack has to go to work that morning, and I call him to let him know I am on my way. When I speak with Jack, he is very blunt.

"What were you doing letting him drive over here by himself? He is in no condition to drive that far."

I agree with him. There is no point in explaining the situation to him. I should have thrown myself in front of the car and not let him drive out. I am feeling responsible and plain tired. The harder I try the more blockades come up. There is one hurdle after another. With pitfalls all along the trail, anyone of them could be fatal.

I had done my best, and my best was not good enough. I should know by now to trust myself. I am angry; I let myself be talked into something I knew was wrong. The men in my family have such strong opinions and such drive that it is hard to stand your ground sometimes. I had always been the kind of person who resisted peer pressure and had no problem standing firm. That is who I thought I was. I am beginning to realize that I am not that person.

His car is in the shop for the next six weeks waiting for parts. When I speak with the man working on repairs to Bryant's Jetta, he tells me that he believes the accident was the result of rain and bald tires. Bryant hydroplaned and crashed into a mile marker, deploying the side airbags. The force pushed him into the grass and dirt causing both of his axles to bend. In my mind the accident seemed far worse than he makes it sound. My imagination had Bryant's head bouncing around, air bags out everywhere, and him unable to see over the airbag to drive.

"He hit really hard," he continues. "Since the car is almost new, and it is leased we will not total it out, we'll fix it."

I shake my head in amazement. With everything else we had happening, checking the tires on his less than one-year-old car never crossed our minds. I thought it was Bryant's driving ability, never dreaming it was the tires. Bryant does not have a mark on his face. It does not look like he hit his head, but he has been shaken up pretty hard, as have we all.

The car accident makes Bryant seem a little more cautious for a while, but he bounces back quickly, much faster than Steve and I are bouncing back. Our relationship is strained. I think I read somewhere around eighty-five percent of all marriages suffering a traumatic event with a child end in divorce. Our foundation is good, but the last few years have been shaky to say the least. I do not know where we are heading, but our relationship will go nowhere if we do not get on the same page. The fall from the cliff has brought all of our cracks to the surface. If it had not been for the accident at the Gorge, maybe we would have gone along with our separate lives. That is no longer acceptable to either of us. It appears that what is wrong with "us," both together and apart, is now becoming blatantly obvious to us both. I want more; he wants more. We really do not know how to get there.

I am grateful Bryant does not have a car to drive until we get his car repaired and back home, and I am not in any hurry for that to happen. Each week he is progressing faster and faster. Now that Paul has moved and Elizabeth is moving out, Bryant no longer wants to live at home with us. He is still in denial and proclaims there is nothing wrong with him. I know this is going to be a problem down the road. I am hoping it is still a little further down the road, but probably not. At the rate things are going, and at the speed of his recovery, I feel like I am on a rocket ship headed for the unknown.

Chapter
Good-byes 45

"I am convinced that life is 10% what happens to me and 90% how I react to it. And so it is with you...We are in charge of our attitudes."
– Charles Swindoll

It is suddenly the middle of August and we are on our way to San Diego. Steve, Bryant, Elizabeth and I are in her car. This is my first trip out West and I am really excited. I had insisted we spend every vacation in Florida visiting with Steve's parents. I wanted my children to know their grandparents and since they did not make it up North often, this was a sacrifice I was willing to make. Steve was all for the Florida vacations because they were free room and board. I always wanted to see the West and really did not want to miss out on this trip.

I am grateful to be here. At the last moment I thought Bryant and I would not be able to make the trip. He is still in his neck brace. The last x-rays show he still needs more time to heal. The doctor almost did not release him for this long car ride. Apparently car rides are hard on necks, who knew? Bryant will only be in the car one way. We are leaving her car there and flying home. The doctor reluctantly gave us the clearance only hours before we left. I can hardly believe that we kept him in this neck brace for almost three months. I am constantly telling him to put it back on.

I need closure before I can say good-bye to my one and only daughter. I need to see the college, her dorm, and the area. James is staying behind with friends, and we are making the long drive to Elizabeth's new home. Steve has planned out the whole trip. I am simply along for the ride.

We are going a little out of our way to visit the Grand Canyon. This is Steve's idea and I do not give it much thought. It sounds like a place I should see, and since we are right here, why not? I am sitting in the middle seat in the back of the Saturn Vue. The far back, the floorboard and the seat next to me are filled to the top with Elizabeth's belongings. I feel claustrophobic and short of breath. I don't know what is wrong. My heart is racing, and I don't feel well. I am sweating profusely. I feel like I might throw up.

"Steve, pull the car over, pull it over now," I tell him.

The car hardly stops before I jump out. I am sucking air and sweating. It feels like my heart is going to beat right out of my chest. I really don't know what my problem is. I walk around for a while, catch my breath, slow down my heart and give myself a pep talk, "this is silly, get back in the car."

After a while I get back into the car. I am concentrating on the fabric on the seat. Looking at the back of the front seat and at Bryant's head bobbing around, trying to stay focused on anything. I have never been one to get carsick. I am currently in the back seat. We are rotating drivers and views and I tell myself it must be the back seat. I see a sign that says we are almost to the Grand Canyon. The tightness in my chest is getting more intense. I am so relieved when we get to the parking lot and I can get out of the car. I am feeling better.

We make our way over to the canyon. Everyone around me is "ahh-ing" and "ooh-ing" over the beauty of the canyon. I look out and all I can see is a huge drop off. I see small children close to the edge. I look over this way and there are signs warning people of possible death from falling. I am feeling dizzy and am having a panic attack. What was I thinking? I try to calm myself down by concentrating on my breathing: one, two, three, four counts in; one, two, three, four counts out.

I want to grab these children and have a long talk with their parents. They don't understand. I feel the need to educate them. I want to tell them to not let their children play next to the edge.

Instead, I shut my mouth and try to hold the panic inside. Elizabeth and Bryant get too close to the edge and I am panicking, yelling at them. We do not stay long.

If you go along in life and don't make plans, and only follow along, sometimes you end up in places you shouldn't be. What was I thinking? Why didn't I put my foot down and pick any of the other beautiful sights to see out West? Did we really need to be at the biggest drop off around? I mean really. My sister later tells me she was wondering what I was thinking. The truth is, I didn't think, I blindly went along. I begin to wonder, *how often do I do that in life?*

It is really hard to say good-bye to Elizabeth. She is such an even-keeled person, so easy and dependable. Today is my forty-sixth birthday, Happy Birthday to me. Bryant and I are scheduled to fly back home this afternoon. Steve is leaving as well to head back to Florida for the next two weeks. I am just plodding along doing what I can. Bryant is still very tender. He is shy and reticent. He is unsure about everything, there is newness and freshness to all he experiences. The plane ride should be interesting.

He is sad and wants his old life back. I understand, so do I. I want my children back, I want my husband back, and I miss my business. Although I am really busy with the family and all of the changes, I miss feeling important, making decisions, having people tell me how creative and talented I am. I don't miss the hours or the work. I miss the accolades. It seems no matter what I do, someone in the family is constantly rolling their eyes at me or telling me I'm wrong. Where is the gratitude in mother-hood?

The plane ride goes well. We develop a bit of a problem when I want Bryant to sit next to the window and not the aisle. He is onto me and makes me explain why. When I explain to him that I do not want the luggage to shift and fall on his head, he rolls his eyes at me, and sits down in the aisle seat. This forces me to climb over him to get to the window. It is a long flight and every time we hit turbulence, I can't help but glance at the overhead bin to make sure it doesn't open. We have suffered so many setbacks, I imagine this is completely possible.

When we get home Bryant, announces he is moving out of the house. He is not willing to live at home with us/me anymore. If I were a stronger woman I would say, "Good luck and have a great life," but I am not. I am too grateful to have him alive. I cannot completely let go of him; yet, I have no real authority over him legally, although we are his only means of support. With Paul permanently moving out East, Bryant wants to move into Paul's old apartment. We discuss his moving out when his father comes home. I already knew what he was going to say; "Sure why not?"

Steve and Bryant met with the school counselor a while back and he has agreed to go back to school. He is not really up to classroom work, but has secured an internship at the zoo. He will be working in the reptile and large cat houses. He has always been great with animals, so this is a positive step in the right direction.

The apartment is right next to the zoo and I don't really have an argument except, I don't think it is a good idea for him to live away from us. I believe it is too soon for him to leave. He is so tender, so vulnerable, as am I. He has his father's support; I am outnumbered and no one is listening to me. I finally agree. At least in our own apartment house, we keep some measure of control. If he moves in with friends, we will not keep any control.

Sadie runs away and disappears for a few days, we finally find her at the pound. We are so happy to retrieve her. I did not want to let Paul down by losing his dog! We bring her and a few friends home with her. Unknown to us she is covered in fleas. We have Sadie and Ali dipped, but not before the entire house is full of fleas. I "bomb" the house, and dip the dogs several more times before we get it under control.

Paul comes home for a quick visit. He cleans out his apartment at the end of August, and takes, Sadie, back to the East coast with him. Bryant moves into Paul's old apartment the first of September and takes, Ali, with him.

In and out, back and forth, it's a revolving door. Steve is now more involved since the car accident. He handpicks two of Bryant's good friends to move into the two other open apartments. We are not efficient landlords. Being soft-hearted parents always seems to get in the way. Our kids live there while we collect rent on the other apartments. We have a hard time collecting rent and deposits; one sad sob story from a young renter and we cave. I know financially renting makes a great deal of sense; personally I think it stinks. Oh my, until you clean up college-kid dirt out of an apartment that you failed to get a deposit on....you have not lived.

Chapter
Testing **46**

"Trust in the Lord with all your heart. Do not depend on your own understanding. In all your ways, remember Him. Then He will make your paths smooth and straight."
– Proverbs 3:5-6

After Bryant moves out and Steve is back in Florida, I stand in my living room surveying the damage. It is void of furniture and people. In the last few months it has been a home, a business, an apartment and now empty. I do not have any idea what to do with the space. I dismantled my business to be a full-time mother to my handicapped son. Now, here I am just a few months later, alone in the house except for James who avoids me, and I'm unemployed. My roles in life are changing so fast, not even a dog to keep me company anymore. I really do not know what I am going to do with myself.

I struggle, trying to remember the different stages of grief. My son has not died, but the son I knew and loved is not really here anymore. Someone else is here with a different smile, personality and walk. Maybe my son will reemerge, and maybe he will not. I did not get to grieve for the loss of my son, and I miss him. He was the son that always came in with a smile and said, "Mom, tell me about your day, how are you?" He always treated me like a person, not just a mom.

Now, I am entering my angry stage. At least I think that's what's happening. Steve gets to go on with his life, like nothing has happened. My whole life has been turned upside down. He is siding once again with the boys, and here I am left holding the bag. I am sad, I am angry, and I feel like a victim to my own life. I know if I change myself I can change my world, I know that. It would take energy, and I am tired, bone tired. Right now, all I want is to feel sorry for myself. I want pity, I want love, and I want intimacy. I do not want to be alone anymore.

I do exactly what I always do, stuff those emotions down deep inside myself and start baking for the holidays; comforting myself the only way I know how. I regained at maximum speed almost all of the weight I had lost. Nothing says love to me like a hot chocolate chip cookie. I make breads, peanut butter cookies, snicker doodles and double chocolate mint cookies. I have acquired really good recipes over the years, and I am a good baker. I am dropping cookies off all over town. People marvel at how one woman can make so many different varieties.

I try to go back to work. I go out on a couple of calls with previous customers. Funny, I cannot do it. When I physically shut the door on the business; clearly, I shut a creative door in my mind. It is more than I can comprehend, but I cannot access that part right now. I do not know if it will ever come back. Besides, I want to be here for James and for Bryant.

I drive over to the apartment often to get Bryant out of bed for his internship. He is so tired and groggy in the morning. It is a constant battle. I think he is drinking, but I cannot prove it. He has stopped taking all medications. He has not improved at all since he left home. I think he may even be backsliding a bit. I am worried and do not know if it is because of the injury or his lifestyle choices. I am afraid it is the combination.

Several times I ask Steve to intervene. It is a really heated situation when Bryant's old girlfriend starts dating one of his friends, who is living in the apartment house. Not a good move. I am afraid Bryant could hurt him. He is angry with his friend for the betrayal. Although his outbursts are fewer and less frequent, he is completely thrown off his game having to deal with this. His friends divide up on the matter. They are either her friends, or his. It's difficult to be both. Steve sweeps in and takes Bryant back to Florida with him, all for the cost of a last minute plane ticket.

I could talk to Bryant about anything before the accident, but not now. The new Bryant is closer to his father. He gets angry when he is around me. I seem to bring out the worst in him. I feel so helpless at times.

Steve is frustrated as well. Bryant will absolutely not listen to me. Something in our relationship has changed. I do not know if it is because only a few months ago I had to be the bad guy, time and time again, or if he is different now and prefers his father. We were always so close, and it is a real loss for me.

James is also struggling with our new life. His high school soccer teammates are indifferent to his struggles. He discovers that what they find important, he no longer thinks of as important. He is "lost." When a teammate tells him that he wants to go out in a blaze of glory and is going to jump off a cliff instead of growing old, James is upset. Later James confronts him over this crude remark after what happened to his brother. The young man not even thinking remarks "Who gives a fuck about your brother," and James is over the lunch table beating him into the ground. James has never been violent, and we are all concerned. He has always had his brothers and sister to go to with his problems. They are no longer here. Bryant is caught up in his own problems and would not understand how hard it is for James. James is lost. James and I make an emergency trip out to visit his brother, Paul. It helps for a while. I obtain counseling for him after we get home.

Steve and I have a "come to Jesus meeting." I tell him I need him to step up and take control of Bryant and be here for James. This situation is not working, and I simply cannot control it. I am watching Bryant spiral out of control. We need Steve home, and we need him home now. He is planning to stop traveling in January. We do not know what it will do to our income, but it will not be good. He is taking Bryant with him one week a month to Florida. At least it is a way to get him away from his friends and his environment. It's the only thing we know to do right now. Unfortunately, we do not have any legal rights over him. However, we do have a

Visa card and we keep taking him away every chance we get.

We refer to our life events now as BA, (before the accident), and AA, (after the accident). Nothing is the same. Everything has changed.

Steve is coming and going. He is focused on work and paying off bills, along with all of the constant drama with Bryant. Life is not fun. But, hey, our son is alive. We are attending church regularly. I am really beginning to enjoy it.

I ask God to use me, to show me the way. So far I am a little disappointed. Waiting on God is not an easy thing to do. I put my name on the volunteer list for countless projects at church. They have so many people volunteering that no one even calls me back. I finally pitch a fit and get on the Thanksgiving food drive. What a bummer, I want to be used. I even try to volunteer at a homeless shelter and am told they do not need any more help. *Look God, here I am, use me. What are You waiting for?*

I decide to be patient. He must have a purpose for me that I do not see yet. Maybe I am still in the "oven of life," not quite fully baked. Yeah, I'm feeling half-baked. I smile to myself over that one. What kind of cookie will I be when I'm done? I'll probably be an ooey- gooey, soft butter cookie if I don't make some changes. Every day I wake up telling myself I will eat good today, and each night I go to bed knowing I failed. I really don't understand myself.

While driving my car to the apartment house, I look around at the landscape. Spring has turned to summer, and summer to fall, and Thanksgiving is around the corner. Bryant has stopped going to therapy, but we do keep him and James going to different psychologists. They have so much emotional baggage after the accident and the carnage to their lives.

I am picking Bryant up today to take him for cognitive testing. I arrive at his apartment and knock and knock with no answer. I have a key and let myself in. The house is dirty, and dark. Ali is back in the bedroom with Bryant, where Bryant is out cold. Great I think to myself. This is not going to be fun.

Clearly he has been up all night and is not ready for conversation, let alone testing. He is tired. It is a real challenge for me to get him up and dressed. He argues with me the whole time. He is angry with me for waking him up. I remind myself once again to be patient. He has not fully recovered and these things take time. However, I am tired of this. I am tired down to the core of my bones. I am tired of the yelling; this is not easy.

I know I should be going for counseling as well, but I put myself last on the list. I avoid that one. I know I need help, but I focus on trying to control and change my family instead of changing me. I am convinced I am doing it right, that I have all of the answers. I do not even know the questions anymore, let alone the answers. I am hanging on by my fingernails, and I am slipping.

Thankfully, the testing center is not far from his apartment. It is in a beautiful old building, which once upon a time must have been quite a mansion. However, the testing facility is in a low-ceilinged basement with no windows. It is dismal down here. It has been a real challenge to just get my groggy, bleary-eyed son here. He is not in any mood to be here but true to form, the moment we walk through the door his entire attitude changes. He is immediately sweet and meek with all of the employees. The mean, nasty, argumentative boy can turn it on and off on a dime. He is charming and quiet to the receptionist, and she takes him back to meet the doctor. They disappear down the hallway.

They tell me it will take at least two days to finish the testing, and I can leave and come back later.

Ha, I think. They do not know me very well.

I am sitting in a chair in the waiting room, or waiting hallway. I sit here for two hours watching and listening to this doctor. I am not impressed with him at all. Bryant is down the hall working on a computer. I saw him when I went to the bathroom. I may not know much, but I do know my son, and he has never been good on computers not even before the accident. Part of his issues with computers is transference. Transferring information is difficult for him. It does not mean he does not know it; it means that he cannot transfer it in the "normal" method. I am pretty sure he is hung over and am convinced this is part of the problem.

After only two hours the doctor tells me there is really no need to continue. We are standing out in the hallway, and this doctor does not even show enough class to take me back to his office. This reminds me of the harsh lesson I learned during therapy and discussing his progress in the hallway. He puts his hands up over his head and informs me my child is functioning at such a low level there is really no point.

"He will never learn anything new," he tells me. "What he has is what he is going to have. This is all the better he will ever be."

I am distraught, frustrated, and cannot accept this. I don't believe him. I promised Bryant that day in the rehab center that we would get through this and we will, somehow, someway.

I walk over and get Bryant. He does not understand what is happening. He is in a fog today. He seems to be digressing since he has moved out of the house. He wants to know why we are leaving and I cannot get the truth out of my mouth. I tell him I was wrong, and they will not need to continue with the testing; it is all finished.

We stop at McDonald's and eat lunch; we are in a really bad part of town and two different homeless people come up to us begging for money. I look at homeless people in a different light now. I understand now that many of them may have had traumatic brain injuries and are unable to fit into society; without a loving family and insurance, perhaps this would have been the fate of my child. After all, these are all the children of somebody. I know in my heart I am losing him once again. He is spiraling downward and I do not know how to stop it. At this moment, I do not know if I can.

I want a better life for him than the life this doctor is suggesting. Perhaps this doctor suspects alcohol use could be the problem, or perhaps he thinks it is the brain injury. He didn't speculate with me why he performed so low. Bryant is planning to do class room work again in January. I do not see that happening, not the way he is right now.

He has started working nights at a local club. He is telling us he is not drinking, but I am not buying it. Partying is the worst thing he can do for his brain. It cannot recover if he does these things. Can this really be what all of the miracles we witnessed are for, for him to work in a bar, end up a party boy out on the street? I cannot accept this. I asked his psychologist the other day, begged him, to put him in a rehab clinic and take him away from the influence. I want to slow his world down. He said, "No not without Bryant's permission." Bryant will never give permission to lose his freedom again. I really do not know how to help him anymore. I am feeling really low and useless.

Chapter 47
Conquering the Cliff

"Love never fails."
– 1 Corinthians 13:8

Christmas comes and goes. Bryant shows up with acne and a Mohawk, quite hung over and acting like a pubescent smartass. It was difficult enough the first time, but imagine a young teenager with the ability to drive and drink. Paul and Elizabeth come home and that is a highlight. Steve's parents are at our house for the first time ever for Christmas. I should be elated, all four of my children are home.

Rose walks around Christmas Eve crying into her glass of wine and telling me what a miracle it is and how happy she is. She has no idea of how absolutely awful things are. I go into the bathroom and cry. I want to shove Christmas cookies in her mouth to shut her up. My world is falling down around me, and I do not know what to do. I cannot save my son. I heard from his friends he is drinking and driving, and it is only a matter of time before he either kills himself or someone else. I am not seeing the miracle right now.

Christmas is always a big deal at our house. I want the Robert Kincaid, Martha Stewart Christmas all rolled into one; the one I did not have as a poor child. I decorate the mantles, the staircase; everything is strung with garland and lights. Christmas looks good on our beautiful old farmhouse. We always open our gifts in the morning, after Santa has arrived. We are big on traditions. Paul gives Bryant a breathalyzer to measure his alcohol level, and I guess to let me know he is drinking. I do not really know why. He encourages Bryant to breathe into it right after he opens it and sure enough he still has enough alcohol in his system for it to register. Merry Christmas, Ho, Ho, Ho and all that goes with it! I want to be in denial. He has been with us all night since he came home from work at the club. Either he is sneaking it or he is still drunk from the previous night.

I go into the kitchen to prepare our Christmas breakfast after opening the gifts. My stomach is in such knots it is all I can do to get through our Christmas celebration. I resist the urge to throw the waffle batter against the side of the wall. I imagine what it would be like to really let go and show everyone how I really feel. Would they care? I doubt it. So I do what I always do, shove my emotions down and prepare the meal.

Only a couple of days after Christmas we discover Bryant has returned all of his presents to purchase a rappelling rope. He has a 200-foot rope and intends to go tomorrow to rappel the cliff he fell from! I am in a panic. We plead with Bryant, but there will be no stopping him. We cannot be with him every minute and his mind is set. He intends to go back and conquer that cliff. He does not know how to tie off so his friend, who has had one rappelling class, is going to go with him.

I am frantic. Later that evening, after an emergency phone call to his psychologist, the doctor agrees to meet with us. We go to his office, and he tells us this is highly unusual. Bryant is his patient, not us. He is only doing this because he can tell we are in a panic.

He looks at us, "You're angry aren't you, I can tell by your body language."

"Yes," Steve answers him, "I am really angry. We have reached our limit. Maybe it's time for tough love. We cannot be a part of this anymore. We are going to take his car away, make him move out of the apartment house, take it all away. Let him live with his bar friends for a while. Maybe that will be a wakeup call for him."

The doctor thinks about it for a while, taking in Steve's crossed arms and stance and answers him.

"If you think you are angry, think about him. Think about your son. He is one hundred times angrier than you are. His entire life has been taken away from him. He can no longer go to school. He cannot play soccer, his friends do not treat him the same. Everything he is and was is gone. He is really angry. If you think throwing him out to show him how angry you are will help, well you are wrong. All you can do is love him. Just love him." He looks at both of us.

He has taken the fight right out of us. We realize what he is saying is right. We feel really stupid right now, selfish.

"The only way for him to get his life back is to beat the cliff that took his life away from him."

He pauses to let the thought sink into our hearts. "Now this is highly unorthodox for me to be speaking to you and I need to ask you to leave. Love your son, just love him."

With that he ushers us out the door. We thank him. He gives us hope that night and some really good advice.

That night, sitting in our dark, cold car in the driveway of the psychologist's office, Steve and I have a change of heart. We see it through the eyes of our son for the first time. Yes, it has been hard on us, but it has been really, really hard on him. Steve calls him up and asks if he is still planning to go to the Gorge the next day. Bryant says yes, and Steve asks if he can go with him. Bryant is quiet for a while, and he then says that would be great.

The next day, they take off. I am a nervous wreck. I spend the day praying and crying, crying and praying. I can't believe this is happening. What if he falls once again? I tell myself I need to have faith. I am praying for Steve and Bryant, if Steve has to witness him falling to his death it will be the end of everything. The gravity of this day is monumental.

Steve calls me right before Bryant goes over the edge. He has the video camera ready and running. He tells me they tied the rope off, and then Steve panicked: What if the rope wasn't quite long enough? What if there were twenty or so feet without a rope? He tells me he walked around the horseshoe bend and down into the canyon. He checked the rope and it is barely long enough. They brought a 200-foot rope; minus the tie off he estimates it is at least a 180-foot drop! All this time we have been amazed that he survived 150 feet. Another thirty feet is a lot! Down in the bottom of the canyon looking up, he finally realizes the distance and is amazed, how Bryant could have possibly survived. Before it was imagination, this is reality. He cannot believe James was able to find him. It is now the middle of winter and the vegetation is sparse. Without knowing that his brother had gone off the side, it is simply unbelievable. The horror of it all comes rushing at him. He is overwhelmed with emotions while standing at the foot of the cliff. I can hear the panic in his voice. I can tell by his quivering voice that he is shaking.

"Do you think Bryant's friend knows what he's doing," I ask.

"I think so, but we're about to find out."

He then yells up to Bryant and tells him to call me before he comes down.

My phone rings, it is my son. "Mom, I'm here I'm ready to go."

He sounds so excited, almost happy. I can't stop myself, I beg him not to do it.

"Mom, I am hanging up now. I will call you when I get down, I love you." With that the line goes dead.

If you won't bend your knees to God, He has the power to drop you to them. Maybe I didn't get on my knees when Bryant was in the ICU, maybe I didn't get to them when he was in the rehab center, but I have now been dropped to my knees.

I feel the hard wood of the plank floor under my knees. The tears are streaming out of my eyes and down my face. Snot is pouring out of my nose. I wipe it away with the back of my hand. I cannot get off my knees or let go of the phone. It is the only lifeline I have with my son, my husband, and my future. It all hangs in the balance. I cannot stop crying and praying. If the rope breaks, or the knot fails, it is all over. I don't know how we can live with ourselves.

Please God, please let the knot hold, please let this be the moment, the miracle we must have. Let this crazy plan help him find himself. I am begging, I am pleading. I bend over even further, placing my forehead on the floor. I collapse. I lie prostrate begging God for a new beginning, the phone still snug in my hand. I do not move from this spot.

Finally the phone rings, it is probably only fifteen minutes later, but it feels like an eternity.

I grab the phone crying into it, "Yes, what happened?"

I am expecting Steve, but it is Bryant. He is alive.

"Hey, Mom, it's me. I did it. I did it. I beat the cliff. I did it. I wanted you to know I am safe and I don't want you to worry. I'm going to let you go now. Dad took a movie of the whole thing and you can see it when we get home. I love you, bye."

I can barely get the word bye out before he hangs up. He is so happy. I have not heard happiness or excitement in his voice since before he fell. I am hoping the psychologist is right and this is the beginning of a new life for him.

Not even eight months after he fell, he has gone back to beat the cliff. His won't-be-beaten spirit that kept him alive in the canyon, the one that fought to get to the top before anyone found out he had fallen, that fought to wake him up out of the coma, that fought to make him walk, talk, and use the bathroom like a man, this spirit of his that just won't quit, is undeniably strong. He knew what he had to do, he had always known. His drive is unbelievable. Living with children who won't be kept down is hard. At times it is pretty awesome, and right now at this moment it feels awesome. The problem is directing their drive in the right direction; sometimes it's pretty destructive.

I get up off my knees and dance around the room. Thanking God for granting me just one more miracle. Later that night, when Steve comes home, I throw my arms around him. Bryant is following behind and cannot wait to show me the video of his descent. Steve is down at the bottom and if I thought his voice sounded shaky I can hardly see the screen his hand is shaking so badly. I watch the entire descent, and it seems to only take minutes. No time at all. How is it possible? It seems like nothing at all on the video screen, minus all of the emotional baggage. I laugh out loud at these words, from Bryant's friend, yelling out loudly enough for us to hear below: "Call your mother, now," and he does.

Steve and I are both elated. We are finally on the same page. We are now one, I don't know where or when it happened, but what is important is that it did happen. We believe in the miracle of the cliff, we believe in the miracle of love. We are sure there will be a huge turn around now that he has beaten the cliff, that everything will be suddenly different.

Chapter What About Us 48

"When you get to the end of your rope—tie a knot in it and hang on!"
– Eleanor Roosevelt

We are wrong. We find out days later that things have not changed. We let him risk his life, and for what? He is still hanging with the wrong crowd and drinking. We know his brain cannot recover with the alcohol in there, and the chance of him hurting himself or others while drinking is even greater than the average person. At least Steve and I are in this together, but it does not seem we are making any difference.

Steve and I remember the words of the psychologist and decide to face this problem head on, with love. Steve is going over there to his apartment tonight. Bryant gets off work at three in the morning, and Steve is going to be there to greet him when he comes home; to catch him drinking. He does not know what he is going to say or what is going to happen, but we are not going to be lied to anymore.

I seem to anger Bryant, so I am going to be the prayer partner. I am now bending my knees to God. I realize I cannot control anything. He is in complete control of this situation, and He will change things on His time, not mine. I will stay awake while Steve is there, on my knees, praying for the right words to come out of Steve's mouth and for Bryant to listen and receive.

The hours tick by slowly. Once again the minutes seem like hours. I am sitting on the couch in the family room watching television, killing time; I don't know what room Steve is occupying in our huge empty house. It is pitch black outside, cold and wintery. Neither of us will sleep tonight. I aimlessly flip channels. When I stop on the local news, I catch the tail end of a story about a father from Bryant's former soccer team. He has been indicted for manslaughter. While drinking and driving he has killed an innocent woman. I am in shock. I run into the office and search Google, I have the story, complete with a horrible mug shot. Printing out the story, thinking maybe this will be a good conversation starter. Someone Bryant knows and cares for has done exactly what we fear. I take the printout in my hand and send a prayer up to God, please, please let this tragedy help our son to see the light. Let this tragedy serve some good.

Armed with this information, Steve goes over to the apartment to wait for Bryant. This time I go up to my bedroom and kneel beside my bed. I pray and pray for an answer. I pray for Steve to find the right words. I pray Bryant will be receptive. I pray for God's will to be done. We do not know what we are doing. We hope God has a plan. Steve surprises everyone and finds the "select friends" Steve chose to live with Bryant sitting in Bryant's apartment playing cards and drinking shots. They are not even embarrassed and offer a drink to him. Steve is feeling sick to his stomach, things are worse than we thought. Steve realizes he, too, has made some grievous mistakes, mistakes that are contributing to the problems we are now facing. How were we expecting our son to live under these circumstances and thrive? Bryant comes home that night and yes, he has been drinking and he drove himself home.

Steve and Bryant need to go into his bedroom to talk because his friends are drinking it up at Bryant's kitchen table. They do not have the sense to take the party upstairs. Steve uses the copy of the manslaughter story to open the conversation. He tells him how much we love him and how worried we are for him. Clearly, he has been drinking and driving tonight. He could not only kill himself but someone else as well. Bryant sits down with his dad and admits things are not working out. He would like to get away. He is thinking about walking the Appalachian Trail alone with his dog for six months. Steve knows Bryant is probably still too tender to be out there on his own and that I would have a complete and total meltdown. Out of nowhere a thought pops into Steve's head. He discusses an outdoor leadership school with Bryant; he has heard they have great programs.

Steve asks Bryant, "If I could find one, would you be interested in one?"

Bryant's eyes light up, he agrees. "Sure, but it might be expensive."

Steve said, "I'm not worried about how much it costs, let's just see if I can find a good trip for you."

It is early in the morning when Steve comes home. He Googles the programs and finds a three-month semester program starting in one week. They have one opening left. We get his doctor to sign off on it and away Bryant goes. It all happens so fast that he does not have time to change his mind. We keep him occupied all week with purchasing the new and amazing accessories he needs for his new adventure. We need to outfit him to live in both forty degrees below zero weather, and to the other extreme, desert life. He will be out in the wilderness with a group of people and instructors. They will educate him on how to climb safely, lead dog sleds in the snow and ice, and most of all, there will be no drugs, no alcohol and no outside stimulation, only peace and quiet. It is our only hope. We would mortgage everything we have to pull off this one. We are praying this will give his brain the time it needs to heal.

The day we take our son to the airport is a really cold, snowy, icy January day. I am holding my breath the whole time, waiting for him to change his mind and bolt. I am afraid to let him go, afraid to not let him go. I have no idea if he is ready for this adventure or not, I only know what is not working, and that is his life here. The thought of letting my tender, vulnerable child go into the wilderness and the harsh elements for three months scares me to death. He is so happy, so excited to go. I kiss him good-bye and watch him walk away with his huge pack.

When we get home from the airport, I put on my coveralls and go outside. Steve walks out to see what I am doing.

"I need a project," I tell him, as I start to whack at a thorn bush. "Do you see those vines growing way up in those pine trees?" I point about thirty feet into the woods and seventy-five feet into the air. "I am going to clear out this brush, cut down that wisteria and you are going to build me something for it to grow on, I need a project. *I need this, and I need you to do that, for me.*"

He looks at me in puzzlement and he turns and walks back inside. I whack, I cut, and I carry. I take out all of my frustration on that brush and it feels good to my unused muscles that have been longing for a work out. The cold air fills my lungs and it is good. I have no idea if what I am doing makes any sense or not, but I am driven. I work out there for days, only coming in when it is too dark to see. Finally the weather turns so cold and wet it forces me back inside.

Steve heads back to Florida for his last trip. He has decided to finish up the month of January. He is in the process of training someone else to take over. His business partner has accepted a three-year mission assignment from his church. He told us about it in early December right before the office Christmas party. He is busy making plans for Brazil, and he is practically dancing around the office.

In contrast, Steve knows nothing will ever be the same between them. We are both really upset with him. We need him right now and we feel abandoned. Both of us are at the lowest point in our lives, hanging on by a thread and now his partner is planning to leave us. Our future is uncertain, both financially and emotionally.

What we couldn't appreciate at the time is that this was all part of God's plan as well. Steve's business partner accepting this mission trip to Brazil was an offer he could not refuse. Steve would begrudgingly need to give up developing people in the work arena to develop his brokerage business. His attention would now be at home. Without splitting the proceeds, we actually have a chance for financial growth.

Steve is unable to get the emotional high of being the center of attention that his training and development programs gave him; he now turns to his family, what a shift. This is the beginning of our financial and emotional recovery. A friend told us that God would bless us for allowing Steve's business partner to have this opportunity with his church. At the time all we could think of was, "What about us?" As it was, we were truly blessed for this sacrifice.

I developed a new respect for not always following the rules. Rules are simply guidelines to protect people, sometimes they don't pertain to you. That is my new way of looking at them. I have a new respect for Steve. I know that because of his allowing Bryant to follow his own urges, he helped Bryant to grow and change at a far faster rate. I still keep a healthy respect for rules, and I guess I always will. That being said we still have the problem of Steve always siding with the kids and never with me.

Of course, I cannot see this right now. I am simply angry at the world. I am standing inside the house Monday morning after Steve leaves for Florida. James is at school and he has taken up acting. He has found a new group of friends and a new path. He has quite a talent, all of the pent up emotions pour out on the stage. People marvel at his depth, what a gift for someone so young. He is now an old person inside a young man's body. I am so grateful to the director who saw all of this raw emotion and has given it an outlet. He is in class all day and rehearsals all evening, leaving me alone for the first time.

Paul is now in Officer Candidate School at the base in Washington, D.C., being abused and loving every minute of it. He has always been a badass and loves to see how far he can push himself.

Elizabeth is in sunny San Diego becoming a vegetarian and recycling everything.

I am standing here alone, except for the dog, Ali. Since Bryant will be gone for three months, the pit bull and I are together again.

Chapter
The Cleansing

49

"Fine old houses make fine friends. Beyond providing sturdy shelter, they turn daydreams into creative endeavors, illuminate history, and speak to your soul.
– Unknown

I am still having an adrenaline surge. I am worried about so many things that I cannot sit still. The weather has turned way too cold to work outside. I turn to an inside project to keep my mind busy and to burn off excessive energy.

I stand on the same stone floor in the room of "the party that never was." This room has such a negative feel to it now. It is time for a change. I empty the room of everything but a long white wicker couch for Ali to lie on and watch me work. He is now my buddy, and I cannot let him lie on the cold, stone floor.

It feels good to have my worn painting clothes on again. I laughingly think back to a memory. Elizabeth once said to me when she was a little girl, "why don't you look like the other moms, you always look like you're painting even when you're not."

These are the clothes in which I am most comfortable. Leaving the cold, stone floor, I walk through the hardwood of the foyer and down to the small door under the staircase that leads to the cellar where I packed away all of my painting supplies and everything left from my store. Working my way through the boxes, snake skins and cobwebs, I pull out cans of paint, stencils, glazes, artists' brushes, faux finishing brushes, a complete cornucopia of items left over from my previous life. I had loved these brushes at one time. I bring them all upstairs and make a huge pile in the middle of the hardwood floor. I leave dusty footprints across the floorboards as I make my way up and down the steps.

I stand in the room, interlocking my fingers and stretch my arms out. I do not have a plan. I am afraid of what I do not know and I do not want to think. I am going completely on instinct. I often tell my clients I do best without a plan...that the walls speak to me...my "gift" comes from somewhere else and not from my brain. I am completely working on autopilot. A woman possessed, I let go of my thoughts and relax my mind.

First, I prime and paint all of the walls, never going out to buy paint, using only paint I have left over. This is my final good-bye to that part of my life. I hated the idea of these mediums being stored away in my cellar without a proper good-bye.

I antique the original clapboard on one long wall. I faux finish the other three walls, taking my time going over each detail, pulling out each type of medium, mementos left over from my store, from my former life. I stencil, I free hand paint, and I paint like a mad woman, doing whatever moves me at the moment. My hands are moving without consciousness. My emotions are howling along with the snow outside, and I sit inside for two weeks and paint, all day and night, and I cry. I cry and cry and cry, the tears and the painting are flowing out of my body together in a symphony. One cannot function without the other.

I finally let myself grieve: for my marriage, for my two sons, my emptying nest, the loss of my business, and for a dysfunctional childhood family. I cannot stop myself. My hair is tied up in a ponytail with wisps of my unruly curls escaping the band I use to keep it in place. I am in jeans and a T-shirt, covered with paint. Ali stays right by my side, my protector. Sometimes I am crying so hard I need to stop painting. I sit down on the white wicker seat. Ali lets me borrow his bed and he lays his head on my knee while I sob. Tears pour out of my eyes, snot drips out of my nose and many sobs crack out of my throat and wrack my body.

I did not know one person could hold so much sadness, so many tears, and so much pain. I cannot stop. I sit with one hand on the arm of the worn wicker chair, looking down where the paint has slowly chipped itself off over the years of use, the only thing in the room not covered with paint. The other hand is holding onto Ali's soft, short fur. This dog that I had never wanted, that I only took in over pity, is my one comfort. He sits for hours protecting me, loving me and watching over me. He looks into my eyes where I sit holding onto him, wrapping my arms around him, sobbing into his fur. He is so patient with me; he seems to understand, and we share a bond. Nothing will ever be the same for either of us.

If I could look down at myself, I would look like one of those women from a 1940's movie that sobs and sobs until someone slaps her in the face, or throws a bucket of cold water on her. It would be the scene where the broken and beaten woman has her "break-down." I guess I am broken and beaten. I understand, but I can not stop. I like to think of this as my "break-through." My only regret is that James is living in the house, and he is a witness to the great sadness.

He looks at me one day and says, "Mom, you are too sad for me."

It breaks my heart, but I can not stop crying even for him. I guess my sadness must have broken something down in him as well. He calls me into the living room and proceeds to tell me about his drinking. I am shocked. I have been so naive. He asks me to help him with it. He wants me to monitor his actions more closely and help him, he is afraid. What he is asking for is a parent, the same parent my other children had, and the one I had not been for a while.

I pull it together for him for a couple of hours. When he leaves I cry for him. For his loss of innocence, for his fears, for the working mother I had become. I had not been there for my child over the past three years. I put my own wants and desires to be a successful businesswoman ahead of his needs. Sure, I had done many things right, but at the end in the fourth quarter, I had not had the staying power to finish up my mothering job. I cried for all of these things as well. I was feeling very much like a failure.

Finally, one day the water works and the painting stop simultaneously. I gaze at my creation. The walls are a light tan with a
mottled faux finish over the top to give them an aged patina. The
original clapboard siding, which ran along the wall that was originally the outside of the house, is now painted and antiqued to show
off all of its dings and pits. Under the five large windows in the
room, I stencil a "frieze" of stone-like fruits under the entire width
of each window. Painted vines and flowers encircled the doorways,
and the finishing touch is a lion fountain with a plant in the water
basin. Wiping my still running nose with the back of my hand, I
am pleased and quite drained. The emotions and painting have run
their course.

James' play is coming up and I offer the use of the wicker
furniture that goes into this room, including Ali's bed as props.
A mother stops by to pick it up. Her daughter had gone to school
with James way back in grade school. I have not seen her in years.
She takes a long look at me, I am sure I look like hell. It would have
been so easy for her to walk away and keep her mouth shut. Luckily
for me, she cared enough to say something.

"I know that I don't know you very well," she says. "I know
about Bryant's accident and you must be in a pretty rough place. I
was in a rough place once, and I went to a local seminar. You might
want to call them. They really helped me. Not a single day goes by
that I don't use what they taught me. You can find them in the
phone book."

Right after she leaves I walk into the kitchen, open the pine
hutch and pull out the phone book. I find the number and call.
A seminar is starting next week. I sign myself up. I have less than
ninety days to get myself together. I do not know in what condition
Bryant will return, but I cannot help him unless I help myself first.
James needs me to be a mother to him as well. I need to get myself
together. Like they say on the airplane, put your oxygen mask on
first. You cannot help others if you are passing out.

I hold onto this idea for the next week, happy to have a plan.
This is all I need to make it through another week. One moment

at a time, one day at a time, sometimes that is the best you can do.

I drive by the building of the seminar three times that night. I am so afraid. I am afraid to go, I am afraid not to go.

I tell myself, if Bryant can withstand forty below cold and sleep outside under nothing but a tarp on the frozen lakes of Minnesota in the middle of the winter to make a change, I can do this. If James can come clean with his problems, rescue his brother, and discover a new outlet, I can do this. If Paul can face the rigors of Quantico right now in the freezing cold at Officer Candidate School, I can do this. If Steve can leave a life he loved, and stay home to run the business alone, I can do this. If Elizabeth is fearlessly living a new life in California, then I can face the unknown demons inside me.

After my "break down-through" I am now an empty shell ready to be refilled and refreshed. My entire life has been changed by the year of the Cicadas. It's so funny, we have been so focused on changing Bryant, that we are oblivious to the changes in us. I am not the person I was before. I prayed for change, and I got change. My children inspired me to move forward. The therapist is right after all; love is the difference. I pull into the parking lot, walk through the door and start the new journey of discovery about myself.

Chapter
Bryant's Story **50**

"Until you make peace with who you are; you will never be content with what you have."
– Doris Mortman

A wonderful fresh newness once again fills our spring world. That beautiful spring green that speaks to my heart with a promise of new things to come. Bryant is finishing up with his outdoor journey and is currently in Mexico in the Copper Canyon. We are coming up on the one-year anniversary of the accident, and are looking forward to his return home before then. He learned to journal while he was on this trip and here is an excerpt, from the last days of his ninety-day adventure.

I am currently sitting on top of one of the most beautiful places on earth. I highly doubt that I will ever again witness a view like the one I am looking at right now. Grand Canyon, wow, the Gorge, wow, Texas and Minnesota, wow. The Copper, wow, wow, I think by far tops them all. I could sit, think and write in this very spot all day. Up here my world makes sense. Up here I don't need companionship. Up here I don't need drugs of any kind, money, or a car. This rock, the one I'm sitting on, staring into this canyon, this is all I need.

I wish this was the beginning of my trip but it's not, and it's coming to an end really soon. I miss my car, house, money and friends but this is all I need. This has been a chance for me to realize that my life is good in so many ways. Tomorrow is really the last day.

I look down at my body, I have bumps, bruises, cuts, cactus wounds and much more. None of these things matter at all to me, not at this moment. I am sitting on a rock jutting out over the Copper Canyon. I am looking down on the Tarahumaran homes in the bottom of the canyon, and as I look at them it is all clear to me. Everything is so clear to me. It doesn't matter how much money I make, it doesn't matter how expensive my clothing is. All that matters is happiness. Right now I am happy. I am at peace.

He never gave up, broken, but not beaten he has succeeded. He climbed to the top of the mountain he fell from and rappelled off it. He has gone on to conquer higher mountains. He is on his mountain-top and the conqueror of his own world. Bryant spends the first anniversary of his fall camped right below where he fell. Facing his adversary square in the face.

Chapter 51
Coming Out
of the Darkness

"Our deepest fear is not that we are inadequate. Our deepest fear is that we are powerful beyond measure. It is our light, not our darkness that frightens us. We ask ourselves, "who am I to be brilliant, gorgeous, talented, and fabulous? Actually, who are we not to be?"
– Unknown

Five months before the accident, I prayed to God, I asked him to change my life. I wanted something and I didn't know what. Up to that point I had wanted change, but what I really wanted was for everyone else to change. I did not want to change myself, there was nothing wrong with me. I was quick to judge and point out what was wrong with everyone else. What was wrong with them? Couldn't they see how much better life would be if they would only change? When I made the decision to live a purposeful life, I made a change in me. A one-degree small shift but it turned my viewpoint enough for me to see things a bit differently.

I had ninety days before Bryant came home from his outdoor experience. I was not in any shape to help my son, unless I helped myself first. I went to the seminar and I changed my life. I attended two additional seminars before Bryant returned home. It was not easy, change never is. I couldn't change "us," I could only change me. When I did find the light again and I had a glow and peace about me and in my heart. I discovered I was worthy. I wanted and needed the intimacy in my life that I had been missing. The feeling of having arms wrapped around me and telling me that I am loved, or a hug. An average person needs twenty hugs a day to thrive. I am planning to thrive, not survive.

I went to the program and while I was away at a retreat, Steve and James built me a pergola for the wisteria. What a pergola it is: the size of a four-car garage. Steve feared the worst and thought I would come home and decide to end our marriage. He knew he had to do something, something big. It is the only thing he had ever built up to that time, and it is massive and beautiful. He did not know I had decided to work on our marriage a while back, before the accident, and had no plans to end it. I love my pergola, and it is covered with wisteria now, and blooms with an abundance of beautiful lavender flowers. The scent is heavenly. We laughingly call it *The Pergola that Saved Our Marriage.*

I have heard it said that some people would rather be right than happy. I now choose happiness. I do not need to be right all the time anymore. I do not judge people like I did before. The older I get, the less I know. The more I peel back the layers on this old onion, the more I discover that we all have layers, upon layers of "stuff" in our lives burying us under the darkness. To forgive and to love is really the most important thing of all. To forgive ourselves and to love ourselves is the key to forgiving and loving others.

The one thing I knew was, I was still in love with my husband, and I rededicated myself to work on my marriage. Another one-degree shift was that I started looking at my marriage and seeing it for what it was, not for what I wanted it to be. My viewpoint of life once again had been shifted. Then I thought, "What else have I been missing?"

I thought about family and my friends not being there for me, perhaps it was not because of them but because of something in me. I seriously and intentionally started journaling and looking at my own actions and how they had contributed to keeping people away from me. I owned my own part of the responsibility, another one-degree shift. Of course, they have their own baggage and their own reasons and they own those, but I had done things as well. I had been hurt in my life, and I did not want to be hurt again. I have a quick mind and a razor sharp tongue; I can be an assassin with my words. I had been unpredictable, ninety-eight percent of the time I go along and am a really loving, caring, giving person, but, when threatened, my default is to protect myself. I can slice and dice people with my wit and tongue. Sarcasm and put-downs are my weapons of choice. I had used my God given gift of intuition to recognize a person's weakness and exploit it. I also excelled at judging people. I thought I knew so much. I loved to tell them how "they" could change and be better. I do not have the power to change anyone but myself, another one-degree shift. Now my viewpoint on life is looking quite a bit different.

A large shift, maybe even a two-percent shift came for me when I came to the realization I had spent my entire life giving, not without strings attached, but giving with one string, if I give to you, you will love me. I learned as a small child, if I gave enough I would get love, so I gave, and gave and I gave. That is how I survived a tough childhood. It worked for me then, but it is not working for me anymore. I believe we are created with two abilities, to give and to receive. I always thought of people as two different kinds, the givers and the takers. I thought to be a taker was a bad thing. Once I shifted the words to givers and receivers, I saw it in another light. To be the person who is always giving and never receiving is actually selfish. To allow someone else to give to you is one of the greatest gifts you can give them. I always gave; my ability to receive had atrophied like a mangled arm with no muscle left in it. I never allowed any member of my family, my children or my husband to give to me. I denied them the gift of giving, and the gift of learning how to give. I did not see how much I needed to receive until "The Accident." I am worthy of receiving as well as giving.

I love to paint walls. I am also the artist of the life I am living. The choices I made in my life have all brought me here to the point I am at now. I say to you, if you do not like the canvas you have painted, change it. I have taken a brutal inventory of my life and realize I gained weight intentionally. I was angry with my husband and did not want to be a cute "arm piece." I was sure he would dump me if I gained weight. He did not, and he still loved me. I discovered he loved the person inside of me, not the outside. I found that being overweight was working for me. Women were nicer to me; no one wants to be friends with the hot mom whose husband is never around. Men did not hit on me anymore, and I loved to bake and eat. Sure it had its drawbacks, but it was giving me what I wanted.

Then one day it was not working for me anymore. I had health issues that had to be dealt with: high blood pressure brought allergic reactions because of the medications necessary to control it. This brought additional weight gain from the medications, along with a threat of diabetes on the threshold. Permanent damage to both of my knees from the excessive weight brought changes in my ability to exercise, even more weight gain. My family started taking hiking and camping trips that I could not go on because of my bad knees. I made another one-degree shift and started focusing on wellness instead of illness. I have had to change not only my diet but one-hundred different things, all of them working in unison to help me lose the weight. I wish one diet plan would have worked for me, but none of them did, I had to make numerous decisions, searching for answers, taking control of my own destiny. I visited doctors, weight loss clinics, nutritionists, metabolic doctors, wellness doctors, and trainers. I took something from each of them and formed my own plan that works for me, one hundred different things all working in unison.

Another one-degree shift was recognizing I have the ability to make decisions for and about myself. It is a wonderful thing to ask for people's opinions, realizing that is all they are, simply someone's opinions. My heart, my mind, my soul, my body already know the answers, they are within me. If I ask enough questions of other more knowledgeable people; they may stir the answer inside of me, or not. I am unique and my answers for me are not the same as for anyone else. I have learned to slow down and listen to myself. Quieting my mind and listening to my inner voice has been a great one for me.

Turning from being spiritual to joining a religious community, better known as a church, has been a big shift for me. Sometimes I still find it difficult to go along with everything that they represent.

I think that's O.K., or at least it is for now. I am a better person because of my affiliation, even if I do not always agree with everything.

Steve decided he liked the new me and wanted some of what I had going. He decided to attend the seminars himself. The changes he has made to himself have been awesome. He is helping so many people in his journey through life.

We decided we were worth it and attended marriage seminars and gave our marriage a new boost. I love our creation. We still struggle with some things that life throws at us, and we always will, but together we can move mountains.

The night before Bryant fell he told James and Ace, that he wanted change in his life, and he did not know how that change would look. I believe Steve needed his life changed as well. We were all in need and, although I do not believe God pushed Bryant off that cliff, I do believe He gave us the chance to make the changes we needed. All of our ugly bumps, bruises and warts were all brought to the surface during this stressful time. God showed us in a heartbeat what was important and what was not.

What a rare gift we were given. Yes, I do mean gift. We saw ourselves and our lives, for what they were and He showed us the way. He could not do it for us, but He gave us the key. It was for us to go through the door and down the path. We are, after all, spiritual beings having a human existence complete with free will.

My childhood family, because of our dysfunction was simply not able to give that to me. It does not really matter why; they simply could not. I am now reaching out to others, building a circle of influence, a functional group to turn to in good times and bad. They come from many walks of life, different states and different backgrounds. That's all right, it's up to me to reach out and make a difference in other people's lives, to help them to change as well.

Steve and I have been blessed with three new grandsons in the past year. Our marriage has survived and thrived. I love him as much now as I did when I first met him. My heart pumps faster every time I hear his voice or see his face. My now wrinkled eyes shine brighter whenever he is near. To think I was almost ready to throw that all away really amazes me. Our marriage and family were worth the fight.

I look down at the small, frail; yet very strong hand wrapped so tightly around mine. The fingers are holding on instinctively. It is amazing. I have been here before. I cannot help but think back seven years ago when Bryant's larger hand was wrapped around mine in the ICU, just as tightly, and just as frail.

I am holding Bryant's son in my lap, right here in this long porch room, the room of the "party that never was." The room painted by the "mad woman" seven years ago. I look down at the white blonde hair, and the face that so reminds me of my son as a baby, and I cannot help but to think, *I am so blessed.*

So many ripple effects, so many changes. I heard the quote before, *"The only way out, is through,"* and for me nothing could be truer. We were all faced with an enormous test, and somehow, someway we came through it. I am a better person, wife, mother, daughter, sister and finally grandmother, because of this journey. I changed as a person in so many ways. We all have.

I am grateful every day for the changes in my life. I still have regrets that my son had to suffer for me to face these needed changes. This will always tug at my heartstrings. Without his journey I would not be the person I am today. My wish is that this story can bring hope to someone who has lost his or her way, like I had. When life gives one tough choices, find the strength to make it through to the other side and, remember, no matter what the odds, or what obstacles you face, climb to the top of your mountain. Never give up.

Bryant returned from his outdoor leadership experience a new person. His brain had time to heal. He found peace and serenity, simply put, he found God within himself. The anger, aggression and depression were gone. He grew up and is a different person. He is a bright, mature, happy, loving, giving individual. He is funny, kindhearted, and very capable of learning new things. You could have a long-term relationship with him and never guess he had an accident of any kind. He is a good looking, normal man, in every sense of the word.

He has his insurance license and went back to graduate from college. After working with his father for years, he is now responsible for and manages the family business while Steve is off doing consulting. Bryant met the woman of his dreams and married her and now they are parents. He is strong, athletic and no longer walks with a limp. He has been healed in every way. He has one small scar behind his right ear and a weak ankle. He still has memory issues, but he has leaned to compensate and record everything. He has gone back to playing recreational soccer, hikes, rappels, and several times a year goes back to the spot from which he fell.

He goes there to camp, to center and to realign his life. Sometimes the world comes at him too fast and too loud. It does for all of us, only he recognizes it. When things get chaotic for him, he finds peace and tranquility in the woods. He returns to the Gorge, the place he still loves. He reconnects with what is really important in life and the woods, rocks and the streams all speak to him; they quiet his mind and recharge his battery. I believe it will always be a sacred spot for him and for James.

James has grown up to be a handsome, strong, healthy young man. He had to find himself, and did two outdoor experiences and traveled the world with a back-pack. He is an avid hiker, camper and rock climber. James is quite the adventurer and ran with the bulls in Pamplona among other things.

We are happy to have him back with us. Although James is a positive person, quick with a smile and a joke, I believe that day will forever be with him. The year of the Cicadas was a formative year for James and for all of us.

He learned to channel all of those raw emotions into acting, and double majored in theatre and history. He accepted a contract with the local Shakespeare Company after graduating and is also working in the family business along with Bryant. He is very positive and has a light about him that makes him the center of attention wherever he goes. He continues to be close to Bryant, and struggles with an over zealous mother who sees danger at every turn.

Elizabeth came back home to go to school after a year in California. I was so glad to have my daughter back again for a while. She has her interior design degree, married and has a son of her own. She is very talented and creative and spends her time working in the church nursery, being a mom and using her creativity as a photographer creating beautiful memories for all of us. She is clearly our rose among the thorns.

Paul and Leigh married and recently became parents. Paul is planning to be a career Marine. He is working on his masters and we are very proud of his accomplishments and the lives he has protected. If ever I am in a foxhole and being shot at, he is the man I would want with me. He is strong, calm, capable, strategic, and sharp as a tack. He moves without fear.

I have been praying for one more miracle, after three deployments, I want my oldest son home, healthy and alive. I know I have received so much, but I am hoping for one more miracle. I look around the room; all of the kids are here, except for Paul, I pray for him daily, morning, noon and night.

Years have passed and once again it is Father's Day, and we have received word that Paul has touched down in Washington D.C.; after twelve long months of intense combat in the mountains of Afghanistan, earning him a bronze star. Although a Marine, he was also awarded an Army commendation for combat valor. He is home safely once again on U.S. soil. Of course we want to be there with him, but he wants this time reserved just for him and his family. I have learned to accept his wishes and not to control everything. After he has time with his wife and son, he will come home for a visit. Won't we all *have a jubilation* then?

My fondest wish is that this story will give you hope. Hope that there is another side, and that the other side hears your prayers. I know this to be true, they heard me, answered me, spoke to me, and in the form of a wolf, helped me. To give hope if you have a loved one struggling with a traumatic brain injury, hope if your marriage is not thriving, hope when relationships within your family are not what you think they should be, hope if your drug of choice is food, hope that whatever you are burying will dig it's way out.

Mother Nature has a plan for everything, and I thought that the only purpose the Cicadas could possibly have was to aerate the ground. Now, I think there is a greater purpose for the Cicadas. I believe the Cicadas are here to teach us that even the dark things buried deep inside of us need to eventually see the light; to emerge and find their voice. Then and only then can we sing. This book has allowed me to not only find my voice, but to sing.

The words Brad spoke over our son, when he gave the blessing, seemed so vague, impossible, and somewhat unfair, "*he will heal himself, but it is dependent upon the two of you.*" Wow, no truer words were ever spoken.

We had quite a year this year, Steve's father and my mother both passed away, watching over us from the other side. I know that tough, hard Bernard was there with Paul in combat. He could not have had a better guardian angel with him. I know both of our parents will be here with us in spirit when we celebrate our next jubilation.

We are sitting here in the porch room talking about how the Cicadas are emerging right now in my hometown. Cicada's are cyclical and will not emerge in our city in mass again for another ten years. Bryant was disappointed they were not out during my mother's funeral back in my hometown, for you see, he is looking forward to seeing them in mass. He can't wait until they come back, he doesn't remember the "Year of the Cicadas"...but we, we will never forget.

Catie's favorite quote:

"People are often unreasonable and self-centered.
FORGIVE THEM ANYWAY

If you are kind, people may accuse you of ulterior motives.
BE KIND ANYWAY

If you are honest, people may cheat you.
BE HONEST ANYWAY

If you find happiness, people may be jealous
BE HAPPY ANYWAY

The good you do today may be forgotten tomorrow.
DO GOOD ANYWAY

Give the world the best you have, and it may never be enough.
GIVE YOUR BEST ANYWAY

For you see, in the end, it is between you and God
IT WAS NEVER BETWEEN YOU AND THEM ANYWAY"

– Mother Teresa

For more information about The Year of the Cicadas, please visit our web site **www.TheYearoftheCicadas.com** or like us on Facebook, The Year of the Cicadas.

You will find photos, speaking engagements, book signings and where to purchase the book, along with answers to your most frequently asked questions.